About the Author

Melissa Tipton is a Structural Integrator, reiki master, and tarot reader who helps people live their most magical life through her healing practice, Life Alchemy Massage Therapy in Columbia, MO. She's also the author of *Living Reiki: Heal Yourself and Transform Your Life*. Take online classes and learn more at getmomassage.com and yogiwitch.com.

LLEWELLYN'S

COMPLETE BOOK OF

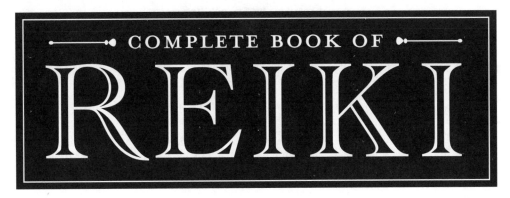

REIKI

Your Comprehensive Guide to a Holistic Hands-On
Healing Technique for Balance and Wellness

MELISSA TIPTON

LLEWELLYN PUBLICATIONS
Woodbury, Minnesota

FIRST EDITION
First Printing, 2020
Cover design by Kevin R. Brown
Interior illustrations by Mary Ann Zapalac, sigil art by the Llewellyn Art Department

Excerpt(s) from *Hands of Light: A Guide to Healing Through the Human Energy Field* by Barbara Ann Brennan, copyright © 1987 by Barbara A. Brennan. Used by permission of Bantam Books, an imprint of Random House, a division of Penguin Random House LLC. All rights reserved.

The Inner Heart of Reiki by Frans Stiene © 2015 Ayni Books.
All rights reserved. Used by permission.

Llewellyn Publications is a registered trademark of Llewellyn Worldwide Ltd.

Library of Congress Cataloging-in-Publication Data
Names: Tipton, Melissa, author.
Title: Llewellyn's complete book of Reiki : your comprehensive guide to a
  holistic hands-on healing technique for balance and wellness / Melissa
  Tipton, Lauryn Heineman.
Description: First edition. | Woodbury, Minnesota : Llewellyn Publications,
  2020. | Series: Llewellyn's complete book series; Volume 15 | Includes
  bibliographical references and index. | Summary: "Providing an in-depth
  look at the history, study, and practice of reiki, a Japanese system of
  energy healing, this is a comprehensive guide for students and
  practitioners of every level, covering hand positions, symbols and
  mantras, attunements, conducting sessions, and professional practice"—
  Provided by publisher.
Identifiers: LCCN 2019055141 (print) | LCCN 2019055142 (ebook) | ISBN
  9780738761831 (paperback) | ISBN 9780738761879 (ebook)
Subjects: LCSH: Reiki (Healing system)
Classification: LCC RZ403.R45 T575 2020 (print) | LCC RZ403.R45 (ebook) |
  DDC 615.8/52—dc23
LC record available at https://lccn.loc.gov/2019055141
LC ebook record available at https://lccn.loc.gov/2019055142

Llewellyn Publications
A Division of Llewellyn Worldwide Ltd.
2143 Wooddale Drive
Woodbury, MN 55125-2989
www.llewellyn.com
Printed in the United States of America

Also by Melissa Tipton

Living Reiki: Heal Yourself and Transform Your Life

For Jake, my favorite.

Contents

Contents

Exercises

• • • • • • • •

Exercises

· · · · · · · ·

Chapter 15

Chapter 21

. . . .

Disclaimer

The material in this book is not intended as a substitute for trained medical or psychological advice. Readers are advised to consult their personal healthcare professionals regarding treatment. Both the author and the publisher recommend that you consult a medical practitioner before attempting the techniques outlined in this book.

Foreword

As someone working nonstop to bring reiki into allopathic medicine, I am beyond grateful to Melissa Tipton for her book *Llewellyn's Complete Book of Reiki*. As the title describes, this is truly a complete presentation of all things reiki, and I look forward to presenting this book to the surgeons and doctors who show an interest in understanding reiki and what it can do for their patients.

As a practitioner working alongside surgeons, I know for a fact that reiki is a crucial complement to serious surgeries of modern medicine, including heart surgery, mastectomy, organ transplant, and others—all of which test the human capacity to withstand harrowing surgeries that can save lives but also leave patients feeling shattered. Reiki is an antidote to the fracturing of the human spirit when such serious medical interventions are necessary.

Llewellyn's Complete Book of Reiki is an eye-opener for every person with an interest in finding out how reiki can help them advance in their life, whether they are in the throes of illness, needing to find peace in a hectic world, seriously seeking their life's purpose, or just curious about energy healing modalities. Tipton's book is also invaluable to us reiki practitioners working with clients in the fulfillment of our destinies, and, furthermore, I believe it should be required reading for the students of any reiki master-teacher who is taking on the responsibility of raising new practitioners. This important book fully describes and honors the incredible and limitless healing art given to us by Mikao Usui.

My favorite parts of the book are getting back to basics and delving into everything about Usui's reiki. Tipton's explanations of the seven types of energy, ending with reiki as the seventh type, is fascinating as well as informative. Since there seems to be a never-ending exploration of the history of reiki by scholars of Usui's life and practices, I appreciate the clear descriptions of what is known, what is fact, and what is fiction. It is also illuminating to understand how and why some of the myths about Usui came into being. I find this section to be of great personal comfort, as it offers the truth of what Usui left us as a healing practice.

The clear explanation of the levels involved in reiki training is helpful to anyone wishing to study reiki, particularly the information on choosing a teacher. In my work of training reiki masters who want to bring their work into medicine, finding the right teacher is of paramount importance. This important work requires reiki masters with in-person training, as it has been demonstrated to me that those who have trained online do not have the skills or the understanding necessary to function in an operating room.

Tipton shares many helpful suggestions for incorporating reiki into one's daily practice of self-care and addresses the difficulties we face in the modern world, accompanied by solutions that are grounded in reality. In the end, it all comes down to how we would like to experience reiki, whether as a client, as a full-time or part-time practitioner, or as a hobbyist. Thankfully, Melissa Tipton's book gives us so much information that each reader can comfortably make the choice without self-judgment, knowing that whatever is decided upon is for the highest good, and that fact has the power to make any heart sing!

Raven Keyes
Author of *The Healing Power of Reiki* and founder of Raven Keyes Medical Reiki International

INTRODUCTION

Healing is your birthright. When you stub your toe, your first impulse is to reach out and hold the pain, bringing soothing and relief. Reiki as a healing system is a powerful way of tapping into and refining your natural healing abilities, and in this book, we'll look at the history, spiritual teachings and philosophy, and hands-on healing techniques of reiki. More than learning *about* reiki, though, the idea is to *experience* reiki, because it is through the embodiment of this spiritual energy in your day-to-day life that you will reap the most benefits, from physical healing and emotional balance to heightened intuition and a greater feeling of purpose and meaning.

I came to the practice of reiki after experiencing years of self-generated drama and destructive habits that left me feeling disconnected from my inner wisdom and frustrated over the aimless path that I was trudging along. Despite trying everything from yoga and psychedelics to talk therapy and systematic goal setting, I wasn't able to make positive, lasting change in my life. A series of fortuitous events, bolstered by my previous yoga and meditation experience, led to the realization that my energy was *seriously* out of whack.

From as far back as I can remember, I've always had a great deal of energy. Sounds good, right? Well, yes and no, for as I was becoming painfully aware, this energy could fuel healthy, soul-affirming pursuits, or I could channel it into unhealthy patterns that were damaging to myself and the people around me. In other words, the energy itself was neutral, but because I didn't have the self-awareness and energetic know-how to channel it effectively, the results were not always pleasant.

After yet another drama-filled year of self-induced social implosions and personal chaos, I heard about this thing called reiki, and a small, barely audible voice within urged me to look into it. Lo and behold, there just happened to be a teacher nearby, so, not really understanding why, I signed up for a level one workshop. In the months and years that followed, reiki helped me understand my own energy so that I no longer felt like a puppet being yanked by invisible strings, and now, as a reiki master with a full-time healing practice, I have been blessed with the opportunity to help others rediscover their own inner healer through hands-on and distance healing sessions, online and in-person reiki classes, and the writing of my first book, *Living Reiki: Heal Yourself and Transform Your Life.*

Reiki means "spiritual or universal energy," and the word also describes a healing system, originating in Japan, that utilizes this spiritual energy for hands-on healing and spiritual growth. "Hands-on healing" refers to methods in which the hands are placed on the body or hovering slightly above it to direct the healing. This book is designed to give you a solid foundation in this healing system. Part 1 offers an overview of energy anatomy from a wide range of perspectives so that you can better understand what makes you tick, where your energy is flowing freely or where it might be obstructed, and different ways to heal any imbalances you find. We'll look at fields and layers of energy, such as auras and koshas; energy centers or bodies, like the chakras; and energy pathways within the body, such as meridians and sen lines. Through a series of exercises, you'll hone your ability to sense energy through both the physical senses and your subtle senses. Don't be concerned if some of these practices come more naturally than others—that's very common. You can focus a bit more effort on the senses that seem weaker to you, but there's also nothing wrong with tapping into your strengths and working with the senses that are naturally more accessible.

In part 2, we'll dive into the specifics of the reiki healing system, including its origins in Japan, the use of symbols and mantras, working with reiki precepts, hands-on healing and breathwork techniques, and how to incorporate reiki practice into your daily life with fun, effective programs tailored to specific goals, such as enhancing divination skills, boosting prosperity, and building a meditation practice. You'll also learn how to create your own reiki program based on your unique goals. We'll cover how to find a qualified reiki practitioner and tips for getting the most out of your healing session. And if you're interested in studying reiki, we'll talk about the different levels of instruction, reiki attunements (and whether or not they're necessary), and how to choose the right teacher.

In part 3, we cover reiki as a profession, including how to set up a successful reiki practice, conducting healing sessions, teaching reiki, and much more. Finally, in part 4, we look at a variety of complements to your reiki practice, from herbs and crystals to sound healing and movement practices, along with a wide range of other healing modalities that you might choose to explore. If you're brand new to reiki, this book provides a solid foundation in core reiki teachings, the ins and outs of receiving a reiki attunement, and choosing your first class. For readers with more experience, use this book to deepen your practice, perhaps through further exploration of the reiki precepts and symbols, finding new ways to incorporate reiki into your day-to-day life, or establishing a professional healing practice.

· · · · · · ·

Your energy affects every aspect of your being, from the physical to the spiritual and everything in between, so regardless of your experience level, throughout this book you'll be learning techniques that approach healing from a holistic point of view. Rather than artificially dividing you into little bits and pieces that must be "fixed," the practice of reiki views you as a dynamically divine whole that already contains all the necessary information to self-heal.

You can think of reiki as a powerful tool for remembering the healing wisdom that you already possess and putting this valuable knowledge to good use in order to create your best life. Reiki has the power to reconnect you with your True Self, a self that knows *precisely* what makes your soul feel vibrant and alive, and can guide you in making choices that are in alignment with this higher truth. Use this book to discover *your* True Self, and awaken the gifts, energies, and wisdom that are your birthright.

PART I
Introduction to Vibrational Healing

In part 1, we build the foundation of the study and practice of reiki by looking at different aspects of the human energy system: energy fields, channels, and bodies. We then look at possible ways of explaining the healing power of vibrational medicines, and we conclude in chapter 5 by learning how to enhance your energy-sensing abilities with a variety of fun exercises. Think of this section as a crash course in energy work, enabling you to enhance your understanding and practice of reiki or any vibrational healing modalities you choose to explore.

CHAPTER I

Energy Fields

The word *energy* is tossed around in spiritual circles so often that it's easy to assume we know exactly what it means, but as I sat down to research this book and attempted to commit a definition to paper, the word *energy* felt more slippery than I expected. What *is* energy? Are energy healers and physicists talking about the same thing? And how does energy differ from matter? Given that energy healing is, in part, about using energy to affect matter, how do energy and matter interact? These are just a few of the questions we'll be exploring in this chapter and this book as a whole, and as I soon discovered after wading into the deep end of classical physics, quantum mechanics, biology, and other fields, science is often stranger than fiction. Getting a solid footing with the basics can help us appreciate just how miraculous and magickal the so-called mundane world truly is.

While the focus of this chapter is energy fields, to understand a field of energy, we first need to grapple with the concept of energy itself. In physics, energy is defined as the capacity to do work, and it's interesting to compare this to a common definition of magick: the ability to create change in accordance with one's will. In both cases, we're talking about the ability to *do* something.

Energy is available in various forms, and these forms determine what sort of work or change is possible. As you turn the pages of this book, you are making use of mechanical energy, the energy of an object's position and motion. Your cup of tea contains thermal energy, the motion of molecules within an object, and chemical energy comes into play as your body breaks down the bonds between the molecules in the tea. Other forms of energy exist as well, and energy can be converted from one form into another.

It was once thought that energy and mass were distinct, but Einstein, in his famous $E=mc^2$ equation, showed that mass is, in fact, another form of energy, which brings us to one of our

· · · · · · · ·

questions at the chapter's start: How does energy differ from matter? If matter is simply another form of energy, we need to look at what makes it different from other forms, and to do this, it's time now to talk about energy fields.

One way to think of a field is as a zone of influence. To use a common example, a magnetic field is the area in which a magnet can exert its magnetic effect. In this scenario, we're accustomed to thinking of the magnetic field as something that is being generated by an object—the magnet, in this case—but the Standard Model of particle physics turns this thinking on its head by describing fields as the source and particles arising from the field. Particles are (very) small objects that have physical or chemical properties, such as mass or volume. You can think of particles and other matter as local concentrations of energy within the field, but they are not independent of the field, just like a knot arises from tying a string but cannot exist independently of the string. It *is* the string, just as particles are the field.

According to quantum theory, each type of particle has its own field, which gives rise to individual particles. This explains why every particle of a type is *exactly* the same. For example, every single electron in the universe is exactly the same as all the other electrons, because electrons are "knots" in a continuous "string" called the electron field. When a field gains energy, it begins to vibrate or undulate, like ripples on the surface of a pond, and these ripples are particles. Individual particles might come and go, but the field giving rise to them is permanent.

There is a parallel between this indestructible field giving rise to temporary forms and the teachings of numerous spiritual traditions, which describe an eternal divine energy or consciousness that creates and reabsorbs the fleeting forms of mortal life.

Some particles arise and disappear so fast that we can't observe them, but scientists know they exist due to their collective effects, which *can* be detected. These particles are called "virtual" particles, which is a bit of a misnomer, because they are no less real than observable particles, and they have been shown to play an important role in natural forces, such as the electromagnetic and weak nuclear forces. It's interesting to think that some of the phenomena in the field of energy medicine could be a product of these unseen, virtual particles.

Earlier we defined energy as the capacity to do work, which means that energy is a process rather than a static entity, and if mass is energy, then mass, too, is a process. Think about this for a minute. The chair you're sitting on, the body that's doing the sitting—these are dynamic processes. The spiritual teachings of Hermeticism, an ancient philosophical and magickal tradition based on the writings of Hermes Trismegistus, espouse that everything vibrates; Buddhism teaches that things are impermanent and ever changing, and physics shows this to be true. These energetic processes can create the *appearance* of solid substance, but the fundamental truth is one of constant movement and ceaseless change.

An important takeaway is the underlying interconnectedness of everything. If all the particles in my body are ripples in the same field that gives rise to the particles in your body (and in the trees, the stars, and everything else), it's hard to assert that we're as separate as we tend to believe. And therefore, the idea that I could affect you by laying my hands on your body during a reiki treatment is entirely possible.

Human Energy Fields

Let's expand our view beyond physics to encompass perspectives from the field of energy medicine. Surrounding and interpenetrating the human body is a multilayered energy field commonly known as the aura. Many energy healers perceive seven primary auric layers, which are associated with the seven main chakras (vortices of energy that reside within the body and the aura, each of which processes different types of energy), although additional layers have been perceived as well. Here, we'll focus on the first seven.

EXERCISE: Perceiving the Aura

This exercise outlines how to practice aura gazing with people, but you might find that you are better able to perceive the aura of crystals, plants, or animals, so if this exercise is challenging, feel free to experiment with gazing at different types of auras. You'll need a black background, like a piece of black cloth or poster board.

Find a comfortable place to sit where you can relax without being disturbed, and take a few minutes to close your eyes and focus on your breath. Allow the inhales and exhales to deepen as you settle into a state of calm and relaxation.

When you feel ready, open your eyes and place the black cloth or poster on your lap. Rub your hands together vigorously for a full fifteen to twenty seconds, and place them on the black background, fingertips an inch or two apart. Soften your gaze as you look at your hands, as if you're trying to look *just* past them. Your vision might blur a bit—that's totally fine.

Look for a soft glow or "fuzz" around your skin. You might notice it more strongly at the fingertips or near the palm. Continue to explore for a few minutes before releasing your focus and closing your eyes for a few breath cycles to let them rest.

You can also try this exercise with a partner, and I find it helpful if the person is sitting in front of a solid background, ideally black or a darker color, but a plain white wall works as well. Follow the same steps to come into a state of relaxation before gazing at your partner with a gentle focus, like you're trying to look past them. Slowly scan around their body, as you might find it easier to see their aura in certain areas.

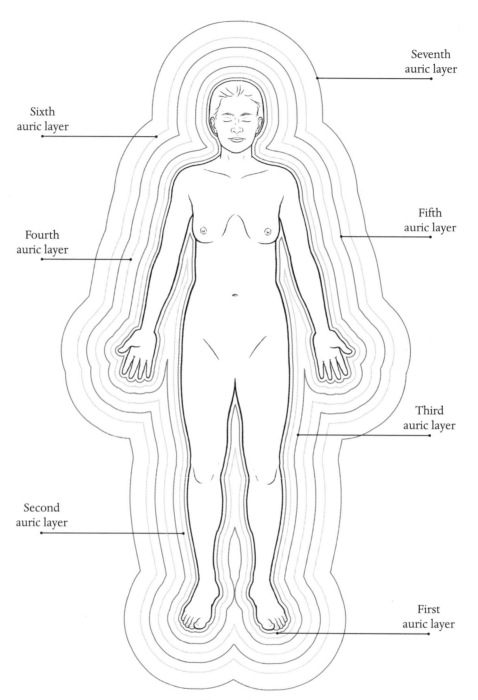

Seventh
auric layer

Sixth
auric layer

Fifth
auric layer

Fourth
auric layer

Third
auric layer

Second
auric layer

First
auric layer

Figure 1: Aura

First Auric Layer

The first three inner layers of the aura are associated with the physical plane of reality, and the one closest to the body is associated with the physical body and the root chakra (the energetic center related to our experiences of safety, stability, and physicality). Energy healer Cyndi Dale sees this layer as being synonymous with the skin, serving as the boundary between our insides and the outside.[1] When this layer is intact and well functioning, we will find it easier to feel grounded, stable, and safe, among other benefits. This layer helps us draw in the energy we need to sustain the core functions of daily living and to establish the necessary boundaries that support self-esteem and healthy interactions with others.

The first auric layer has been perceived as mapping the structure of the body, complete with the forms of individual anatomical features, such as organs and bones. Barbara Ann Brennan describes it as "a definite structure of lines of force, or energy matrix, upon which the physical matter of the body tissues is shaped and anchored."[2] I find it interesting to compare this auric layer with the continuous web of fascia (a type of connective tissue) that interpenetrates, provides structure to, and transmits information and force throughout the entire body. If you were to remove all the other tissues in the body, leaving only the fascia, what remained would be quite recognizable as a human body, down to astonishingly minute details.

Various spiritual traditions teach the importance of maintaining the health of your aura, and the innermost layer in particular is closely tied to your physical health. Working with this layer can be thought of as the epitome of preventative medicine, because you are interacting with the state of your energy before it condenses into physical form. Recall the concept of a field, the undulations of which are particles of matter. By initiating healing in the field, you can change the nature of the undulations and therefore the resulting matter, rather than attempting to shift the quality of the matter after it has already formed. I liken this to making edits to the blueprint for a chair, rather than trying to make changes after you've already cut and assembled the wood.

EXERCISE: **Exploring the Physical Template**

Find a quiet place to sit where you won't be disturbed, get comfy, and close your eyes. Bring your focus to your breath, noticing the inhales and the exhales for a few cycles. Begin to slow your breathing down by gradually lengthening each inhale and exhale, feeling yourself becoming more and more relaxed.

---

1. Cyndi Dale, *The Complete Book of Chakra Healing: Activate the Transformative Power of Your Energy Centers* (Woodbury, MN: Llewellyn Publications, 2011), 180.
2. Barbara Ann Brennan, *Hands of Light: A Guide to Healing through the Human Energy Field* (Toronto: Bantam Books, 1993), 49.

· · · · · · · ·

In your mind's eye, conjure up an image of your body. You might see an outline or a more three-dimensional visual; allow impressions to arise naturally. Say to yourself three times, "I now perceive the first layer of my aura." Notice if the image changes in any way or if other forms of information come to you, such as intuitive knowings that pop up, seemingly out of nowhere, or sounds, smells, or sensations. When you experience one of these changes, focus on it. For example, if you see a glowing blue light around your left shoulder, focus on this light in your mind's eye, and allow any additional sensations or insights to come through. You can also ask questions such as "What is most important for me to know about this blue light?" or "How does this blue light affect my physical health?"

If you're more tactile, you can run your hands slowly over your body, a few inches from your skin, sensing any changes, such as hot or cool areas, tingling patches, sticky or tacky areas, "breezy" spots, and so on. Follow the same process as above for focusing on these areas, allowing additional insights to come through. When you're finished, return to the mind's eye image of your first auric layer, and see a clear stream of healing energy entering this layer, filling the energetic shell with a cleansing, balancing light.

Second Auric Layer

The next layer of the aura is the emotional body, associated with the sacral chakra (the energy center related to emotions, sexuality, and intimacy), and it is related to the energy of emotions and feelings. Returning to the concept of a field in physics, let's use the example of a magnetic field to understand how auric layers function. Just as a magnetic field exerts an influence specifically on magnetized materials and not, say, a chunk of wood or a piece of fabric, each layer of the aura attracts or repels specific types of energy. The second layer transmits your emotional energy to the outside world, while also drawing to you emotional experiences that resonate with the energy present in this layer and repelling dissonant experiences. For example, if your aura has been patterned over time with the emotional energy of fear, you may be predisposed to find yourself in fear-triggering situations, or you might be more attuned or hypersensitive to fearful experiences. On the flipside, if your aura has been patterned with the emotional energy of joy, you will be more likely to experience and notice joyful experiences.

This is not about limiting ourselves only to positive emotional experience, however. Ideally, we are able to experience the full range of emotions without being overly attached to any one emotional state, and one way to support this is to tend to our second auric layer (see also Navel Healing Technique, page 230). When this layer is functioning optimally, we are able to remain fully present with and feel our emotions without clinging to the emotions we like or rejecting the ones we don't. Emotions contain energy and information; thus, when we allow them to flow organically, our energy is permitted to move, which is vital to our health, and we also benefit from the useful information "encoded" in our emotions. If, on the other hand, we resist uncom-

· · · · · · · ·

fortable emotions, such as shame, we halt the natural flow, which can lead to pockets of trapped, stagnant energy. These pockets can emerge from the aura in physical form, manifesting, for example, as anything from sore, achy muscles to chronic illness.

We will also be left with blind spots connected to, in this example, shame-triggering experiences, because we aren't accepting the information carried by the emotion of shame. This can lead to impaired decision-making that continues to generate predictable experiences, in the same way that we would continue to make the same, predictable math error if we never absorbed the information necessary to master multiplication. I find this analogy to be particularly useful, because it lessens the charge of a blame-oriented attitude. When we view recurring experiences simply as indicators that there is something new to learn, it's easier to adopt an attitude of openness and curiosity, which is a very powerful pathway to health and change, rather than getting hung up on self-judgment.

Allowing our emotions to arise naturally is not synonymous with acting on our emotions. I like to approach the emotions as a self-knowledge tool, viewing them as messengers from my otherwise hard-to-access unconscious realms and giving me clues to how various aspects of myself are responding to a situation. When I allow my emotions to flow and I permit myself to fully feel them, my experience is that they always, quite naturally and of their own accord, ebb and fade. Once that cycle has run its course, *then* I can make decisions based on the information delivered via my emotions, but I try to avoid taking action while the emotional tide is still coursing through me; it's like waiting for the entire message to download before attempting to respond. When our first and second auric layers are healthy, we are able to stay present and grounded (first layer) with the emotional tide as it arises (second layer), bringing with it valuable information and a flow of energy.

EXERCISE: The Flow of Emotions

This exercise is a practice in allowing emotional energy to flow through you, rather than resisting this flow and causing energy to become trapped and stagnant.

Find a quiet place to sit where you won't be disturbed, get comfy, and close your eyes. Bring your focus to your breath, noticing the inhales and the exhales for a few cycles. Begin to slow your breathing down by gradually lengthening each inhale and exhale, feeling yourself becoming more and more relaxed.

Bring to mind an animal or person for whom you feel love. Allow the emotion of love to arise, building in intensity for a few breaths. Visualize this emotional energy flowing through your body and energy field, perhaps as a river of colored light. Release attachment to the image of the animal or person and allow the emotional energy to run its course as you remain present with the sensations.

• • • • • • •

Notice as the intensity of the emotion naturally starts to fade. Recall the memory of the animal or person once more and explore your ability to bring in another flow of emotional energy. When this round of emotions fades, slowly come back to your breath, and when you're ready, open your eyes.

Following this exercise, notice in daily life how your emotions rise and fall of their own accord. If an emotion is lingering, bring your awareness to your thoughts: Are you calling in additional waves of this energy by thinking about the initial trigger, perhaps by replaying events in your mind? Recognize this inner power to conjure up emotions long after the original event, and know that you can choose when to engage in this pattern. The more you practice exercising your power to choose, the easier it will become to allow your emotions to fade naturally.

Third Auric Layer

The third auric layer is associated with the solar plexus chakra (the energy center tied to the directing of our will through the choices we make), and in various traditions it is also linked to the mental body, which includes the thoughts and beliefs that shape our reality. Just like the emotional energy of the second layer, our thought energy can attract or repel experiences, and depending on the health of this layer, those experiences will be more or less in line with our well-being. Dale describes this layer as emanating from the third chakra to create a "mind field" around us, which can connect to the mind fields of others, creating a "holistic network of data that stretches beyond our current time/space continuum," an idea that echoes the concept of morphic resonance discussed later in this chapter.[3]

It is in this third layer that we may encounter thoughtforms, which are energetic constructs created through the power of thought, and over time, we can reinforce a thoughtform through repetition. For example, in childhood we may have internalized the message "I am unworthy," creating an unworthiness thoughtform. The more we put stock in that thoughtform by telling ourselves "I'm not worthy," the stronger the thoughtform becomes, running like a computer program in the background and influencing how we see ourselves and the world, just as trapped, stagnant emotions in the second layer continue to exert an influence long after the original emotion has passed.

Tending to the third auric layer would include clearing out unhelpful thoughtforms, much like brushing your teeth, and I see this as tending to your daily thought landscape as you would a beloved garden. While it's probably not possible to completely root out *all* unhelpful thoughts, we can plant the seeds of many beneficial thoughts, and over time, these thoughts will outcompete those that are not in line with our highest good. Just as with the emotions, this is not about

3. Cyndi Dale, *The Subtle Body: An Encyclopedia of Your Energetic Anatomy* (Boulder, CO: Sounds True, 2009), 187.

trying to think happy, light thoughts 24/7; life is a rich tapestry not limited to any one zone of experience, but we can learn to expand on the thoughts that support us in making healthy decisions while learning from and releasing the thoughts that leave us feeling immobilized by, for example, fear, shame, or judgment.

I like to approach unhelpful thoughts by first allowing myself to be aware of them. This might sound obvious, but oftentimes these thoughts run in the background like white noise, and various practices, such as regular meditation, journaling, and therapy, can help bring them to light. When I become aware of a thought, I adopt an attitude of openness and curiosity, approaching it with the assumption that it has something valuable to teach me. For example, if you identify the thought "I am unworthy," you can ask your higher self, "Can you show me a time when I first had this thought?" and "Can you show me some examples of how this thought affects me in the present?" before meditation or journaling. See what arises. Allow this inquiry to expand your self-awareness. Then, proceed to the next exercise to release the thoughtform.

EXERCISE: Clearing Thoughtforms with Healing Energy

Find a quiet place to sit where you won't be disturbed, get comfy, and close your eyes. Bring your focus to your breath, noticing the inhales and the exhales for a few cycles. Begin to slow your breathing down by gradually lengthening each inhale and exhale, feeling yourself becoming more and more relaxed.

In your mind's eye, conjure up an image of your body. You might see an outline or a more three-dimensional visual; allow whatever comes naturally to arise. Say to yourself three times, "I now perceive my aura and any harmful thoughtforms." Slowly scan the image, looking for thoughtforms, which often appear as dense or tangled, darker-colored or gray blobs of energy, floating in or attached to your aura. You can also run your hands over your body if you're more tactile, setting the intention to locate any harmful thoughtforms.

When you locate one, see yourself grasping it with both hands and allow healing energy to flow into the thoughtform, filling every fiber of it with white light. Push the dissolving thoughtform out of your aura, where it will continue dissolving completely. If any holes or tears have appeared in your aura, seal them with healing energy by placing your hands over the damaged area and allowing the energy to flow. Repeat this process with any additional thoughtforms, and then release the image of your body and aura and slowly return to a normal state of consciousness.

Fourth Auric Layer

The fourth auric layer is associated with the heart chakra (the energetic center of love of self and others, relationships, and interconnectedness), and it serves as an intermediary between the lower and upper chakras. Brennan describes it as "the transforming crucible through which ... the

• • • • • • •

spiritual energy must pass through the fire of the heart to be transformed into the lower physical energies" and vice versa.[4] We might think of this layer and of the associated heart chakra as a communication tower, relaying information and transmitting influence between the other auric layers and energetic centers, as well as with the environment.

Because the fourth layer acts as a relay between the upper and lower energy centers, we will find it easier to translate energies from the upper chakras, such as the desires of our higher self and guidance from Source, into our mental, emotional, and physical experience when this layer is healthy. This has interesting parallels to research conducted by the HeartMath Institute, particularly in regard to coherence. Without coherence, the workings of the body would be an ineffective jumble of activity performed by independent parts, rather than the synchronized, efficient processes of a living system, and the heart appears to play an important role in establishing this coherence: "when functioning in a coherent mode, the heart pulls other biological oscillators into synchronization with its rhythms, thus leading to entrainment of these systems."[5]

The fourth auric layer is sometimes referred to as the astral body, and as such, it is our interface with a plane of existence known as the astral plane, which contains blueprints of all potential shapes and forms, whether or not they are currently manifested in physical reality. This again has interesting parallels with the physics conception of an energetic field from which matter arises, and this in turn aligns with Brennan's view that the fourth layer acts as an interface between physical and non-physical reality. When people talk of astral travel, it is thought that this energetic body is the part of us that can travel on the astral plane, connecting us to beings and realms beyond the constraints of time and space.

This theme of connection brings us to the topic of energy cords, which are energetic conduits tethering you to other people, places, things, or entities. Most energetic practitioners maintain that cords are not an optimal way of interacting with others and the world, because they bind us to people, places, or situations, making it more difficult to create and maintain the boundaries that support healthy connection. Cords between people allow for energy draining or "dumping," and cords to places or events can drain our energy through repetitive thoughts of the past, preventing us from fully living in the present.

The most common resistance I've encountered around cord clearing is the fear that by dissolving cords, the connection with whoever or whatever is on the other end will be lost. And yes, sometimes that does happen, but more often, my experience is that I am able to relate more fully and authentically when I am no longer bound up with cords that are siphoning off my energy or allowing someone else's energy to flow, unmitigated, into my system, both of which can

---

4. Brennan, *Hands of Light*, 51.

5. "Chapter 4: Coherence," HeartMath Institute, accessed March 07, 2019, https://www.heartmath.org/research/science-of-the-heart/coherence/.

• • • • • • • •

lead to all manner of ickiness, including resentment and codependence. Think of it like being in relationship with someone because you both genuinely want to be versus forging a connection because you're both chained to the same rock. A bit melodramatic, perhaps, but truly, the feel of a connection grounded in mutual love and respect is worlds apart from the feel of a tangled web of cords.

EXERCISE: Clearing Cords

Find a quiet place to sit where you won't be disturbed, get comfy, and close your eyes. Bring your focus to your breath, noticing the inhales and the exhales for a few cycles. Begin to slow your breathing down by gradually lengthening each inhale and exhale, feeling yourself becoming more and more relaxed.

In your mind's eye, conjure up an image of your body. You might see an outline or a more three-dimensional visual; allow whatever comes naturally to arise. Say to yourself three times, "I now perceive my aura and any energetic cords." Slowly scan the image, looking for cords, tendrils, ropes, or beams of energy running through or out of your aura. You can also run your hands over your body if you're more tactile, setting the intention to locate cords.

When you identify a cord, see yourself grasping it with both hands. You will sometimes receive information regarding who or what the cord is attached to, but this isn't necessary to complete the healing. Pay attention to where in your energy field the cord is attached, as you will often see connections with your health, physically, emotionally, mentally, or spiritually. For example, a cord attached to the heart can generate issues related to love, intimacy, and relationships. While grasping the cord, allow healing energy to flow through your hands, filling the cord with light, dissolving its attachments so you can gently and completely pull the cord out. Push the cord out of your aura and see white light traveling to the other end of the cord, dissolving it as it does so with love and light. Repeat this process with any additional cords.

When the process feels complete, allow healing energy to wash over your entire aura, sealing any holes or damaged areas with light. Let this energy fill the interior of your energetic shells, permeating every fiber of your energy field. Let the image slowly fade from your mind's eye, and when you're ready, open your eyes.

Fifth Auric Layer

The fifth auric layer is associated with the throat chakra and our etheric template. It is similar to the first auric layer but differs in that it is the perfect blueprint from which the first layer derives its form. I see this perfect blueprint as a set of downloaded operating instructions, so to speak, from our higher self. In my experience, the more we consciously seek to commune with sources of higher guidance, the more often this blueprint is refreshed, like updating your phone software to ensure that things run smoothly.

· · · · · · ·

In quantum theory, there is an idea called the "many worlds interpretation," which claims that anything that is possible already exists in some plane of reality.[6] In other words, if something isn't impossible, then it's already real, and the possibilities that we're not seeing in our immediate reality may be unfolding in parallel universes. If that's the case, could it be possible to access these alternate realities via the astral plane to glean information from the paths not taken by our current self? Many energy practitioners believe that this is, indeed, possible and that the fifth auric layer is a primary conduit for accessing this information.

This auric level is most responsive to sound healing, which is apropos given the energetic theme here of communication.[7] While there are countless ways to incorporate sound into your healing practices (see chapter 21), in the following exercise we'll use a simple yet powerful chant to cleanse and balance your energy field.

EXERCISE: Healing with Sacred Chants

Sit or stand in a comfortable position, grounding through all points of the feet if standing, lifting up through the spine and crown of the head. Close your eyes and focus on your breath, taking as much time as you need to bring yourself into a state of calm and centeredness. Chant the word *om* three times, pausing when done to sense where you feel the vibrations in your body and energy field.

The meaning of om is complex, but we can loosely translate it as the union or oneness underlying all things. By chanting the mantra, you can unite all aspects of your being into a coherent whole, while also enhancing your connection to the world around you. I like to use chanting whenever I need an energetic reset, and with continued use, you will likely be drawn to use different mantras for specific situations. Follow your intuition!

Sixth Auric Layer

The sixth auric layer is associated with the third eye or brow chakra, which is related to our ability to see things clearly, both in the physical world and in a spiritual or psychic sense. Many healers perceive the sixth layer as being composed entirely of light, and it has been associated with the halo often depicted around holy people, such as saints. When this layer is connected to and in harmony with the heart center, we rest in the knowing that we are one with the divine, giving rise to unconditional love, both for ourselves and others, and when we make decisions from this place, our life becomes an expression of this love.

The connection between clear seeing and unconditional love reminds me of an experience I had a few years ago while driving. As I pulled up to a stoplight, I glanced over at the woman in

6. George Musser, *The Complete Idiot's Guide to String Theory* (New York: Alpha, 2008), 194.
7. Brennan, *Hands of Light*, 52.

the car beside me, and quite suddenly, it was as if a light switch had been flipped, illuminating her from within. I could still see her physical form, but it was transparent to reveal light layers within and overlays of light webs extending from her body. A young man jogged past me on the crosswalk and he, too, was a radiant being of light. I felt overcome with love, humbled by the stunning beauty of everyone and everything around me. The visuals faded within a couple of minutes, but ever since, when working with clients, particularly during energy work or tarot readings, or in moments of heartfelt connection with friends and loved ones, I will often see glimpses of what I call their "radiance," and it's always accompanied by an intense feeling of love. I believe that when we are able to truly see each other, without the layers of persona and life baggage obscuring our soul's light, we can't help but feel unconditional love.

Tapping into this light-love energy can help us see deeper layers of truth, beyond the obfuscations of the ego, which makes it a wonderful tool to use when we need guidance, a process outlined in the following exercise.

EXERCISE: Enhancing Clear Sight

Find a quiet place to sit where you won't be disturbed, get comfy, and close your eyes. Bring your focus to your breath, noticing the inhales and the exhales for a few cycles. Begin to slow your breathing down by gradually lengthening each inhale and exhale, feeling yourself becoming more and more relaxed.

Bring your focus to your third eye. Feel energy concentrating in this area; you might experience this as a hum or slight pressure between your brows. Now, imagine yourself looking out through your third eye, like a picture window. Notice if the window is hazy or obscured in any way, perhaps by curtains or other objects. Get curious about what you find. For example, if there are curtains, look at them more closely. Is there a pattern to the fabric, and if so, what does it remind you of? Ask any questions you might have, such as "What do these wooden boards over my window represent?"

When you're finished exploring, see yourself holding a white cloth in your mind's eye, and bring healing energy down through your crown and into the cloth, filling it with bright, white light. Use this cloth to wipe your third eye window clear, making multiple passes if needed. When this process feels complete, let the cloth dissolve into light, and look out of your window once more.

If there's a situation in your life that you wish to see more clearly, ask any questions you have and see what insights arise with your newly cleared sight. When done, let the images fade in your mind and slowly come back to a normal state of consciousness.

· · · · · · · ·

Seventh Auric Layer

The seventh auric layer is also known as the causal body or ketheric template and contains all the inner auric layers in its durable sheath, while providing a grid for the physical body, chakras, and energy channels. It contains bands of colored light, each corresponding to different past lives, and connects us with Spirit.

When healthy flow and energetic dialogue between this and the inner layers is obstructed, we will feel a dissonance, because the various levels of our being aren't able to exchange energy freely with Source. Without this exchange, we may experience any manner of challenges, such as lack of purpose, energy, health, or creativity. By reopening the dialogue with Source, we will be guided to the changes and shifts necessary to regain our sense of purpose, energy, and so forth. In my experience, this healing is most effective when we step up to cocreate with Source, rather than passively waiting for Source to "fix" us. You might be given insights into action steps that need to be taken, such as having an honest conversation with someone in your life, looking for a new job, or starting a daily walking practice. Source works *through* us, and our active participation is required. That said, there is a distinction between taking purposeful action as we partner with Source versus actions rooted in fear and the false belief that everything rests on our shoulders. The latter usually has an urgency to it and anxiety over what might happen if we don't take action. Source-supported action, on the other hand, is inspired by genuine desire and curiosity. When you're acting from fear and a desire to control, you will often feel depleted, drained, or confused, whereas Source-led action, while sometimes requiring hard work, gives back more than it asks of us; you'll feel a sense of satisfaction and nourishment during and after engaging in these activities.

Learning how to discern between the two allows you to do self-inventory to determine whether the majority of your recent actions stem from a place of fear or Source. Make a list of the decisions and actions you've taken over the past three days. Which actions carry a mark of urgency, fear, or a need to control the outcome, and which were motivated by a genuine desire and a curiosity of the results? If you find yourself taking more fear-based actions, use the following exercise to open to a healthier flow between Source and your entire energy body.

Exercise: Connecting to Source

Find a quiet place to sit where you won't be disturbed, get comfy, and close your eyes. Bring your focus to your breath, noticing the inhales and the exhales for a few cycles. Begin to slow your breathing down by gradually lengthening each inhale and exhale, feeling yourself becoming more and more relaxed.

Envision a stream of healing energy, descending down into your crown, washing over the entire outer layer of your aura, including down your back and underneath your body, coating it with pure, white light. Bring your awareness back to your crown and feel this energy penetrate to the next layer of your aura, once again washing over the entire surface with a pure, white light. Return your awareness once more to the crown area, and feel as healing energy penetrates into the next auric layer, the fifth layer. Continue this process, letting each auric layer fully soak in the energy before moving progressively inward. When you reach the innermost layer, allow healing energy to permeate your entire body. Breathe here for a few cycles.

Expand your awareness to encompass your entire energy field, glowing with pure, white light. Sense how the energy moves throughout the various layers of your aura, creating dynamic flows and webs of communication. If there are any areas that feel resistant to this flow, bring your awareness here and allow the healing energy to gently dissolve any obstructions. Pay attention to any insights that arise, perhaps indicating choices or changes that need to be made in your day-to-day life. When the process feels complete, allow the imagery to fade, return your awareness to your breath, and come back to a normal state of consciousness.

Koshas

A parallel to the aura in yogic tradition are the five *koshas*, or energy sheaths.

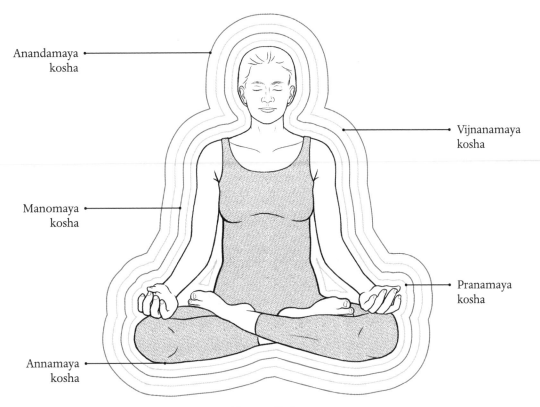

Figure 2: Koshas

• • • • • • •

The First Sheath (Annamaya Kosha)

The koshas start with the physical sheath, or *annamaya kosha*. This layer is connected to the element of earth, and we nourish it, in part, by taking good care of our bodies: eating healthy food, getting plenty of movement and restful sleep, managing stress levels, allowing ourselves healthy sexual expression, and enjoying a wide range of physical experiences, from the feel of a supersoft sweater to an impromptu dance in the rain.

It is at this level that we manifest the content from the other layers of our being; for example, it is here that our thoughts and emotions crystallize into physical form. When working with the annamaya kosha, it's helpful to ask ourselves, "What do I want to embody?" Are your thoughts, actions, and other expressions an accurate embodiment of these desired qualities, or are you devoting thoughts, time, and energy to things that aren't in alignment with your goals? If you sense a mismatch, through this layer you can introduce more harmony by returning to your physical self-care practices. After all, it's much harder to live in alignment with our highest self when we're eating under-nourishing foods, denying our bodies healthy movement, and falling short on sleep. I think of this layer of experience as a foundation, the ground on which my other levels of experience rest, so when life feels out of whack, come back to the basics and treat your body like the sacred temple that it is.

The Second Sheath (Pranamaya Kosha)

The second sheath is the energetic layer, or *pranamaya kosha*, and it is composed of *prana*, or vital life force. Without this energy, we wouldn't be alive, which explains prana's connection to the breath, another indispensable thing for us living beings. Thus, working with the breath is a primary way of working with the pranamaya kosha, and this can be as simple as bringing your awareness to your inhales and exhales, something that we rarely do throughout the course of a busy day. By focusing on the breath, we can activate the parasympathetic nervous system, the "rest and digest" complement to the sympathetic nervous system's "fight, flight, or freeze" mode.

Another word for the *inhale* is *inspiration*, and this certainly ties in with the pranamaya kosha's connection to our vital life force. To keep this force strong and flowing, we must devote time and energy to practices that inspire us. If we're constantly doing things that leave us feeling blah and drained, it should come as no surprise that our life force is dampened. Too often, we do things we love only after we've checked everything off the to-do list, but in order to have energy to carry out the tasks of daily living, we must stoke our inner fires by doing what we love on a regular basis. Pencil in time every day to focus on something that inspires you, and treat this like the non-negotiable wellness practice that it truly is.

The following breathing technique is called *nadi shodhana*, or alternate nostril breathing, and this practice never fails to leave me feeling clearer, calmer, and more focused. It's great for bal-

• • • • • • • •

ancing the left and right hemispheres of the brain, as well as harmonizing our internal polar energies (energies like active and receptive, doing and being, etc.).

EXERCISE: Alternate Nostril Breathing (Nadi Shodhana)

Find a comfortable seated position, and begin with a few rounds of calming inhales and exhales. Do this until you find a steady, smooth rhythm to your breath. With the thumb of your right hand, gently but firmly seal your right nostril closed and exhale through the left nostril. With the thumb of your right hand, gently but firmly seal your right nostril closed and take a deep breath in through the left nostril. Pause at the top of the inhale.

With your pinky or ring finger, seal your left nostril, exhaling out through the right. Pause, then breathe in deeply through the right nostril. Pause at the top of the inhale, then open the left nostril and seal the right nostril once more with the thumb. Exhale through the left nostril, ending where you began.

This is one round of nadi shodhana, and you can repeat for a few rounds or up to ten to fifteen minutes. If you feel light-headed or otherwise unwell, stop and return to normal breathing. This is a great practice to do in the morning or before bed to refresh and reset your energy through the breath.

The Third Sheath (Manomaya Kosha)

The third sheath is the emotional layer, or *manomaya kosha*, which regulates and expresses our emotional energy. We've already talked about the flow of emotions in regard to the second auric layer; here, let's explore some of the ways the emotions influence our physical form. For starters, we experience our emotions through the vehicle of the body, perhaps as a fluttering in the belly, heat in the face, or a sudden wave of gripping cold. The work of researchers like Dr. Candace Pert has shown the emotions to be an interface between the mind and the body; thus, by working with our emotions, we can influence the physical.[8]

As a bodyworker, I am also fascinated by the parallels between chronic emotional states and physical patterns in the body, one of the most common being a state of depression or fatigue with a "sunken chest" and rounded shoulders. In a study by social psychologists Dana Carney, Amy Cuddy, and Andy Yap, participants were given a specific pose to adopt for a few minutes, such as slumping in a chair with arms folded across the chest or hands on hips with chest held high. Saliva samples were taken before and after the poses to look at levels of hormones such as testosterone and cortisol. The study showed that physical postures can change the cocktail of

8. Candace B. Pert, *Molecules of Emotion* (New York: Scribner, 2003).

· · · · · · · ·

chemicals coursing through your system, dramatically affecting how you think about yourself and how you interact with the world.[9]

While we're likely accustomed to emotions affecting how we feel in our body (racing heart, flushed cheeks, etc.), in the following exercise, you'll reverse this process by using various physical postures to affect your emotional state.

EXERCISE: Emotional Healing through the Body (Manomaya Kosha)

Cultivating safety and calm: Start out in a kneeling position on the floor, using a yoga mat, blanket, or any necessary padding. Open your knees to a comfortable distance, such that as you fold your upper body forward, your chest can rest in between the legs. If this pose isn't accessible, you can fold forward onto a chair, resting your head on your arms, or onto a pillow or bolster. Close your eyes and feel the cozy containment of this pose as you let your inhales and exhales deepen and lengthen.

Cultivating love and possibility: In a comfortable seated or standing position, start by placing your palms over your heart. Close your eyes and focus on the sensation of the breath and your heartbeat. Tap into a sense of gratitude for your miraculous body, for your beating heart and life-giving breath. When you feel ready, open your arms up and out, tilt your face to the sky, and broaden your heart space, beaming out love and opening to possibilities.

The Fourth Sheath (Vijnanamaya Kosha)

The fourth sheath is known as the knowledge or wisdom layer, or *vijnanamaya kosha*, and it governs our ability to discern. This layer has been connected with the inner witness, that part within us that can observe our internal states without judgment or attachment, thereby increasing our self-awareness and our ability to respond mindfully instead of reacting. It's difficult to tap into this layer if we're constantly immersed in distractions, like buzzing phones and mental chatter, so practices like meditation, solo walks in nature, and soothing baths can help us carve out the space and relative silence to connect with the vijnanamaya kosha.

The vijnanamaya kosha is a blend of the intellect and the five senses, so one way to work with this layer is by engaging all those faculties with awareness. The following exercise draws on ritual elements from my practice, and you're free to adapt it as needed to make use of whatever tools you have on hand. The important part is to engage each of the five senses: touch, taste, sight, hearing, and smell.

---

9. Dana R. Carney, Amy J. C. Cuddy, and Andy J. Yap, "Power Posing: Brief Nonverbal Displays Affect Neuroendocrine Levels and Risk Tolerance," *Psychological Science* 21, no. 10 (September 2010): 1363–68, doi:10.1177/0956797610383437.

EXERCISE: Cultivating Awareness through Sensory Delight (Vijnanamaya Kosha)

For this exercise, you will be taking a hot bath, and you'll need a few supplies:

- Dried lavender or scented bath sachet of your choice
- Candle (scented, if desired)
- Salt
- Good-quality chocolate or other favorite food

Once in the bath, take a few minutes to feel the sensations of the hot water on your skin; perhaps closing your eyes to heighten your feeling sense and listening to the sound of the water's movements. Add the dried lavender or sachet to the water, and breathe in the scent, crushing the herbs a bit to engage the sense of touch and smell. Light the candle and gaze gently at the flame, focusing on the sense of sight (and smell, if it's scented). Look at the water, the floating herbs, and your body with the same gentle gaze, taking in any details. Take a handful of salt and gently exfoliate your skin, really tuning your awareness to the sensations and sounds. Finally, take a piece of chocolate and, before eating it, really take in the details: look at it, noticing the sheen or color; smell it; feel the texture. Then, take a bite, noticing the sounds, and absorb every nuance of the flavor and texture as the chocolate melts in your mouth. Give yourself plenty of time to engage all your senses, treating each movement, each scent, each visual, sound, and taste as a fascinating universe unto itself.

When you feel ready, pause and notice the state of calm and centeredness you have cultivated simply by engaging your senses with mindful attention. In this space, if you are seeking guidance on any area of your life, ask a question to your higher self. Stay in this state of calm openness and allow any insights to arise. Know that you can tap into this state anytime you wish by slowing down and using the five senses to bring you powerfully into a state of presence and awareness.

The Fifth Sheath (Anandamaya Kosha)

The fifth sheath is known as the blissful layer or *anandamaya kosha*, and it is here where the experiences and awareness of the other layers weave together to help us remember our True Self: the self that is eternal, divine, and resonating with the energy of bliss. In my book *Living Reiki: Heal Yourself and Transform Your Life*, I outline a seven-step process of transformation to help you remember this True Self, even amidst the busyness of day-to-day life. Here, we'll focus on one of the most powerful shortcuts to bliss: helping someone else feel awesome. When we're caught up in the drama of our own life, it's easy to lose perspective on what really matters. We're so focused on our irritating boss that we can't connect to a sense of gratitude for our work. We're frustrated by the number on the scale, and we forget how amazing our body is. And so on it goes. By stepping outside the story in our head and making a positive impact on someone else's day, we reconnect with a sense of connection and the energy of gratitude.

What's one thing you can do today to bring a smile to someone else's face? Some ideas include the following:

• Surprising your coworker with a cup of her favorite tea

• Holding a door open for someone with a smile and a hello

• Asking the checkout clerk how their day is going and really listening

• Volunteering for the local soup kitchen, nursing home, trash pick-up team, etc.

• Leaving a little gift on a park bench or other public space with a cheery note

Morphogenetic Fields

Biologist and researcher Dr. Rupert Sheldrake has developed a theory describing another kind of field relevant to living organisms: morphogenetic fields. Sheldrake asserts that genetic information alone is insufficient to direct development, as evidenced by, for example, the fact that arms and legs contain the same genes, yet the body somehow "knows" that an arm must have a different form than a leg. In the 1980s, the discovery of homeobox genes, which were shown to determine the location of body parts within a developing embryo, could have been the missing puzzle piece, but when further research showed that the homeobox genes of widely different animals were nearly identical, it was again underscored that genes alone cannot account for the amazing differences between living organisms and the heritability of these "operating instructions." Sheldrake proposed that in conjunction with genes, morphogenetic fields, specific to each individual species, store this added layer of information, similar to C. G. Jung's conception of a collective unconscious that stores and transmits cultural information.

Like genetic information, morphogenetic transmissions can range from helpful to harmful. By working at this level of our energy field, we can effect healing surrounding faulty beliefs and ideas, physical health issues, emotional patterns, and spiritual issues that we have inherited from family and the human community as a whole. The following exercise uses healing energy to dissolve harmful programming in your morphogenetic field.

EXERCISE: Morphogenetic Healing with Energy Healing (Anandamaya Kosha)

Find a comfortable place to sit where you won't be disturbed. Close your eyes, and bring your awareness to your breath, gradually lengthening the inhales and exhales. Continue this pattern until you feel calm, centered, and focused.

In your mind's eye, see your body. It might appear as an outline or a more three-dimensional shape; you might also see various layers of your aura. Say to yourself three times, "I am perceiving my morphogenetic field," and wait for the image to shift. For me, the field appears as a rather dense web of light, permeating and extending outward from my body in all directions. Slowly scan the web in the vicinity of your body, looking for any areas that appear different in color, density, or vibration. Focus your awareness on one of these areas, and ask, "How does this affect my well-being?" You might receive insights in the form of images, memories and thoughts, physical sensations, and so on. Ask any clarifying questions as needed.

When the exploration process feels complete, place your physical or energetic hands on this area and allow healing energy to flow through your crown and out through your palms, saturating the web with pure, white light. For me, the area will change in color, density, and so on, and I receive an intuitive sense of restored balance and harmony. Repeat this process for any other areas that appear. When done, allow the images to fade, and gently bring yourself back to a normal state of consciousness.

Now that you have an understanding of the fields of energy surrounding and interpenetrating your body, it's time to look at the energetic channels that distribute energy within these fields. A proper flow of energy is vital for health on all levels of your being, and understanding these energetic pathways, the subject of the next chapter, will help you maintain this dynamic energy flow.

CHAPTER 2

✦

Energy Channels

To carry out its functions, the energy within and around your body must be able to travel where it is needed, and one way people have perceived and measured these energy flows is as a network of lines or channels, like energetic rivers and streams. These lines go by different names, such as the *meridians* in Traditional Chinese Medicine (TCM), *nadis* in Hindu spiritual science, and *sen* in traditional Thai medicine. In this chapter, we will be focusing on the meridians and nadis, but know that there are other valid approaches to perceiving how energy travels throughout the human system.

In physics, in order for energy to flow there must be a difference between one point or area and another. For example, heat will flow from warm areas to cooler ones, and electrically charged particles will flow from areas of high potential to areas of low potential, creating an electric current in the process. In addition, particles typically cannot move through all materials willy nilly; there are conditions that limit the path and quality of this flow. Again using electricity as an example, the material in question must be a good conductor in order for an electric current to be established. You won't have the same effect using a piece of rubber as you would a copper wire. So, too, in the body, there are distinct pathways through which different types of energy are conducted more easily, and these are the meridians (or nadis, sen, etc.).

If you look at diagrams for meridians and other energy lines in books, it's easy to walk away with the impression that everyone's meridians are exactly the same, and indeed, it does appear that there is a great deal of consistency from person to person. However, just like with our flesh and bone anatomy, differences can and do exist, and beyond congenital variations, we can also alter our physical and energetic makeup based on usage patterns. When working with the meridians, energy medicine looks at how energy is flowing through these channels, and practitioners use

• • • • • • • •

abnormalities in this flow to pinpoint underlying issues. Reestablishing healthy flow, which involves balancing over- and under-energized areas, can support healing on many levels.

Meridians

Meridian therapy has a long history in Chinese culture. The Chinese word for meridian is *ching-lo*. It is sometimes written *jing-luo*, and it can be translated as "to pass through" (*ching*) and "to connect" (*lo*).[10] The meridians allow for the passage of *chi*, also spelled *qi*, or vital life force energy, which is synonymous with *ki* in Japanese healing. Along the meridians are precisely mapped points or entryways to the meridians. These are commonly called acupuncture or acupressure points and are the site for needling or manual pressure during a meridian-based treatment.

There are twelve major meridians that create a network of energy channels throughout the body, supplying and removing chi to and from the various organ systems. The meridians are as follows:

- Lung (yin, metal)
- Large intestine (yang, metal)
- Stomach (yang, earth)
- Spleen (yin, earth)
- Heart (yin, fire)
- Small intestine (yang, fire)
- Urinary bladder (yang, water)
- Kidney (yin, water)
- Pericardium (yin, fire)
- Triple warmer (yang, fire)
- Gallbladder (yang, wood)
- Liver (yin, wood)

10. Dale, *The Subtle Body*, 161.

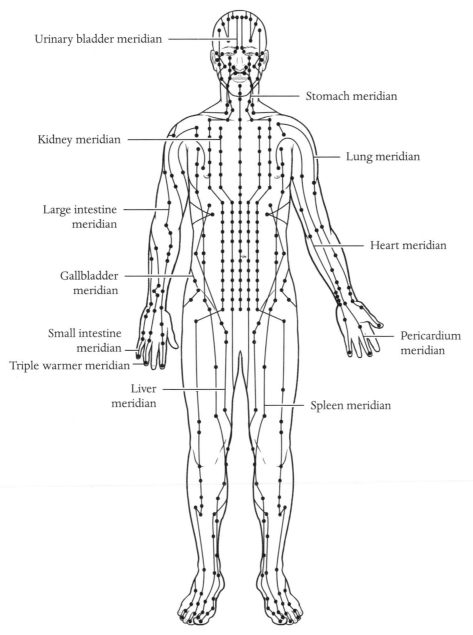

Urinary bladder meridian

Kidney meridian

Large intestine
meridian

Gallbladder
meridian

Small intestine
meridian

Triple warmer meridian

Liver
meridian

Stomach meridian

Lung meridian

Heart meridian

Pericardium
meridian

Spleen meridian

Figure 3: The 12 meridians, anterior view

Each meridian is associated with the energetic quality of yin or yang (as well as one of the five elements, which we'll discuss below). Yin-yang theory states that there are two basic forces: the yang force is associated with qualities like excitatory, dynamic, and stimulating and is traditionally described as male, while yin is inhibiting, static, calming, and traditionally described as female. These dual energies are like two sides of the same coin. Yin becomes yang and yang becomes yin in a dynamic flow, and the union of the two creates a supreme energy that gave rise to the universe and continues to flow through all things. This is strikingly similar to our discussion earlier in the chapter, in which we saw that an energy current is generated by a difference in state between one point or area and another. It's possible that the polarity of yin and yang establishes the same sort of energetic differential on a subtle level, giving rise to a current or flow of energy throughout the body via the meridians. Balance between these two forces does not imply a constant equilibrium but rather dynamic checks and balances between doing and being, stimulation and inhibition, and so on. Sometimes life calls for more yin energy lest we become burnt out and depleted, while other times we need a little more get-up-and-go to prevent us from spending all our time binging Netflix.

In addition to the exchange between yin and yang, there is also a dynamic flow between the elements of earth, metal, fire, water, and wood, each of which corresponds to a season: late summer, autumn, winter, spring, and summer, respectively. Each season and element give way to the next in an unceasing cycle, and the elements are seen to interact either by generating and increasing one another or by destroying and inhibiting. For example, wood increases or feeds fire, while water quenches fire. These relationships can be used to reintroduce balance: inhibiting elements can be used to decrease an overabundance of another element, while generative elements can increase the potency of weaker elements within the system. There is a complex mapping of symptoms and qualities associated with each element that further enables practitioners to diagnose and treat imbalances, such as anger and irritability suggesting an excess of wood, or cold feet indicating a water issue.

The elements are also paired with different atmospheric states, and different organ systems prefer a particular state (similar to, in astrology, a planet being in an exalted, or more favorable or powerful, state when it enters a particular sign). These atmospheric states vary somewhat by source, but they are generally listed as wind, cold, heat, wetness, and dryness, with heat sometimes being parsed into heat and summer heat.[11] The organ associations are as follows:

Wind: Liver and gallbladder

Cold: Kidney and urinary bladder

---

11. Subhuti Dharmananda, "The Six Qi and Six Yi," November 2010, http://www.itmonline.org/articles /six_qi_six_yin/six_qi.htm.

Heat: Heart and small intestine

Wetness: Spleen and stomach

Dryness: Lung and large intestine

As chi courses throughout the body's meridians, it does so in a regular, twenty-four-hour pattern, and this, too, can aid in diagnosis of imbalances. While I studied the five-phase theory of TCM in massage school, this was one of the topics that really hit home. I was astounded to see that the hour at which I had been routinely and inexplicably waking up every night corresponded to the organ system (and corresponding emotions) with which I was experiencing health issues!

Lungs: 3 am to 5 am

Large Intestine: 5 am to 7 am

Stomach: 7 am to 9 am

Spleen: 9 am to 11 am

Heart: 11 am to 1 pm

Small Intestine: 1 pm to 3 pm

Bladder: 3 pm to 5 pm

Kidneys: 5 pm to 7 pm

Pericardium: 7 pm to 9 pm

Triple Warmer: 9 pm to 11 pm

Gallbladder: 11 pm to 1 am

Liver: 1 am to 3 am

In addition to the twelve major meridians, there are the eight extraordinary channels or vessels:

- The Du
- The Ren
- The Dai
- The Chong
- The Yin Chiao
- The Yang Chiao
- The Yin Wei
- The Wang Wei

Figure 4: Body clock

In contrast to the twelve major meridians, the vessels do not correspond to specific organ systems and are instead responsible for connecting the major meridians to the organs and other parts of the body, helping supply, store, and drain chi as needed. Two of these vessels, the Governor or Governing Vessel, which runs up the back of the body, and the Conception Vessel, which runs up the front of the body, are considered by some practitioners to be part of the main meridian system, giving a total of fourteen meridians.

Interesting research has been conducted on the meridians and acupuncture points in an attempt to see whether they can be mapped using scientific tools and to reveal how acupuncture and acupressure treatments facilitate healing. In a study by Darras, Albarède, and de Vernejoul, radioactive tracers were injected into the body at acupuncture points, and a device known as a scintillation camera, which detects and records radiation emissions, was used to map the migration patterns. These pathways were shown to correspond with the meridians.[12]

12. J. C. Darras, P. Albarède, and P. de Vernejoul, "Nuclear Medicine Investigation of Transmission of Acupuncture Information," *Acupuncture in Medicine* 11, no. 1 (1993), 22–28, doi:10.1136/aim.11.1.22.

• • • • • • • •

Another study demonstrated a higher concentration of cell gap junctions, which are connections between cells that allow for the passage of various molecules, ions, and electric charge, along the meridians, suggesting higher levels of communication via these pathways. Other researchers have found a close relationship between the locations of peripheral nerves and meridians, and yet another study has demonstrated that the electric potential measured at acupoints was significantly different from surrounding areas, with lower electrical charge in ill patients.[13] These data suggest that there are veritable structures related to the meridians, but there is still much to be learned, with some facets perhaps forever remaining beyond the bounds of science to reveal.

Nadis

The word *nadi* can be translated as "stream," and like the meridians, they are a network of channels for subtle energies. The first written record of the nadis comes from the Upanishads written in the seventh to eighth centuries BCE, which mentioned 72,000 nadis. Other sources vary from 1,000 to 350,000 nadis. According to tantric yoga, there are two classifications of nadis: subtle (which is further subdivided into *manas*, mind or mental energy, and *chitta*, feeling energy) and gross. The subtle nadis are invisible channels for energy, while the gross channels are visible pathways, such as nerves and lymphatic vessels, but both types of channels can transport *prana,* or life force.

There are three primary nadis, which are integral to kundalini practice, and they are the *sushumna*, or central channel, the *ida*, and the *pingala*. The sushumna travels up the spinal column, along which the primary chakras are arranged. The chakras are energetic centers tasked with receiving and processing energy, which is then transmitted to the rest of the body and energy field via the nadis. The sushumna begins at the base chakra, *muladhara*, and passes through the crown chakra, or *sahasrara*, where it splits into two streams: one that passes through the brow chakra (*ajna*) before reaching the seat of consciousness (*Brahma Randhra*) between the left and right brain hemispheres, and one that passes behind the skull before entering the seat of consciousness. The sushumna is composed of different nadis, layered like wrappings around an electrical wire. The outermost layer is the sushumna, considered to exist outside of time, and it is wrapped around the *vajrini*, associated with the sun. The vajrini, in turn, is wrapped around the innermost layer, the *chitrini*, which is associated with the moon. The trilayered sushumna is responsible for delivering prana to the chakras and other subtle energy structures (in cooperation with the entire network of nadis), and it partners with the ida and pingala to activate the rising of kundalini (more on that follows).

13. Andrew C. Ahn et al., "Electrical Properties of Acupuncture Points and Meridians: A Systematic Review," *Bioelectromagnetics* 29, no. 4 (May 2008): 245–56, doi:10.1002/bem.20403.

· · · · · · · ·

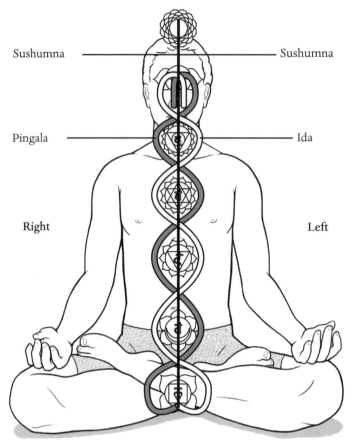

Sushumna ———— Sushumna

Pingala ———— Ida

Right   Left

Figure 5: Nadis

The ida nadi is seen as primarily feminine and associated with the moon, and it is said to be dominant from the new to the full moon. It has calming, peaceful, magnetic, and nurturing qualities and constitutes the left channel of the nadi system. As with TCM's yin-yang theory, the ida is partnered with the pingala on the right, which is associated with masculine energy and the sun, and the qualities of vitality, power, mental alertness, and taking action. It is dominant from the full to the new moon. The ida and pingala are often depicted as coiling around the central channel of the sushumna, mirroring the image of the caduceus, the medical symbol of the staff entwined by two snakes.

Working with the sushumna, ida, and pingala, kundalini practitioners seek to awaken a type of energy known as kundalini energy (*kundalini* translates to "she who is coiled"[14]), which rests in a dormant state at the base of the spine, often depicted as a coiled serpent. Using the breath and trained will, this energy can be guided upward, through the ida and pingala channels, flow-

14. James Mallinson and Mark Singleton, trans. and eds., *Roots of Yoga* (London: Penguin Books, 2017), 178.

• • • • • • • •

ing through and stimulating the chakras as it rises, reaching the brow (ajna) chakra, where the energy streams join the sushumna and crown chakra, initiating what has been described by practitioners as a state of enlightenment or liberation (*moksha*), which can include mental and psychic clarity, physical healing and renewed vitality, and the awakening of *siddhis*, which are considered to be supernatural or otherwise elevated powers. It is said that without proper training, this awakening can be dangerous, triggering mental or psychic instability, while others claim that rather than causing harm, the experience will simply be short-lived and difficult to translate into lasting change without sufficient preparation.

In addition to the three primary nadis, there are additional pathways that aid in the transmission of energy throughout the body. As with other systems, health is seen to arise from a healthy flow of energy throughout these channels, and various tools have been developed to aid in this balancing process, such as the physical postures of yoga (*asanas*) and breath control (*pranayama*).

While systems for mapping energetic channels throughout the body vary to some degree, what is agreed upon is the need for energy to flow without obstructions, in the right amounts, and to the proper locations to support health. In the next chapter, we'll explore one more feature of our energetic anatomy: energy bodies, also known as chakras, that lie along the various channels and are responsible for processing energy both from the external environment and from within.

CHAPTER 3

❧

Energy Bodies

We've covered energy fields and channels in previous chapters; now it's time to talk about energy bodies, another important facet of our subtle anatomy. While there are numerous chakra models, we'll be using the Hindu chakra system as our main focus here, exploring the role of the system as a whole and the specific functions of the individual chakras.

Just as our physical body has organs to process substrates for use by or excretion from the body (among other tasks), our energy system needs a way to process, assimilate, and release different energies, and the chakras fill this role. The Sanskrit word *chakra* means "wheel," and many cultures and practitioners visualize the chakras as spinning wheels or vortices of energy, often with a specific color of light associated with each chakra.

Energy worker Barbara Ann Brennan perceives each chakra as a double cone-like shape with the pointed ends facing inward.[15] For the primary seven chakras, with the exception of the first (a single downward-facing cone) and seventh (a single upward-facing cone), one half of the double cone opens to the front of the body, with the other half opening to the back. Homeopath and chakra healer Ambika Wauters sees the outer lip of the cone acting as a filter, exchanging energy with our environment throughout the day. If we aren't able to express or process these energies in a healthy manner, they collect along this filter and create a congestion. The body of the cone is composed of our collective attitudes and beliefs like an etheric fabric woven from the strands of our thoughts and beliefs, and the tip of the cone contains what Wauters calls "the seeds of our destiny." She believes that we cannot access these seeds until we process and clear out the

---

15. Brennan, *Hands of Light*, 46.

limited beliefs and other negativity that obstruct our energy.[16] When we affirm our self-worth and honor our True Self, these seeds begin to germinate and our destiny takes root and flowers.

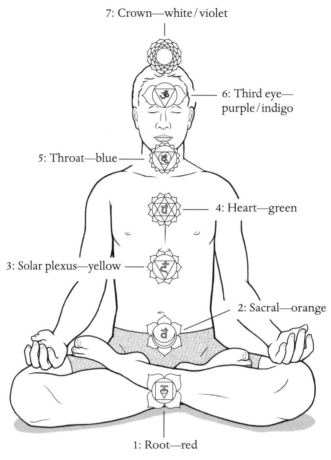

7: Crown—white / violet

6: Third eye—purple / indigo

5: Throat—blue

4: Heart—green

3: Solar plexus—yellow

2: Sacral—orange

1: Root—red

Figure 6: Chakras

Cyndi Dale associates the front side of the chakras with conscious awareness, facets of tangible, day-to-day reality, and our current lifetime, while the back side is related to the unconscious self, awareness beyond the bounds of space and time, and information from the past, including past lives.[17] While much chakra healing is focused on the more easily accessible front side, it's important to work on the back side as well, because the unconscious mind exerts a powerful influence on our everyday experience, and by working with these energies, we can shift seemingly intractable issues and long-standing patterns. The back-side energies also give us access to

16. Ambika Wauters, *The Complete Guide to Chakras: Unleash the Positive Power Within* (Hauppauge, NY: Barrons, 2010), 23.

17. Dale, *The Complete Book of Chakra Healing*, 154.

• • • • • • • •

alternative realities beyond the path we are currently walking, and opening to these energies can create change in seemingly miraculous ways that don't necessarily conform to the laws of physical reality.

Within the body of the cone, Brennan perceives small, rotating vortices, which she believes are synonymous with the lotus petals in Hindu descriptions of the chakras. These vortices spin at very high but slightly different rates, and it is this difference that generates the unique color signature of the individual chakras, while also allowing them to process different types of energy.[18] Just as our body relies on regular intake of food, water, and oxygen to survive, we also require universal energy (chi, prana, etc.). The chakras absorb this energy, processing it into forms usable by the different systems within our subtle and physical body and releasing it into the energy channels for distribution. The chakras also pull in other energies from our environment, including energies from fellow human beings. Not all these energies are beneficial or usable by our system, and their intake can contribute to imbalances, which are outlined in the individual chakra profiles below.

The chakras are said to exist primarily in the first auric layer, which is the layer most closely affiliated with the physical body, but they penetrate and can affect all layers of the aura. Energy healer Donna Eden sees the chakras spiraling down through the auric layers, with successive layers yielding different information, with the most superficial layer containing as-yet-unintegrated energy from recent events, which she describes as "more like a debris than a coherent energy."[19] By the fourth layer, she is able to perceive incidents from the person's childhood and other past experiences, with personal stories and images emerging in the fourth through sixth layers. By the seventh layer, Eden is able to access information pertaining to each chakra that was learned and assimilated in previous lifetimes. She believes that as we develop and mature, we bring more alignment and harmony to the chakric layers, which engenders a deeper sense of who we are and our life's purpose.[20]

As with the auric layers and the energy channels, each chakra is associated with a different domain of existence. For example, the root chakra is closely associated with your physical experience, and it processes energies regarding your physicality on different levels: physiologically, psychologically, and spiritually. The physiological level can include organ and endocrine gland function, with each chakra influencing a particular subset of physiological processes. On a psychological level, each chakra aids us in integrating our experiences into a cohesive self-concept and narrative, while trauma can interrupt this process. Each chakra pertains to a facet of our

18. Brennan, *Hands of Light,* 48.

19. Donna Eden and David Feinstein, *Energy Medicine: Balancing Your Body & Energies for Optimal Health, Joy & Vitality,* 10th anniv. ed. (New York: Penguin, 2008), 155.

20. Eden and Feinstein, *Energy Medicine,* 156.

maturation or psychological development process, such as survival and sexuality at the root chakra or wise perception and inner sight at the third eye chakra. And finally, on a spiritual level, the chakras help us assimilate energies from various metaphysical sources, which could include the collective unconscious and archetypes, past-life content, and communication with non-physical beings.

Imbalances in a particular area of life can often be mapped to certain chakras and vice versa, and a simple tool for diagnosing chakric health is using a pendulum to determine the movement of energy within each chakra.

EXERCISE: Pendulum Dowsing the Chakras

I've successfully used this technique with a homemade necklace made from rocks found on a hike, so you needn't get a fancy pendulum to experiment with this method. Ideally, use something with a bit of weight to it, like a small rock or even a washer from the hardware store, looped onto a cord or chain that hangs about six inches or more from your hand. I loop the chain once around my fingers so I can release any sensation of gripping or holding without dropping the pendulum.

Bring yourself into a calm, focused state with a few minutes of steady, conscious breathing. Hold the pendulum over the energy center you wish to explore, typically a few inches away from the body (I feel a sort of energetic tug or gentle "locking in" sensation when I've found the proper distance). And now for the tricky part: release expectations and clear your mind, as best you can. It might take some time, but the pendulum will begin to move, with the pattern generally becoming more pronounced and easier to determine as the movement builds. When a chakra is closed, indicated by no movement, I experience this as the energetic line "going slack," like a dropping off in sensation.

If you detect an imbalance in any of the chakras, you can use the healing exercises outlined in the individual chakra profiles below or this very simple yet effective method: visualize the imbalanced chakra glowing with brightly colored light (find color indications in the chakra profiles or follow your intuition), and say to yourself three times, "My [chakra name] is healthy and balanced on all levels." Alternatively, or in addition, place your hands over the chakra and let healing energy flow, clearing away obstructions and returning the chakra to a state of optimal health. You'll also find chakra-healing techniques on page 237.

The Seven-Chakra System

Let's look more closely at the chakras by outlining some of their individual functions and qualities, using the seven-chakra framework (we'll talk about alternative models at the end of this chapter). This is not a comprehensive cataloging of the chakra system, but it will give you a solid foundation from which to work with these energy centers. It's important to remember that none of the chakras operates in isolation, and it is their ability to work as a coherent system that is vital to our health and sense of wholeness. Know, too, that the qualities listed here, while in common usage, are not unanimously agreed upon by all healers, and you may experience or see different qualities when working with yourself or others. Use this material as a guide, but don't let it quash your own intuitive experience.

Root Chakra

Location: Perineum at the base of the spine

Color: Red

Sanskrit Name: *Muladhara*

Element: Earth

Sense: Smell

Primary Functions: Root, support, safety, security

Associated Glands: Adrenals

Associated Body Parts: Blood, skeletal system, kidneys, legs, teeth

Seed Sound: Lam

Crystals: Ruby, garnet, bloodstone, lodestone, hematite

Archetypes: The Mother (positive), the Victim (negative)

Astrological Association: Earth, Saturn, Capricorn

Physical Connections: Development of physical structure, survival functions, DNA and inheritance, food and physical nourishment, physical movement, grounding

Mental/Emotional Connections: Trust and a sense of safety; self-worth and deserving; feeling a right to be here; ability to be present; passion, rage, joy, and other primal feelings; survival instinct

Spiritual Connections: Seeing the sacred in the physical, ability to manifest in the physical realm, commitment to life / will to live

Signs of Health: Feeling embodied and present, balanced physical health, nourishing diet and movement practices, connection to nature, healthy relationship to finances

Signs of Imbalance: Addiction; sexual dysfunction; urinary and colorectal issues; reproductive health issues; instability regarding basic needs, such as housing and food; chronic financial instability; overeating or undereating; body dysmorphia; family-of-origin issues; childhood abuse; foot problems

The root chakra is our root, our seat, of physical existence; thus, when this chakra is healthy, we are able to survive and thrive in the physical realm, which includes having a safe and comfortable place to live; access to nourishing food and clean water; a healthy lifestyle, including diet, movement, and sleep; and a stable relationship with our finances. When this energy center is out of balance, we can experience upheaval in any of these areas, including addiction, chronic financial instability, unsafe or otherwise unhealthy living conditions, and a feeling of not being present in our bodies or actively engaged in life. It may be difficult for us to manifest our thoughts, ideas, and desires into tangible reality, and we may struggle with feeling that we don't deserve to be here.

EXERCISE: Root Chakra Forest Bathing

There are many meditative practices for healing the root chakra that work beautifully, but one of my favorite practices that heals not only the root but also our entire self is the practice of forest bathing. Quite simply, this involves spending time in nature, even if that's the park up the street, provided it has at least one tree in good health. While in this space, do your best to be fully present, and a great way to do this is to engage the five senses, just as you did in the Cultivating Awareness through Sensory Delight Exercise in chapter 1. What do you see, smell, and hear? Touch the bark of the tree, the soil, the leaves. What do the different textures feel like? While there might not be anything that you can safely taste, can you detect a "flavor" to the air? As much as possible, resist the urge to play over events of the day in your mind or otherwise get caught up in your thoughts. You don't have to obsess over emptying the mind, but when thoughts arise, treat them like dryer lint: little blobs of thoroughly uninteresting material that need not have any impact on the current moment. Let them blow away.

After spending at least ten minutes in this natural space, as you walk or sit, bring your attention to your root chakra at the perineum. Let any intuitive knowings arise regarding the health of this chakra, such as images, memories, thoughts, and physical sensations. Ask your higher self any questions you have about this chakra, including how to create and maintain its health. Visualize this chakra glowing with a ruby red light, clearing any obstructions and returning the energy to a healthy vibration and flow.

Sacral Chakra

Location: Slightly below the navel
Color: Orange
Sanskrit name: *Svadhisthana*
Element: Water
Sense: Taste
Primary Functions: Desire, pleasure, sexuality, creativity
Associated Body Parts: Genitals, womb, kidneys, bladder, circulatory system
Associated Glands: Ovaries, testes
Seed Sound: Vam
Crystals: Moonstone, coral, carnelian, tiger's eye

Archetypes: The Empress/Emperor (positive), the Martyr (negative)

Astrological Association: Moon, Jupiter, Cancer, Scorpio

Physical Connections: Feeling emotions through the body (crying, laughing, etc.); sensual and sexual experiences; movement; appetite for food and sex

Mental/Emotional Connections: Ability and a desire for healthy change, mental flexibility and emotional resilience, welcoming pleasurable experiences, authentic emotional expression, creativity

Spiritual Connections: Empathy and compassion, honoring feelings (our own and other people's), finding meaning in life, expressing joy

Signs of Health: Ability to experience pleasure, including sexual pleasure; expression of creative energy; healthy emotional expression; nurturing, healthy relationships; ability to create healthy structure and boundaries

Signs of Imbalance: Lower back pain; impotence and reproductive health issues; urinary, bladder, or kidney issues; painful/dysfunctional menstrual cycles, fibroids, endometriosis; chronic and/or pervasive pain issues; creative blocks; codependent relationships; lack of or excessive appetite for food or sex; difficulty establishing healthy limits

The sacral chakra brings us from the solidity, the unity, of chakra one to the polarity of two. Here is where we experience a sense of differentiation that allows us to come into relationship with others and with ourselves. Thus, this chakra is closely associated with the trappings of relationship, including emotions, pleasure and pain, and the need for boundaries and flexibility. This encounter with the other, whether that be another person or the meeting of our inner polarities (such as our yin-yang energies), is a potentially creative act, and in order to manifest what we desire, over generating unwanted experiences, we must bring as much conscious awareness as possible to these encounters.

Tending to the sacral chakra, then, requires taking responsibility for our relationships, both with ourselves and others, and this starts with a robust self-care practice, for it is impossible to offer in relationship what we cannot offer to ourselves, be that love, support, companionship, and so forth. Healthy relationship also requires boundaries, for you and I cannot be in relationship if I don't know where I end and you begin. These boundaries also apply to self-relationship, because a healthy lifestyle requires balance that can only be cultivated when we are willing to set appropriate limits: for example, by turning off the TV so we can get a good night's sleep. And relationships cannot thrive without healthy emotional expression, so practicing our ability to be present when our emotions arise, rather than mindlessly reacting from them, and learning ways to express our emotions authentically in ways that deepen intimacy, even when dealing with more challenging emotions, strengthens this chakra as well. Using the Flow of Emotions Exercise in chapter 1 is a

· · · · · · ·

great way to boost sacral chakra health, as is the following exercise, which uses the power of healing energy to highlight and transform boundary issues.

EXERCISE: Boundaries of Love

Find a place where you can lie down comfortably without being disturbed. If this pose is accessible to you, lie on your back with your knees bent and your feet planted on the floor. If your feet are directly below your knees, move them about a foot away from your butt to create more opening. This pose helps to release a muscle called the psoas, which travels from the lower spine, through the pelvic bowl, to the femur (thigh bone), and I have found this muscle to be energetically related to the lower three chakras.

Place both palms over your lower belly. Imagine there are elastic cords running from your knees, along the tops of your thighs, and attaching to the front of your hip bones, and as you breathe, let these cords start to lengthen and soften. While you may not notice much, if any, external movement, this area can feel longer and more spacious as you relax. Continue to breathe as long as you like here, entering a state of relaxation and calm.

Imagine the area under your hands beginning to glow with a beautiful orange light, like freshly squeezed citrus. Do this for a few rounds of breath, and then open your crown chakra to the flow of healing energy, seeing and sensing a pure stream of white light traveling down your body and into your belly, further energizing and balancing your sacral chakra. Focus on this flow for a few more breaths, and when you feel ready, ask your higher self, "Where in my life do I need to set a healthy boundary?" Spend some time here in contemplation, allowing any images, sensations, memories, and other insights to arise, and ask your higher self any clarifying questions as needed. Ideally, before you come out of this meditation, you will have one clear action step to establish healthy boundaries in your life. When you're ready, set the intention that your chakras are returning to a state that is healthy and balanced for you, release any imagery, and gently roll to one side to press yourself up to a seated position.

Solar Plexus Chakra

Location: Directly below the sternum

Color: Yellow

Sanskrit Name: *Manipura*

Element: Fire

Sense: Sight

Primary Functions: Will, power, self-esteem

Associated Body Parts: Muscles, digestive system

Associated Gland: Pancreas

Seed Sound: Ram

Crystals: Citrine, amber, topaz

Archetypes: The Warrior (positive), the Servant (negative)

Astrological Association: Sun, Mars, Leo, Aries

Physical Connections: Desire to move, to take action, healthy digestion and metabolism

Mental/Emotional Connections: Healthy ego development and self-esteem, healthy decision-making, ability to discern one's will and direct it toward healthy change, courage

Spiritual Connections: Cultivation of inner power as opposed to exerting power over others, connection to divine will, ability to impact the world in a way that aligns with our higher self

Signs of Health: Ability to make conscious choices, functional expressions of will and power, healthy digestion, ability to take action even when the outcome is uncertain (which, in truth, is always the case!), enjoying a sense of agency and self-directedness in one's life

Signs of Imbalance: Over-controlling and micromanaging, chronic indecision, abdicating choice and responsibility to others, inflammation, diabetes, digestive disorders, inertia or excessive busyness, chronic nervousness and fear, feeling powerless, judgmental attitudes toward self and others

The solar plexus is a bit like our chakric command-and-control center, and it governs our ability to express healthy forms of power, which include the ability to make life-enhancing decisions and to take action based on those choices. When this chakra isn't functioning properly, we often experience a dysfunctional relationship to power, which can manifest in excessive or deficient forms. In excess, we might be hyper-controlling, micromanaging our own lives and trying to control other people. It might feel really scary to accept the limits of our control and to be in relationship without trying to change others to meet our expectations. When deficient, we might struggle to exert *any* control, vacillating on decisions and lacking in energy to carry out our choices. We might prefer to leave the decisions up to someone else, while struggling with resentment and feeling powerless when life doesn't go the way we'd like it to. It's not uncommon to experience both, swinging back and forth between rigid control and total loss of will-power, with strict diets and the backlash of binge days being one example of this.

A powerful method for healing the solar plexus chakra involves taking responsibility for our right to choose and realizing that abstaining from decision-making is, in itself, a choice. We cannot avoid choice in life, so it is well worth the effort to learn how to wield this power effectively and in accordance with our highest self. When working with clients energetically, something I often see is a tangled-up wad of energetic threads, like a gnarled ball of yarn, at the solar plexus, and this is always accompanied by a feeling that one's choices are not one's own. Cultural and peer pressure outweigh personal prerogative far too often, leaving the person feeling trapped and bound up with *should*s and *have to*s. The following exercise helps you clear and balance your solar plexus to support healthier decision-making.

• • • • • • •

EXERCISE: Solar Power

Find a place where you can sit or lie down without being disturbed, and get comfy. If you're lying down, you can use the posture from the previous sacral chakra exercise if it suits you. Place your hands over your solar plexus, which is at the base of the sternum (breastbone). Take as many nice, deep breaths as you need to calm and center yourself, feeling your hands rising and falling with the inhales and exhales.

Bring your awareness to your solar plexus, and first, get a sense of its energetic state. Allow any intuitive messages to arise, which might come in the form of images, thoughts, physical sensations, emotions, and so forth. Ask your higher self any clarifying questions you might have. Then, visualize a beautiful golden sun above you, and focus on the image to increase its energy and power. You might even feel the warmth of the sun on your skin or see hints of light beyond your closed eyelids. Draw the energy of this sun into your solar plexus, and allow its golden yellow light to infuse this chakra with health and vitality, clearing any obstructions and returning this energy center to a state of harmonious flow. Know that the clarity and conscious power of the sun has fully activated your ability to choose, and you can now use this in your daily life practice, outlined next.

Pair the Solar Power Exercise with a daily life practice of making conscious choices more and more often. You can start small with choices like "What flavor tea will I have this morning?" and progress to larger decisions, like "Does it feel nourishing to continue going to Sunday dinners with my extended family?" To enhance this process, anytime you need to, reaffirm your connection to the sun by drawing sun energy into your solar plexus, clearing away any energetic cobwebs and enhancing your ability to make wise decisions. The more you use this practice, the easier it will be to navigate life's choices with intelligence and grace.

Heart Chakra

Location: Heart/middle of the chest

Color: Green or pink

Sanskrit Name: *Anahata*

Element: Air

Sense: Touch

Primary Functions: Love, compassion

Associated Body Parts: Lungs, heart, pericardium, hands

Associated Gland: Thymus

Seed Sound: Yam

Crystals: Emerald, rose quartz, tourmaline, jade

Archetypes: The Lover (positive), the Actress/Actor (negative)

Astrological Association: Venus, Libra, Taurus

• • • • • • • •

Physical Connections: Strong heart, healthy immunity

Mental/Emotional Connections: Self-love, ability to give and receive love, seeing life and humanity as generally good in spite of the "ills of the world," desire to connect with others, ability to refrain from temporary wants and desires when they run counter to higher-self goals

Spiritual Connections: Feeling worthy of and connected to love, both human and divine; ability to attract what our higher self seeks and manifest our soul's wishes in the physical plane

Signs of Health: Nurturing relationships, self-love, heart health, strong immune system, ability to love within the context of imperfect human relationships, compassion for self and others, ability to return to a state of balance following temporary illness

Signs of Imbalance: Physical heart issues, bronchitis, pneumonia, compromised immune system, difficulty receiving and expressing love, self-hatred, need for immediate and constant gratification of wants and desires, tendency to withhold love when expectations are not met, chronic health issues (physical or mental)

As the midpoint between the lower and upper chakras, the heart plays a huge role in helping us manifest our higher goals in the physical realm while staying connected to sources of love and guidance that we cannot experience solely through the physical senses. When this chakra is malfunctioning, among other things, we might feel that life requires constant toil and struggle and that we really can't count on anyone or anything to support us. This often fosters chronic overwork, which can lead to this chakra's associated issues of impaired heart and immune system health. By regularly tending to this chakra, we open to the gifts life has to offer; it's easier for us to ask for, recognize, and receive support in many forms; and we're more likely to feel connected, both to other people and to a sense of something larger than our human story. Use this practice whenever you're feeling burnt out or disconnected.

EXERCISE: Basking in the Love Glow

Choose a time when you can relax for at least fifteen minutes without interruption. Brew a cup of tea containing any combination of rose, hibiscus, or holy basil (tulsi). Sweeten with honey if desired. Get cozy and comfortable, perhaps wrapping yourself in a soft blanket, with the option of lighting your favorite incense (some good choices for the heart chakra include lavender, jasmine, and rose, but the most important thing is to choose a scent you love). Holding the cup of tea in both hands, open to receive a stream of healing energy, down through your crown, into your heart, and coursing down your arms, out through the palm chakras. Visualize this healing energy infusing every molecule of the tea with its energy of unconditional love; you might see the tea take on a green or pink glow in your mind's eye.

· · · · · · · ·

Drink in this magickal elixir, and feel the warmth travel into your body, filling you with love. Allow the energy to fill your heart space, and as it builds, the heart energy begins to glow brighter and brighter until you are shining with its luminescence. Give yourself time to bask in the healing energy of love, feeling it pulsing in tune with your heartbeat, bringing your entire being into a state of perfect love and perfect harmony. When you feel ready, release the imagery and bring yourself back to a normal state of consciousness, allowing yourself as much time as you like to do something that brings you joy.

Throat Chakra

Location: Base of the throat

Color: Bright blue

Sanskrit Name: *Visuddha*

Element: Sound

Sense: Hearing

Primary Functions: Communication, creativity

Associated Body Parts: Neck, throat, shoulders

Associated Gland: Thyroid

Seed Sound: Ham

Crystals: Celestine, aquamarine, turquoise, blue agate

Archetypes: The Communicator (positive), the Silent Child (negative)

Astrological Association: Mercury, Gemini, Virgo

Physical Connections: Hearing and speech, thyroid, arms and neck, throat

Mental/Emotional Connections: Speaking and listening; setting boundaries and self-protection; ability to take in new information/learning; associated with writing, reading, chanting, and singing; honesty and acting with integrity

Spiritual Connections: Receiving higher guidance, feeling in partnership with spiritual forces, listening to the intuition

Signs of Health: Ability to communicate effectively; active listening skills; full range of motion in the shoulders, neck, and arms; strong voice; keen hearing; freedom for creative expression; thyroid health; honest communication; healthy emotional expression; connected to intuitive faculties

Signs of Imbalance: Sore throat; voice loss; neck and shoulder pain or other dysfunction; trouble expressing oneself; frequent misunderstandings; difficulty listening; physical hearing impairment; jaw tension; thyroid issues; nail biting or other oral habits; excessive talking; smoking, alcohol, or drug abuse; gossiping or lying

The throat chakra is such an important vehicle for communication, both within ourselves and with the world around us, so when this energy center is imbalanced, we can feel disconnected from our inner truth and from a sense of community and partnership. It can be useful to explore our patterns in conversation to get a sense of how energy is flowing through this chakra, and if you can enlist feedback from a trusted friend, all the better, as these patterns can sometimes be tricky to see ourselves. If you find it difficult to speak up and regularly have the sensation of "holding your tongue" or "biting back your words" or feeling like there's "a lump in your throat," this is a sign that the throat chakra is out of balance. Similarly, if you find yourself interrupting, needing to fill every silence with chitchat, or talking very loudly and rapidly in non-urgent situations, your throat chakra is likely in need of some TLC. Remember that these outward forms of communication are mirrors for our internal dialogue. In the former case, we might often suppress our feelings, authentic thoughts, or intuition, while in the latter case, we might be overrun with mental chatter, feel unable to "get our thoughts straight," or routinely let our ego overrule authentic needs to maintain a certain image of ourselves.

After doing this self-inventory of your conversational habits, with optional feedback from a friend, the following exercise will help to return the throat chakra to a more balanced state. Remember to partner this work with practical action steps based on what you discovered in the conversation inventory. For example, if you noticed that you tend to interrupt, really be mindful of this urge when it arises, take some calming breaths, and wait for your turn to speak. If you tend to hold back what you really think and feel, start practicing more authentic expression with people you trust, gradually expanding this to all your interactions.

EXERCISE: Healing Vibrations

For this exercise, you will need the sound of a singing bowl. If you don't have a singing bowl, don't fret. Simply do an online search for "singing bowl sound," and you will have your choice of countless free options. Find a place where you can sit undisturbed, and come into a comfortable position. Close your eyes, and bring awareness to your breath, gradually lengthening the inhales and exhales, becoming more present and centered.

Bring your attention to your throat chakra at the base of your throat. Begin the singing bowl sound, and imagine your throat chakra glowing with a pure, sky-blue light, clear and radiant. Give yourself at least a few minutes to take in the sound, feeling the vibration, and visualize the sound waves breaking free and neutralizing any harmful energy, particularly in your throat chakra. Say to yourself three times, "My throat chakra is healthy and balanced on all levels." When ready, gently come out of the meditation.

Third Eye Chakra

Location: Slightly above the space between the brows

Color: Indigo

Sanskrit Name: *Ajna*

Element: Light

Sense: Intuition

Primary Functions: Intuition, clear seeing

Associated Body Parts: Eyes

Associated Gland: Pituitary

Seed Sound: Om

Crystals: Lapis lazuli, sapphire, quartz, indigo gabbro

Archetypes: The Sage (positive), the Intellectual (negative)

Astrological Association: Neptune, the moon, Sagittarius, Pisces

Physical Connections: Eyes, sinuses, endocrine system

Mental/Emotional Connections: Ability to see subtle connections between people, situations, events; ability to perceive patterns, internal and external; active imagination, ability to visualize new possibilities and desired outcomes

Spiritual Connections: Honors intuition, feels a sense of purpose and enthusiasm about the future

Signs of Health: Sense of clarity and focus, vibrant imagination, ability to see new options and creatively problem-solve, healthy physical vision, clear sinuses, balanced hormones

Signs of Imbalance: Distrust or lack of connection to intuition, sinus issues, poor eyesight and other ocular health issues, confusion and inability to pick up on subtle cues, lack of imagination, feels like things are impossible or there are limited options, hormonal imbalances

The third eye is our vision center, processing both inner and outer sight. When this chakra is working optimally, we hold a healthy self-image, and we are able to visualize positive opportunities that we feel enthused to translate into action in partnership with the rest of our energetic system. When this chakra is blocked, we often feel muddled and confused, and all of the seemingly available options feel like more of the same old, same old. We all have the ability to access inner wisdom that can realign us with a strong sense of purpose, but it can be easy to forget how in the hustle and bustle of daily life. By regularly carving out time to retreat, even briefly, from the sensory overload of work, family, busy social calendars, buzzing phones and a never-ending stream of emails, we strengthen our ability to recognize our inner voice, making it that much easier to connect when we need it most. The following exercise can be done whenever you need a dose of clarity, and I like to pencil it onto my calendar at regular intervals, such as New Year's Day, my birthday, and so on, to ensure I'm not wandering too far from my soul's path.

. . . .

EXERCISE: Third Eye Visioneering

Go someplace new, like a park you haven't been to before (or in a while) or a new coffee shop. The idea is to get out of your normal groove to shake loose different thoughts, feelings, and other energy. Bring a notebook, whatever calendar tool you use, and colored pens or markers. Take a few moments (you can do this in the restroom if you feel self-conscious or unsafe closing your eyes in a public place) to close your eyes and focus on your breath. Bring your awareness to your third eye, visualize it glowing with a beautiful indigo light, and say to yourself three times (silently, if you need to), "My third eye is healthy and balanced on all levels."

Get out your notebook and pens and start on a clean, fresh page. Start free writing, describing your ideal day from the time you wake up until your head hits the pillow. What are you doing, where are you doing it, who are you with, how do you feel? Write until you've gotten everything out that needs to be committed to paper. How many of these things can you start to incorporate into your life now? Choose one that feels most important to you right now, and write it at the top of a fresh sheet of paper. Make sure the phrasing is specific, and take time now to revise if needed. For example, instead of "I want to be healthier," try something more focused, like "I will run a nine-minute mile by June 1."

If you didn't note many feelings in the first step, take some time now to imagine how you would be feeling while carrying out this priority. Confident? Engaged? Stimulated? Joyful? Is there a theme with certain emotions stated in slightly different ways? If possible, condense it down to one to three desired emotions.

Now that you have a priority to focus on and you're clear on how you want to feel by engaging in this activity, start brainstorming all the ways that you can work this into your day-to-day life right now. When you're finished, choose three specific action steps to move forward with your chosen priority and put them on your calendar, just like any other important engagement. For example, if your priority is to run a nine-minute mile, what could support you in reaching that goal? Getting a running buddy and setting up your first run date? Hiring a trainer and booking your first three sessions? Going on a ten-minute jog three mornings this week? Buying running shoes that actually fit?

Are there things you would need to *stop* doing or do much less of to make room for your desires? Make a list and develop a short-and-sweet action plan to phase out each of these activities, working on one at a time. Pencil these actions steps onto your calendar. When you've successfully phased out an activity, celebrate! Really honor the occasion to generate positive momentum as you pencil in the next phase-out activity. Bonus: concentrate your efforts on the period between the full moon and the new moon, when the moon is waning. This is a great time for releasing things.

· · · · · · · ·

And finally, sweeten the process by going back to your chosen feelings. What are three ways this week that you can cultivate or increase your chances of feeling this way? For example, if your chosen feeling was confidence, you might wear your favorite outfit, the one that makes you feel unstoppable, to this week's work meeting. Or you might carry a carnelian, red jasper, or tiger's eye crystal, looking at it throughout the day and consciously drawing in the energy of confidence. These activities don't have to be directly tied to your chosen priority (in this example, running a mile), but by consciously generating your desired feeling more often, you add a powerful oomph to your efforts even when you're not engaged in your priority activity, while also getting to feel the way you want to feel more of the time. It's a win-win!

Crown Chakra

Location: At or slightly above the crown of the head

Color: Violet or white

Sanskrit Name: *Sahasrara*

Element: Thought

Sense: Thinking

Primary Function: Consciousness

Associated Body Parts: Central nervous system

Associated Gland: Pineal

Seed Sound: Silence

Crystals: Diamond, amethyst, clear quartz

Archetypes: The Guru (positive), the Egotist (negative)

Astrological Association: The universe, Aquarius

Physical Connections: Pineal gland and associated functions (regulation of circadian rhythm, appetite, body temperature, emotions)

Mental/Emotional Connections: Clear thought processes, mental-emotional stability, feeling a sense of life purpose, knowing one's higher values and acting in accordance, an integrated sense of self, healthy connections with others, nourishing spiritual practice of one's choosing, positive self-image, ability to feel bliss

Spiritual Connections: Feeling one with all existence, feeling connected to the Divine, accessing the Akashic Records

Signs of Health: Feeling engaged and purposeful in one's life, ability to make decisions in accordance with one's higher values, healthy self-esteem, cohesion of internal parts (physical, mental, emotional, spiritual), sense of belonging in one's chosen communities, regular experiences of peace and joy

Signs of Imbalance: Learning disorders, headaches, religious fanaticism, psychosis, immune system dysfunction, chronic depression, dizziness and light-headedness, feelings of alienation or persecution and paranoia, difficulty feeling peace or joy

The crown chakra is the energy center most closely associated with Source energy, like our personal electrical socket for plugging into divine consciousness. When this chakra is well functioning, we feel connected to a sense of something that is larger than ourselves, which helps balance and heal the delusions of the ego, which, by definition, are very self-centered. The ego takes everything personally, and while we need our ego to function in physical reality, when it doesn't feel a connection to Source, this I-centered tendency goes into overdrive and throws us off balance. We take things a little *too* personally and we become embroiled in unceasing, self-generated drama.

Among other issues, this can lead to a state of hypersensitivity about what others might think of us, because when we over-identify with our ego, our primary life goal becomes protecting this limited sense of self. From this place, it's common to suppress our natural desires, our honest thoughts and opinions, and our true emotions, which leads to rejecting the work our soul feels called to do. At a certain point, we might forget (on a conscious level) what this work even is and feel aimless and unsure of our life's purpose. We feel dependent on gaining approval from others and spend a great deal of energy pursuing external metrics of success, such as degrees and awards, to "prove" that we're worthy. This is not to say that the pursuit of degrees and awards is, in and of itself, unhealthy—simply that when we do this from a place of trying to assuage a fear that we're not enough, we set ourselves up for suffering.

If this sounds familiar, let's change the soundtrack and reopen an enlivening connection to Source. Think of this as the first step toward weaning yourself off the endless hamster wheel of external approval seeking so you can know, deep down, your inherent worth and value. The following exercise clears and balances your crown chakra, which, again, is your personal hotline to the Divine. Tap into this guidance whenever self-doubt is tempting you to hold back your inner awesomeness in the name of "playing it safe."

EXERCISE: Hotline to the Divine

Find a place to sit comfortably where you won't be disturbed, and close your eyes. Bring your awareness to your breath, and gradually slow and lengthen your inhales and exhales to invite a state of peace and calm. Bring your awareness to the crown of your head, and imagine a beautiful white lotus flower. See as the lotus begins to unfurl, opening layer after layer of petals, bringing you into a deeper state of focus with each unfurling. Continue for a few more breath cycles.

In the center of the lotus, you discover a white-light diamond with almost blinding brilliance. This is your True Self. Bask in your divine nature, breathing here for a few cycles. See a stream

· · · · · · · · ·

of healing energy descend into the lotus, where it fully activates the potential held in your crown chakra in accordance with your highest good. The stream of energy penetrates your central channel and descends to the third eye, activating its full potential for your highest good. Continue this process of allowing healing energy to travel down your central channel, activating each chakra in accordance with your highest good: the throat, the heart, the solar plexus, the sacral, and the root chakras. At the root, allow this energy to swirl into a glowing ball of white light, cradled in your pelvic bowl, and feel the connection, the oneness between body and spirit. Allow this unity to inspire an upward stream of energy, once more traveling through your central channel, flowing freely through your cleared and balanced chakras, until it flowers at your crown, creating a beautiful fountain of light. Rest here for a few breath cycles, enjoying a sense of integration of all your parts into the beauty and brilliance of your True Self.

In this space, if there's anything you need help with, ask questions and open to receive higher guidance in whatever forms arise. Give thanks, and when you're ready, slowly let the imagery fade. Set the intention that your chakras are in a state that is perfectly balanced for you, right here, right now, and bring yourself back to a normal state of consciousness. If you received guidance in this space, write it in your journal and take your first action step based on this guidance within the next three days to keep the energy active and flowing.

Other Chakra Systems

The seven-chakra model from a Hindu perspective is but one way of conceptualizing human energetic bodies, and even within the Hindu framework, there is variation to the number of and location of the primary chakras, with some ancient texts citing four to seven or more of these energy centers. Donna Eden suggests these differences may be due, in part, to the existence of many smaller chakras throughout the body, as well as vortices of energy that appear wherever new energy is needed.[21] I have also had teachers who were resistant to one-size-fits-all models of the chakras, as they felt it was more important to get a felt-intuitive sense of where these energies reside within the individual. My outlook falls somewhere in the middle: I find various chakra models to be helpful guides, and I love to explore my own energy field firsthand. As a bonus, consciously interacting with our energy is one of the best ways to maintain its good health, so these explorations initiate healing and enhance our self-awareness simultaneously.

Now that we've looked at the energetic layers, pathways, and centers in and around the body, in the next chapter we'll look at different theories of how reiki and other vibrational medicines work to initiate healing.

---

21. Eden and Feinstein, *Energy Medicine*, 153.

CHAPTER 4

❧

Energy Healing Mechanisms

Energy medicine practitioners and researchers have long explored various possible mechanisms for energy healing, and while we're not at a stage where all of our questions have been answered—far from it—there have been some interesting developments, which we'll look at in this chapter.

There is a fundamental difference in the way vibrational medicine approaches the body versus allopathic intervention, and we might describe this as a holistic-versus-reductionist viewpoint. Reductionism takes things apart and looks at how the individual components function, and the goal is to break things down into the smallest possible units, the idea being that if you understand how the indivisible particles forming Thing A work, you now understand Thing A. To be sure, this approach has generated massive breakthroughs in our understanding of the world. One of the major shortcomings, however, is that it rarely tells us how the parts integrate to form a whole. For this we need holism, or its cousin, emergentism. The latter posits that when you study all the little bits and add them back together, something new emerges from the whole that you can't explain solely from the individual workings of the bits. It's like trying to explain the complex organization of a bee colony by studying one bee; it can't be done.

Vibrational medicine looks at the body and, indeed, all of existence, as a whole, so while we can explore individual parts and enhance our understanding by doing so, we will always be missing part of the puzzle if we overlook the relationships between the parts and the fact that *all things are in relationship*. As a structural integrator, my work is predicated on the fact that the body, rather than being an assemblage of isolated muscles and tendons and bones, is a complex, continuous web of tissues, none of which can be separated out from the rest. Having pain in your shoulder? That might very well be related to an issue in the sole of your foot, and I could work on your shoulder until the cows come home without ever giving you the relief you're

• • • • • • • •

looking for. And your shoulder and foot don't exist in a vacuum, either; there's a complex world surrounding and interpenetrating your body that informs your state of health. In the same fashion, we can throw surgeries and medications at issues that we've falsely isolated from the rest of the living system (and the environment in which this system exists), but this frequently fails to address underlying conditions, which may reoccur in various forms, from physical issues to mental-emotional and spiritual states of dis-ease.

Holographic Reality and the Implicate Order

Two popular models espousing a more holistic view are the holographic model and David Bohm's theory of implicate order. The holographic model states that each individual part of something contains the whole, and to understand this, let's look at how a hologram works. The process of creating a holographic image involves, on a basic level, capturing the light scattering off of an object and recording it so that this precise scattering of light can be reconstructed later, even when the original object is no longer present. On a more detailed level, let's say you're trying to create a hologram of a teddy bear. One way to do this is to take a laser light and split it into two beams. One of these beams is passed through a special lens and directed at the teddy bear. The bear then reflects or scatters this light, and a special recording plate captures the scattering. The second of the two beams is shone on the recording plate itself, and the interaction between the light scattering off the teddy bear and the light of the second beam interfere. This interference pattern is recorded on the plate, and it looks nothing like the teddy bear—yet. When the original, unsplit beam of light is shone on the recording plate, it acts like a key, decoding the strange pattern and recreating the teddy bear as a hologram.

What does this have to do with energy medicine? Well, if you were to break the holographic plate into smaller pieces and shine the laser at one of these pieces, it wouldn't reproduce just part of the teddy bear—say, its arm or ear—it would reproduce the entire teddy bear. In other words, the part contains the whole. This model is used to explain how our energy fields operate: as holographic plates, each part of which contains the whole. Proponents of this model believe that each part of our energy field and body contains instructions for, among other things, healing at a whole-system level; thus, if you can trigger one part to "remember" this holistic repair sequence, the entire system will benefit.

In a similar fashion, the theoretical physicist David Bohm (1917–1992) proposed an emergent model for explaining the universe, which he called the implicate and explicate order. This model sees a deeper, fundamental ordering of all existence giving rise to all of the phenomena we experience through normal human perception. What we're able to perceive is the *explicate* order, and the underlying pattern is the *implicate* order. In chapter 1, we discussed the nature of energy fields and the idea that matter is merely a local concentration of energy within a field.

In the same way, Bohm proposed that reality as we know it is like a local concentration in the implicate order, and he saw this unseen order as a possible explanation for the bizarre behavior of quantum particles, which is otherwise hard to reconcile with "ordinary" reality. The implicate order reflects the vibrational medicine approach of looking at things holistically, because if all things emerge from an underlying source, each "part" still retains the whole. We cannot separate the parts from the field, because they *are* the field, just like an individual ocean wave cannot be separated from the ocean.

Bioelectricity

In looking at the human energy field in particular, numerous theories have been put forth to explain what this field is made of, and many researchers believe that electricity might play a huge role. In the mid-1900s, Yale professor and bioelectric researcher Harold S. Burr coined the term *L-field* to describe the electric field of living organisms. While studying salamanders, Burr identified an electrical line or axis corresponding with the brain and spinal cord, which was surrounded by an electrical field, roughly mapping out the shape of an adult salamander. In plants, Burr found that the electrical field surrounding a plant sprout mirrored not the tiny seedling but the shape of an adult plant, suggesting that the "blueprint" for the mature organism existed not only as genetic information, but in the electrical field surrounding and interpenetrating the organism.[22]

Perhaps more well known in metaphysical circles is Semyon Kirlian, from which Kirlian photography, which is said to capture the aura of humans, other organisms, and non-living objects, takes its name. To create a Kirlian image, an object is placed on a special photographic sheet, which is then set on a metal plate. A high voltage is applied to the object, and the photographic sheet captures the electrical discharge between the object and the metal plate. When the discharge interacts with the various dyes contained within the sheet, colorful images are generated. One now-famous experiment demonstrates what is known as the Phantom Leaf Effect: a Kirlian photo of a leaf whose top half was torn off still showed the original, intact leaf. Skeptics have claimed that lingering moisture on the surface of the plate resulted in a false image, but this may have been refuted by Chris Wagner of California State University, who demonstrated that the phantom leaf could still be captured even when a plastic barrier prevented moisture contamination.[23]

All these perspectives are pointing toward the idea that all parts of an organism, whether that part is an arm or an individual cell, have access to a greater whole, and this whole can be

22. Richard Gerber, *Vibrational Medicine,* 3rd ed. (Rochester, VT: Bear and Company, 2001).
23. Gerber, *Vibrational Medicine,* 85.

• • • • • • • •

accessed through various means, such as energy medicine, to trigger system-wide balance and healing.

The Extracellular Matrix

A key question in energy medicine is how healing energy or information travels throughout the body. Is it via visible pathways, such as nerves and blood vessels, or invisible-yet-mapped pathways, such as acupuncture meridians and nadis, or is there another network of communication? The answer may well be all of the above, and the work of researcher Albert Szent-Györgyi (1893–1986), biochemist and winner of the Nobel Prize in Physiology or Medicine in 1937, gives us another possibility: connective tissue.

Szent-Györgyi researched reactive oxygen species (ROS), which are molecules with an electric charge due to one or more missing electrons. This makes them highly reactive; they are eager to reverse their electron deficit, and they will steal electrons from other molecules in order to do so. ROS are formed as a natural byproduct of metabolism, but they can also be produced in excess in reaction to UV exposure, pollutants, certain drugs and pathogens, and other triggers, and they can cause significant damage to cell structures, such as DNA, proteins, and lipids (fats). For example, research has implicated ROS in the functional decline of aging, male infertility, and cancer.[24] This damage can be counteracted by substances known as antioxidants, which interrupt the chemical reactions leading to ROS-inflicted cellular damage.[25]

In the 1950s, Szent-Györgyi began researching the potential role of ROS in cancer. He determined that a cell's natural regulatory mechanisms, which prevent the cell from becoming cancerous, were hampered in cells that were no longer in communication with the rest of the body. He intuited that there must be as-yet-undiscovered pathways of communication between cells, and he believed that free electrons and protons were the primary messengers of this intercellular communication. Conventional wisdom of the time held that any flow of electrical charge within the body was accomplished primarily through charged molecules, or ions, but Szent-Györgyi proposed that electrons and protons were also able to travel throughout the body on their own, without an ionic mediator.

He focused his attention on the extracellular matrix (ECM), which, as the name suggests, is the "stuff" outside of cells, a rich network composed of different substances, such as proteins,

24. Florian L. Muller et al., "Trends in Oxidative Aging Theories," *Free Radical Biology and Medicine* 43, no. 4 (2007): 477–503, doi:10.1016/j.freeradbiomed.2007.03.034; R. J. Aitken et al., "The Simmet Lecture: New Horizons on an Old Landscape—Oxidative Stress, DNA Damage and Apoptosis in the Male Germ Line," *Reproduction in Domestic Animals* 47, no. 4 (August 2012): 7–14; Rob A. Cairns et al., "Regulation of Cancer Cell Metabolism," *Nature Reviews Cancer* 11, no. 2 (2011): 85–95, doi:10.1038/nrc2981.

25. Finley Eversole, ed, *Energy Medicine Technologies: Ozone Healing, Microcrystals, Frequency Therapy, and the Future of Health* (Rochester, VT: Inner Traditions, 2013), 48.

enzymes, and other chemicals. This connective tissue was routinely seen as unimportant and discarded in order to study the cells in isolation. Szent-Györgyi found that one of the extracellular matrix components, a type of protein called collagen, was capable of transferring mobile electrons, and the water surrounding the collagen, known as the hydration shell, was capable of conducting protons, providing a transmission route for these particles that didn't require carrier molecules.

The ECM is not restricted to affecting only the external environment of cells, either. The cytoskeleton of the ECM, which is like a living, dynamic scaffolding, is connected to the cytoskeleton *inside* of cells, too, and these connections even extend into DNA. In other words, this connective tissue matrix doesn't just surround cells; it interpenetrates each and every one and maintains intimate contact with the genetic material housed within the cells. Thus, activity in the ECM can have a profound effect, including altered gene expression. The cytoskeleton allows for communication that is much faster than hormones or nerve impulses, and healthy flow within this network may be, in part, what energy workers address when they seek to reestablish a proper flow of energy via vibrational medicine techniques.

Ultimately, we may find that it is beyond the scope of science to entirely explain the mechanisms underlying energy medicine, and it becomes important to honor our subjective experience when determining whether a modality is effective for us. How do you feel after a reiki session? Do you notice any changes to your physical, mental-emotional, or spiritual health? Because reiki works to effect change when and where we need it most in a deeply personal manner, it can be difficult to generalize the effects of reiki treatment. For example, throughout the course of a day, I might see a client who needs to experience deep relaxation in order to see a path through the forest of chronic anxiety, while another client is struggling with gastrointestinal issues and leaves with an intuitive urge to cut dairy from her diet for a few weeks to see how she feels. Given the rich diversity of responses to reiki treatment, it seems likely that the underlying mechanisms for reiki's effectiveness are similarly diverse, and in the years to come, perhaps further research will give us a more complete picture.

In the next chapter, we'll explore various practices for sensing energy, the prerequisite to working more consciously with your own and others' energy fields, pathways, and centers. If you're brand new to this, don't despair! You're sensing energy all the time, and it's simply a matter of heightening conscious awareness of your innate capacities.

· · · · · · ·

CHAPTER 5

✒

Sensing Energy

Whether you see this in yourself or not, you *already* possess acute abilities to sense energy, and in this chapter you'll learn how to tap into those abilities whenever you need them through a series of fun exercises. Sensing energy is something you do each and every day, from grabbing a coat when the temperature drops to feeling your "spidey sense" activate when someone is staring at you from across the room. A popular misconception of energy work is that it always entails dramatic or overt demonstrations of energetic abilities, and sure, those do exist, but they're certainly not necessary to facilitate effective healing. In fact, working with subtle energy is often much more, well, *subtle*, although the effects can be far-reaching and profound.

Another misconception that can hamper our intuitive and energetic skills is the belief that working with energy primarily means accessing what we might think of as supernatural or otherwise outside our normal frame of reference. And yes, this can be part of it, but we musn't overlook the so-called mundane experiences either. As we learned in chapter 1, matter and energy aren't so different after all, so bringing mindful attention to the physical world is a powerful way of enhancing our energetic abilities, because the physical world *is* energy.

Nowadays, we're usually moving through our environment with a million things on our mind and our attention glued to a device, only partly aware of what's going on around us. I'm amazed at how often I see someone out hiking in a stunningly beautiful landscape … and they're on their phone. Is it possible that the "mundane" world feels mundane because we're ignoring the vast majority of what it has to offer? While I think spiritual practice is a vital part of wellness, it also seems that sometimes we're reaching for profound mystical experiences because the rest of our life has been drained of color, and we've largely forgotten how to see the sacred in the world around us.

· · · · · · · ·

It's my belief that disconnection from our environment dulls our energetic perception, so in the following exercise, you're going to hone your energy skills through the five senses. While all your senses work together, here you'll attempt to isolate them, focusing on one sense at a time. There are two reasons for this, and the first is practical: when we're accustomed to tuning out, it's often easier to get reacquainted with our senses if we approach them one at a time. The second is tied to hypersensitivity and boundaries for empaths, which are big topics these days. With the barrage of stimuli and distractions everywhere we turn, it's no wonder. Learning how to focus on one form of sensory input enhances our ability to tune out unwanted "noise," which is an important form of boundary setting and one that will prove immensely useful during healing sessions. As energy workers, we need to be able to mediate our interaction with energy in a useful way; our perceptions are of little use to us or to others if we're simply overwhelmed by them.

EXERCISE: Opening the Five Senses, Part 1

You'll need a piece of fruit for this exercise and a quiet place where you won't be disturbed.

Sight: Set the fruit down and look at it. What color is it? Is it shiny or dull, smooth or rough looking? What shape is it? Are there any visible patterns in the skin, the leaves, or other details? Pick up the fruit and look at it from different angles, up close and at arm's length, from above and below. Look at it through your peripheral vision.

Touch: Start by feeling the textures, the weight, the shape of the fruit. Explore the surface like you're searching for a hidden entrance, and really bring your awareness to the minute sensations you're receiving through your skin.

Sound: Tap the fruit with your fingers; lightly or more firmly tap the fruit on the table. What does it sound like? Continue this exploration as you peel or open the fruit in the next step, and while you taste the fruit, listening to the sounds of your chewing.

Smell: Smell the fruit. If it has a peel or skin, smell it with this layer intact, then open the fruit and smell the interior. Does the scent evoke any memories or images? Can you already taste the fruit simply by smelling it?

Taste: Finally, take a bite. Notice the different flavors unfolding as you chew, taking your time and mindfully chewing until the fruit is pulpy and ready to be swallowed. How do the other senses play into the taste, from the feel of the fruit in your mouth to the sound of your chewing and the smell?

Following this exercise, bring this level of awareness to at least one part of every day, perhaps to your morning tea or the act of brushing your teeth before bed. Use this practice as a way to build your energetic sensitivity, honing your ability to take in details that others overlook.

EXERCISE: Opening the Five Senses, Part 2

For this sensory exploration, you will need to go out in nature, such as a local park or a wilder setting. Use common sense and take any necessary precautions, such as bringing a water bottle and a snack or letting someone know where you'll be.

Start by taking a walk through this natural space and giving yourself a few minutes to simply take in information without trying to focus on anything in particular. Continuing to move, bring more awareness to your body, and prepare to focus your attention on one sense at a time. Feel free to be in stillness at times to take in different details, but spend at least part of each sensory exploration moving in some way.

Sight: What do you see? With so many sights, are there certain features of the landscape that your eyes are drawn to? Choose one of these features and explore it further. Look at it from different angles, perhaps standing up, sitting down, and while moving. Look at it from a distance, then get up close and explore its surface in more detail. Do any textures, colors, patterns, or other features catch your eye?

Touch: Move around your environment once more, and focus on the sensation of your feet touching the ground. Notice which part of your feet you tend to land on first. Experiment with letting your heel touch, then rocking through to the ball of your foot before pushing off. What does the rest of your body feel like in space? What are your arms doing—are they swinging, and if so, does one arm feel freer to move than the other; are they crossed or with hands in pockets? What does the temperature feel like? Is there a breeze? Can you feel the warmth of the sun or is it overcast? Choose something in your environment and explore it through touch more fully, noticing any textures and shapes.

Sound: Move around again, and this time, tune in to the sounds around you. Can you hear any animals or birds? Is there wind or running water, creaking tree branches or rustling leaves? Sounds of human activity? What do your feet sound like on the earth as you walk? Choose a feature of your environment and explore its sounds more closely. Is it something you can safely pick up or interact with in some way, perhaps shaking it or tapping it on the ground to see what sounds it makes?

Smell: Move around again, and now focus on your sense of smell. What stands out? Once you notice the most prominent smell(s), get curious and see if you can detect more subtle smells, such as scent on the breeze or the smell of the soil. Choose a feature of the landscape to explore in more detail. Get up close and take a whiff—what do you smell? If it's safe to do so, rub your fingers on it or rub it between your fingers and see if that produces any new odors. Do the scents conjure any memories or images?

· · · · · · · ·

Taste: It might not be possible to safely ingest anything in your environment, so please use common sense. If there are edible nuts, fruits, or berries that you can identify with absolute certainty, have a taste, going through the same explorations as you did with the piece of fruit in the previous exercise. If not, close your eyes for a moment and breathe in through your mouth a few times. Do you notice any subtle flavors?

Proprioception: Finally, tap into your sixth sense: proprioception, the ability to gauge where your body and body parts are in space. Proprioception is crucial for balance and movement, and we often set up our environment to minimize proprioceptive challenges, thereby weakening this important faculty. If it's safe to do so, close your eyes for a moment, and touch your nose with one index finger and then the other. Was it easy to do without accidentally poking yourself in the eye? If not, practice this over the next few weeks. Then, close your eyes and see if you can lift one foot, even just a couple of inches, off the ground. Repeat with the other foot. Is one side easier than the other?

When you're ready to end the exercise, release focus on any individual sense and allow them to work in concert, enriching your experience of your environment, providing you with layer upon layer of information. Thank your senses for helping you interact with the world and for bringing to your awareness what is most important for you to know. Break the habit of spacing out and ignoring what's going on around you; treat your senses like the finely tuned antennae that they truly are. The more you have full presence in your environment, the easier it will be to pick up on, at will, important details, including those related to subtle energy.

EXERCISE: Electric Hands

In reiki practice, healing is most commonly done through the hands, making it useful to spend time activating and honing your ability to perceive energy through them. One simple yet effective way of doing this is to vigorously rub your palms together for a full fifteen to thirty seconds. Then, slowly start to pull your palms apart a couple of inches, feeling for a sensation a bit like electrified taffy, a gentle tugging sensation between the palms. Explore slowly moving the hands a bit closer and further apart, noticing if the energy feels more pronounced at one distance versus another.

Another variation that can yield rather "trippy" sensations is to once again rub your palms together vigorously, but this time, using the thumb and index finger of one hand, gently pinch the center of the opposite palm, imagining that you're picking up a thread of energy, and slowly draw it up and away from the palm. Can you feel the gentle tug in the center of your palm? With time, you will likely be able to tap into these sensations without rubbing your palms together.

EXERCISE: Opening the Hand Gates

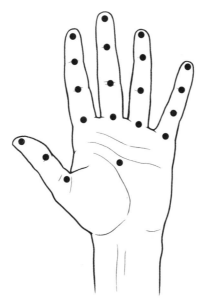

Figure 7: Energy points of the hand

Where awareness goes, energy flows, so by bringing more awareness to our hands, we increase our energetic presence there. One way to do this is to lightly massage the energy gates in the hand, as mapped by the system of *qigong*.[26] One energy gate is in the middle of the palm, where you "plucked" the energy string between your thumb and forefinger in the previous exercise. The remaining gates are in the thumb and fingers, located at the tip and the base (where each digit meets the palm), and at the joints of the digits. There are three in the thumb (tip, base, and one joint in the middle—the interphalangeal joint) and four in each of the fingers (tip, base, and two interphalangeal joints). With a finger pad, gently massage each gate with a clockwise circular motion to free the flow of energy and enhance sensory awareness in the hands.

EXERCISE: Byôsen Reikan Hô (Energy Scanning)

Sometimes referred to simply as *byôsen*, this practice comes from reiki teachings and is the process of energetically scanning the body for illness. You can do this for yourself or with a partner, and the method is quite simple. Take some deep, calming breaths to center yourself and release distractions. Place your hands directly on the body or hovering slightly above, and allow them to be drawn where they will (avoiding direct contact with areas of privacy, of course). Perhaps the trickiest part is quieting the ego and trusting the process, but I have never met anyone who

26. Sandra Kynes, *Change at Hand: Balancing Your Energy through Palmistry, Chakras & Mudras* (Woodbury, MN: Llewellyn Publications, 2009), 7.

• • • • • • •

wasn't able to do this, once they got out of their head and released expectations. You might feel a gentle tug toward a particular area or get an image or other impression of a body part in your mind. As you scan the body, some areas might feel tingly, cold, or hot, drawing you to them. In a reiki session, you would place your hands in these areas, allowing reiki to flow until you get the sense it's time to move to the next spot.

Exercise: Clairvoyance (Clear Seeing)

One of my favorite techniques for enhancing clairvoyant skills is one I learned from Debra Lynne Katz in her book *You Are Psychic*. I was astonished at how dramatically my tarot readings changed after only a week of practicing this technique. Find a comfortable place to sit where you won't be disturbed, and close your eyes. Bring your awareness to your breath, gradually lengthening each inhale and exhale, cultivating a sense of peace and calm. Open your crown chakra to the flow of healing energy, and allow this pure, white light to travel down through your crown, all the way out through your root chakra, grounding you into the earth. Allow healing energy to well up from the earth, entering at your root and ascending all the way out through your crown, connecting you to the heavens. You are now perfectly balanced between heaven and earth with all your chakras open and attuned to divine information.

Say to yourself three times, "My clairvoyant abilities are fully activated in a manner that is correct and good for me." In your mind's eye, conjure up the image of a single rose. Take some time filling out the image, noticing increasingly finer levels of detail. When the image feels secure in your mind, ask a question on which you are seeking guidance. The answer will come in the form of changes to the rose, perhaps a color shift, a change in its health, size, the appearance of thorns, and so on. When you notice a change, focus on it and ask what this means in relation to your question. At this point, you will often be shown images, such as memories or symbolic scenes, that shed further light on your situation. If the rose underwent multiple changes, work with each one individually, zooming out between each one to see the rose as a whole before refocusing on a different alteration.

When done, wipe the image of the rose from your mind's eye, like erasing a chalkboard, and bring your attention back to the stream of energy from earth and sky. Allow the stream to slow and fade, and set the intention that your chakras return to the state that is correct and good for you. I like to hold my palms about a foot in front of my body, starting at the crown of the head, and slowly pass them down the length of my body, ending with my palms flat on the ground, all the while holding the intention that I am returning to a state of perfect balance. Practice this technique regularly to hone your clairvoyant skills.

• • • • • • • •

EXERCISE: Clairaudience (Clear Hearing)

For this exercise, you will need one earplug (yes, just one!) and a place where you can sit undisturbed. Close your eyes and slow your breathing down, one breath cycle at a time, until you feel calm and centered. Cup your palms over your ears and allow healing energy to flow in between your hands, clearing your physical and energetic ears of any blocks and supporting a balanced flow of energy. Say to yourself three times, "My clairaudient abilities are fully activated in a manner that is correct and good for me."

Put an earplug in one ear (if this is uncomfortable, you can skip this step, but I've found it easier to practice this technique with one ear at a time). From the unobstructed ear, imagine an energetic cone beginning to take shape, the point deep within your ear and the mouth widening out into the surrounding space. See this cone constructed from a web of energy, a web that is connected to a universal web that surrounds, interpenetrates, and extends out in all directions from your body. This cone is perfectly adapted to picking up vibrations on this web and decoding them for your clear understanding.

Ask a question, and sit quietly, allowing any relevant energies to condense in your energetic funnel, where they are translated into words. Most likely, you will hear these words as a voice in your head; very rarely will they manifest as something that sounds like someone speaking in the room with you. Gather whatever guidance you need, then retract the energetic cone into your body. Once more, cup your palms over your ears and allow healing energy to flow, sealing any energetic openings that may have been created with the cone and leaving you in a state of perfect balance.

EXERCISE: Clairsentience (Clear Feeling)

A super simple, yet very effective way to tap into clairsentience throughout your day is to check in with your body sensations when making a decision. Let's say you're weighing out options A and B. Close your eyes and breathe for a few cycles to calm your mind and connect with your body. Bring to mind option A and notice how you feel in your body. Then do the same with option B. A "yes" response for me is some variation on open, expansive, or curious. I can sometimes feel a flutter of excitement, too, which might at first glance seem like anxiety, but it's accompanied by a general body sense of openness, a desire to move toward this option even with the butterflies. A "no" response elicits a sense of contraction, closing down, getting smaller or moving away. Try this over the course of the next week—you'll be surprised how clear your body is, even when your mind might be vacillating!

Another clairsentience exercise: Find a place where you won't be disturbed, get comfy, and close your eyes, bringing your awareness to your breath. Really feel where your body is making contact with the chair, floor, and so on, and use these sensations to focus all your awareness in your body. Say to yourself three times, "My clairsentient abilities are fully activated in a manner that is correct and good for me." Take a few more breaths here, really concentrating on the physical and emotional sensations occurring in your body right now. Then, ask your question. How does your body respond? Do you feel a heightened sensation in a particular part of your body? If so, bring your awareness there and ask your question again. Breathe as you wait for a response. Emotional energy is also within the domain of clairsentience, so check in: How do you feel after asking your question? Again, the emotions are often consistent and clear, even when the mind can endlessly debate the pros and cons.

EXERCISE: Claircognizance (Clear Knowing)

This subtle sense typically expresses itself as a fully formed thought popping into our heads. These aren't the thoughts generated by hashing something out in the mind; they arise, quite suddenly, seemingly out of nowhere. Granted, not every spontaneous thought is one we need to follow, but clear knowing has a certain feel to it. When the thought appears, it resonates. It makes sense on a deep, gut level. Our ego might not know what to make of it, but our higher self likes how it sounds and feels.

To jumpstart your claircognizant abilities, try this "spiritual Mad Libs" exercise. Copy the following template, either with a photocopier or by hand, onto a separate sheet of paper. Ideally, if you are copying the words by hand, do this a few days beforehand so the text isn't fresh in your mind. Write your question on the top of the page. Use your breath to calm your mind and bring you into a more grounded state. Say to yourself three times, "My claircognizant abilities are fully activated in a manner that is correct and good for me." Then, without reading the sentences, start filling in the blanks according to the prompts (noun, verb, etc.). Work somewhat quickly to prevent the analytical mind from hijacking the process.

In regard to my situation, my root chakra wants me to _____ (activity) while bringing more awareness to my _____ (body part). My sacral chakra feels very _____ (emotion) about this situation. My solar plexus believes that a wise choice would look like a _____ (animal) that was _____ (verb). My heart chakra knows that if I _____ (verb), I will be able to let go of _____ (difficult emotion). My throat chakra wants me to _____ (school recess activity) to help me express my needs in a mature fashion to _____ (another person involved). My third eye chakra sees a possibility for _____ (positive emotion) if I make more time for _____ (fun hobby). My crown chakra knows that if I let go of _____ (bad habit), I'll find a more productive way of responding to _____ (someone/ something you fear). Generally, I feel _____ (emotion) about this situation. It is an opportunity for me to treat myself with more _____ (quality you would associate with unicorns).

Over the last five chapters, we've learned a great deal about energy, including different ways of conceptualizing and working with various aspects of the human energy system. In the next part, we'll focus our energetic explorations on one particular type of energy: reiki. You'll learn how the system of reiki developed into what it is today and explore fascinating components of this rich healing tradition, from attunements and symbols to precepts and hands-on techniques, and much, much more.

PART II
The Reiki Method

In part 2, we dive deep into the specifics of the healing system of reiki, starting with an exploration of different forms of energy and how reiki fits into this larger context. We'll then trace the system's origins back to 1920s Japan and a man named Mikao Usui, to understand more fully how reiki developed into the practice we know today. We'll talk about the experience of receiving reiki treatments (and how to make the most of your healing session), the various options for studying reiki, and the ins and outs of reiki attunements. We then look at important teachings and healing tools in the reiki system, such as hand positions for healing treatments, symbols and mantras, the reiki precepts, and a variety of traditional and non-traditional reiki techniques. And because reiki is meant to be lived, in chapter 16, we cover simple yet effective ways to incorporate reiki into your daily life, including creating fun reiki programs tailored to your unique goals!

· · · · · · ·

CHAPTER 6

❧

Understanding Reiki Energy

Figure 8: Kanji for reiki

Reiki is a Japanese word written with two kanji. It can be translated as "spiritual energy" and is pronounced RAY-kee. Another common translation is "universal energy" or "universal life force energy," but scholar-practitioners Bronwen and Frans Stiene contend that this is a partial translation of the second kanji only.[27] The first kanji, *rei*, means sacred, the soul, that which contains infinite power, spiritual, the source of wondrous power. The second kanji, *ki*, means energy of the universe, vapor, breath, something unseen. Thus, we might think of reiki as the energy that is in all things, that forms all things, that connects all things. It's the essence or spirit of everything.

27. Bronwen Stiene and Frans Stiene, *The Reiki Sourcebook* (Ropley, UK: O Books, 2008), 5.

• • • • • • • •

Outside of Japan, reiki has come to mean a specific healing system originating with a man named Mikao Usui (we'll learn more about Usui in the next chapter), but within Japan, reiki has been used for many spiritual healing methods. In fact, Usui never called his method reiki, but, as was common practice at the time, the word was written in his teachings to indicate that his methods utilized this spiritual energy. On Usui's memorial stone, erected one year after his death by his students, he is indicated as the founder of *Reiho*, which means "spiritual method" or "spiritual energy healing method."[28]

Different Types of Life Energy

To develop an understanding of what reiki is, I find it helpful to view reiki in context, as one facet of ki, which is a broad term for life force energy. Within this larger category, we can define seven subtypes of energy: *kekki, shioke, mizuke, kuki, denki, jiki,* and *reiki*. These various life forces all derive from a higher energy known as *shinki*.[29]

First Type of Energy: Kekki

Kekki is the first type of energy and is described as "ki of the blood" or "energy of the blood." Living beings require kekki to "maintain their substance" and have sufficient energy to take action.[30] Kekki is the least structured type of energy, and more structured, organized types of energy can use kekki to nourish a variety of structures. In some sense, it's like an all-purpose energy drink that can be utilized to power a variety of processes within a living system.

In order for kekki to provide nourishment, there must be something that needs to be nourished, and this brings us to the second type of energy.

Second Type of Energy: Shioke

Shioke provides structure and form, acting as a container for kekki, and it is described as "Ki of the salt" or "Ki of the minerals."[31] Shioke has a strong connective power, keeping certain energies in relationship to each other in order to create unified forms. Thus, shioke is related to boundaries, because forms are defined by their boundaries, by what is a part of them and what is not. Shioke maintains these boundaries, giving kekki a place to gather and be stored, where it can then be used as nourishment by the structure. Kekki and shioke are both associated with the root chakra, which makes sense given how their functions are the foundation upon which a structure exists.

---

28. Stiene and Stiene, *The Reiki Sourcebook*, 8.
29. Walter Lübeck, Frank Arjava Petter, and William Lee Rand, *The Spirit of Reiki: The Complete Handbook of the Reiki System*, trans. Christine M. Grimm (Twin Lakes, WI: Lotus Press, 2001), 52.
30. Lübeck, Petter, and Rand, *The Spirit of Reiki*, 54.
31. Lübeck, Petter, and Rand, *The Spirit of Reiki*, 55.

· · · · · · · ·

Third Type of Energy: Mizuke

The third type of energy is *mizuke*, the energy of relationship, and "without Mizuke, the Shioke forms would remain isolated … rigid and sluggish without any genuine movement."[32] Mizuke utilizes the kekki within the shioke "containers" and initiates flow and interaction among them, giving rise to the dynamism that characterizes all life. Mizuke also generates emotional experiences, which are the language of relationship and the means through which we experience things like love, trust, and desire, which motivates us to connect with others outside of our shioke-derived boundaries. Mizuke is known as "ki of the water" and is associated with the sacral chakra.

Fourth Type of Energy: Kuki

The fourth type of energy is *kuki*, "ki of the gases" or "ki of the air," and this is the energy that inspires self-fulfillment and self-development. Kuki supports logical thinking and force of will and is associated with the solar plexus chakra, an important energetic hub of our inner power and ability to self-direct our lives. Kuki helps us see what makes us unique and imparts the strength to dance to the beat of our own drum over becoming distracted by the endless *should*s and *have to*s. It helps us discover what is of true value to us and make choices in accordance with those values.

Fifth Type of Energy: Denki

Kuki works best in conjunction with the fifth energy type, *denki*, which integrates our desire for self-fulfillment with the ability to remain in relationship. It is associated with the heart chakra, and Lübeck describes it as "the urge to grow in a way considerate of others."[33] Denki translates to "ki of the thunder," and Lübeck relates this to the power of thunder described in the *I Ching*, an important ancient Chinese text. Thunder can be terrifying and, as such, serves to jolt us out of a state of self-centeredness and remind us that our life is shaped by greater organizing forces, inspiring us to live with integrity. We generate denki when we pursue self-fulfillment while still acting in a way that promotes the well-being of all life.

Sixth Type of Energy: Jiki

To support our quest for self-realization, denki partners with the sixth energy type, *jiki*, which can be translated roughly as "magnetic power" or "gathering force."[34] It is associated with the throat chakra. Jiki draws into our life the energy that is the ideal complement to each moment. This energy can, in many ways, be thought of as a mirror-image version of our current state,

32. Lübeck, Petter, and Rand, *The Spirit of Reiki*, 56.
33. Lübeck, Petter, and Rand, *The Spirit of Reiki*, 57.
34. Lübeck, Petter, and Rand, *The Spirit of Reiki*, 58.

• • • • • • •

giving us access to what C. G. Jung called the shadow self or unconscious mind. Consciousness as we know it could not exist without this polarity of "light" and "shadow," and just like jiki, the unconscious generates and draws toward us experiences that reflect our unconscious landscape. If we use these experiences as a mirror rather than seeing them as things that are simply happening to us, our awareness expands to include more of our unconscious self. Thus, we generate jiki when we take responsibility for our relationships to ourselves and our relationships with others, as these external relationships are, in their own right, a form of mirror as well. Jiki feels similar to the physics concept of antimatter, whereby every particle in existence is theorized to have an antiparticle that is exactly the same but with an opposite charge. For example, electrons have an antimatter "twin," the positron. Perhaps jiki is a form of antimatter that is specifically required by the human energy field.

Seventh Type of Energy: Reiki

And finally, we arrive at the seventh energy: *reiki*. Reiki organizes the interactions between the other six energy types, and Lübeck associates it with the third eye chakra. Lübeck also states that reiki is the highest form of life energy that can manifest in the physical plane, and therefore it acts as a sort of intermediary between material life and the highest form of energy, *shinki*, which is associated with the crown chakra.[35] Shinki is the energy that creates all things and the energy that all things return to when their material existence ends. We could then think of reiki as shinki that has been "translated" into a form that is able to be processed by our energy systems. This also is in keeping with a common reiki teaching, that reiki is guided by a higher intelligence and knows precisely what the recipient needs and where.

How Does Reiki Work?

Given that reiki is able to organize the other six forms of energy, one way of viewing a reiki treatment is much like cleaning your house. Over time, the counters get cluttered, the floors collect dirt, and the stuff in the closets seems to multiply of its own accord (or maybe that's just my house). So, too, as you go about your life, does your energy system pick up a little clutter here and a little debris over there, and with time, this can lead to blockages and areas of stagnation. These blocks can also create areas with too much energy, a phenomenon that can be seen even on the physical level. One example: Let's say your right hip doesn't move as freely as it could, maybe from an injury or from years of sitting all day at work. This lack of movement will need to be compensated for somewhere else in your body. Perhaps your left hip, now, will be moving much more, and this could lead to excessive strain and wear and tear on the joint. Energetically,

---

35. Lübeck, Petter, and Rand, *The Spirit of Reiki,* 60.

certain areas might "pick up the slack" and carry more energy than they're equipped to handle long term, leading to burnout and dysfunction.

In my previous book, *Living Reiki*, I likened reiki to a divine blueprint containing the pattern of our original wholeness. Throughout life, we come to forget some or all of this wholeness, and working with reiki is like downloading the blueprint again, reminding us of our True Self. The more reminders we get, the more our True Self becomes our natural, automatic home base, and when we make decisions from this Self, we live in alignment with our soul's purpose, making full use of our unique gifts that we came into this life to express and share with others.

Reiki has the ability to enter your energy system, clearing away obstructions to allow for a healthy flow of energy in under-energized areas, while relieving the burden on over-energized areas, bringing your entire system into greater balance and harmony. And just as we can't get away with only cleaning house once (sadly), we need to regularly tend to our energetic "hygiene." One way of doing this is through reiki treatments, but it certainly isn't the only way, and in fact, it's great to have a rich tapestry of practices that you employ to keep your energy functioning optimally. For example, I like to meditate every day and get outside as often as possible. When I skip those basic practices, my energy feels sluggish and convoluted. I also give myself reiki daily, and I mix in a variety of tools depending on the day and my intuitive sense, such as carrying a particular crystal in my pocket, running energy through my chakras over my lunch break, or doing some chanting on the drive home. The point is, pay attention to your energetic health. Find the tools that work for you and *use them*. There are plenty of exercises in this book to get you going, and I invite you to pick a few of your favorites and pencil them onto your calendar this week. Your energy will thank you for it!

In the next chapter, we'll look at reiki as a healing system, starting with its origins in Japan with a man named Mikao Usui.

· · · · · · · ·

CHAPTER 7

❧

The History of Reiki

The history of reiki centers around a man named Mikao Usui, who was born on August 15, 1865, in the village of Taniai (now called Miyama cho, *cho* meaning "town") in Yamagata county of the Gifu Prefecture of Japan. Usui lived in an evolving country. During the reign of the Meiji Emperor, Japan underwent significant change, most notably the end of its self-imposed isolation, or *sakoku*, from the rest of the world (outside of limited contact with Dutch and Chinese traders), which had lasted from 1639 to 1854.[36]

Usui was born into a class system that would change dramatically over his lifetime. His family, which included two brothers and an older sister, belonged to the privileged class and were descendants of the Chiba clan, an influential samurai family (the samurai were the military nobility in medieval and early-modern Japan). Specifically, they were *hatamoto samurai*, who were the highest-ranking officers and the personal guard of the *shogun*. Usui studied martial arts, beginning in his youth: *aiki-jūjutsu*, the precursor of modern *jujitsu* and *aikido*, and a form of *yagyu ryu* (the art of sword fighting).[37] Presumably, part of these studies would have entailed learning how to cultivate and use *ki*, as this is a core tenet of many Japanese martial arts, and in *aiki-jūjutsu* in particular, practitioners are trained in redirecting their opponent's energy flow in order to control their actions with minimal effort. For example, one aspect involves meeting and blending with your opponent's energy and tuning in to its rhythm, which enables you to respond with minimal effort and maximum effect. No doubt Usui's many years of martial arts training influenced his development of the system of reiki.

---

36. Stiene and Stiene, *The Reiki Sourcebook*, 53.
37. Stiene and Stiene, *The Reiki Sourcebook*, 54.

According to his memorial stone, which was erected one year after his death by his students, Usui traveled a great deal, both within Japan and overseas. His career was varied (we know at one point he was a private secretary to a politician named Shinpei Goto), and his interests were diverse as well, ranging from history, medicine, and psychology, to Buddhism, divination, and physiognomy.[38]

While he is sometimes referred to as Dr. Usui, he was never a medical doctor, and there are no records indicating that he was called by this title in Japan. It is thought that this was an incorrect translation by Hawayo Takata (we'll learn more about her later) of the honorific title *sensei*.

According to Chris Marsh, a reiki teacher who met some of Usui's students in Japan, Usui was a *zaike,* or lay *Tendai* priest. Tendai is a branch of Buddhism that was brought to Japan in the ninth century by a monk, Saichō, who founded a temple on Mount Hiei, a mountain northeast of Kyoto where there is still a temple today (rebuilt in the 1500s after the original complex was destroyed).[39] Tendai practice centers around the Lotus Sutra and involves the use of *mudras,* or hand gestures, devotional chants, and meditating on mandalas and other sacred geometries. As part of his Tendai practice, it is believed that Usui also studied *Shugendō,* which translates as "the path of training and testing."[40] Shugendō blends Japanese Buddhism, *Shintō* (the indigenous Japanese religion), Taoism, and shamanism, and the influence of both Tendai Buddhism and Shugendō is seen in Usui's teachings, for example, in the *reiju,* mantras, symbols, and other techniques, as well as in his twenty-one-day fast on *Kurama-yama,*[41] which we'll look at in more detail below.

While Usui did not open an official learning and treatment center until 1922 (the *Usui Reiki Ryôhô Gakkai,* or Usui Reiki Healing Method Society, in Aoyami Harajuku, Tokyo), two sources indicate that his teachings existed prior to this time. A woman whom Chris Marsh refers to as Suzuki-san indicated that her formal training with Usui began in 1915. She and her fellow students retained study materials that included the precepts, *waka* (poetry), meditations, and other teachings. And a Japanese article from 1928, "A Treatment to Heal Diseases, Hand Healing" by Shûô Matsui (a student of Chûjirô Hayashi; more on him below) states that Usui's system was founded decades prior to the article's publication.[42] Usui's early teachings as a whole were not called reiki; the name was used in conjunction with his teachings but with the literal meaning

---

38. Stiene and Stiene, *The Reiki Sourcebook,* 55.

39. Paul Groner, *Saichō: The Establishment of the Japanese Tendai School* (Honolulu: University of Hawaii Press, 2002), 65.

40. Shokai Koshikidake and Martin Faulks, *Shugendō: The Way of the Mountain Monks,* foreword by Steven K. Hayes (Faulks Books, 2015), 15.

41. Stiene and Stiene, *The Reiki Sourcebook,* 57.

42. Stiene and Stiene, *The Reiki Sourcebook,* 58.

of "spiritual energy," a word commonly used by healers practicing various modalities. It wasn't until Usui's teachings left Japan that the system became known as reiki.

The aim of Usui's teachings was enlightenment, but healing was occurring as a wonderful side effect, and initially, there wasn't a clear distinction between those coming for hands-on healing and those interested in the spiritual teachings. This changed in 1917. All of Usui's students would receive *reiju*, a spiritual blessing or attunement, designed to help the student remember their true nature, as well as the five precepts (see chapter 13), but those who wished to go deeper with the spiritual practices became dedicated students. The concept of reiju was not specific to Usui's teachings. For example, in Tendai practice, *go shimbô* purification is performed using specific mantras and mudras to prepare oneself for ritual, and the famous Japanese healer Toshihiro Eguchi, a friend and student of Usui, performed a similar spiritual blessing known as *kosho michibiki* (illuminating guidance).[43]

Usui utilized a variety of teaching tools to reach students at different levels, such as meditation practices, and mantras and symbols to help students with less energetic sensitivity tap into particular elements of energy. After the formation of the Usui Reiki Ryôhô Gakkai, the teachings became more codified, and at the society's fifty-year anniversary, a manual was published, the *Reiki Ryôhô Hikkei*, which included a healing guide, the *Ryôhô Shishin*, as well as information regarding the early development of Usui's system.

One of the most legendary founding stories involves Usui's twenty-one-day fast on *Kurama-yama* (Mount Kurama). In one version, Usui experiences enlightenment during his fast, and as he is returning down from the mountain, he stubs his toe. When he placed his hands on his foot, he realized that he had been given the power of hands-on healing. The twenty-one-day practice on the mountain is known as *kushu shinren*, which, in Shugendō, is a form of intense discipline and severe training. This was a well-known practice that was carried out most commonly by the *yamabushi*, or mountain ascetics, who would use these extreme trials to, among other things, test themselves, deepen their personal practice, and achieve enlightenment or revelation of some kind. This was not a quest to be taken lightly by the untrained, and presumably Usui's many years of spiritual practice and martial arts training prepared him for this trial. The memorial stone states that "he suddenly felt One Great Reiki over his head and attained enlightenment and he obtained *Reiki Ryôhô*. Then, he tried it on himself and experimented on his family members. The efficacy was immediate."[44]

While the Gakkai was not formed until a month after Usui's experience on Mount Kurama, it seems clear that he was teaching before this point. *The Reiki Sourcebook* notes that "Divine Inspiration is a must for the founder of any Japanese art," so is this part of the story merely a tool to

43. Stiene and Stiene, *The Reiki Sourcebook*, 59.
44. Stiene and Stiene, *The Reiki Sourcebook*, 61.

• • • • • • •

add credibility to Usui's teachings?[45] We will likely never know for certain what happened on the mountain, but in many ways, it matters little. Usui's teachings were effective prior to his twenty-one-day practice; perhaps they became more so afterward due to a revelatory experience, or perhaps not. Regardless, his methods are still in use over a hundred years later and have helped thousands of people, indicating that they offer something of great substance and value that is worth preserving and passing on.

In 1923, the Great Kantō Earthquake hit Tokyo and Yokohama, causing an estimated 100,000 deaths with 40,000 reported missing. Hundreds of thousands of people were left homeless. According to his memorial stone, Usui "went out every morning to go around the town, and he cured and saved an innumerable number of people. This is just a broad outline of his relief activities during such an emergency."[46] In 1925, Usui moved his clinic and home, selecting the new location in *Nakano ku* by divination. He traveled throughout Japan to teach and give treatments, with the number of students totaling over 2,000. On March 9, 1926, while traveling in Fukuyama, Usui suffered a stroke and passed away. In February of the following year, his students erected his memorial stone at the Saihô-ji temple in Suginami, Tokyo.

Chûjirô Hayashi (1879–1940)

There are numerous figures throughout reiki's history, some of which we'll meet in the appendices when we look at the various branches of reiki, but one especially important figure is Chûjirô Hayashi, a naval officer who was one of only twenty people (some sources cite twenty-one) permitted to progress to the highest level of training (*shinpiden*) within Usui's system. Many of the shinpiden-level students were naval officers, and according to scholar-practitioner Hiroshi Doi, three of the Gakkai's presidents were as well: Jûzaburô Ushida, Kanichi Taketomi, and Hôichi Waname.[47] Hayashi was also a medical doctor, and he is credited with developing Usui's teachings into a system with a slightly greater emphasis on healing over spiritual development.

It is surmised that while he was still a member of the Gakkai, during the year following Usui's death, Hayashi wrote the healing guide included in the organization's fiftieth anniversary manual, as it is very similar to the healing guide that Hayashi wrote shortly thereafter for his own clinic, the *Hayashi Reiki Kenkyû Kai* (Hayashi Spiritual Energy Research Society) in *Shinano-machi*, Tokyo. It was a large clinic with eight treatment tables and sixteen practitioners, two per client.[48] One practitioner would begin treatment at the head while the second practitioner began at the

45. Stiene and Stiene, *The Reiki Sourcebook*, 61.

46. Stiene and Stiene, *The Reiki Sourcebook*, 63.

47. Hiroshi Doi, *A Modern Reiki Method for Healing* (Southfield, MI: Vision Publications, 2014), 36.

48. Tadao Yamaguchi, *Light on the Origins of Reiki: A Handbook for Practicing the Original Reiki of Usui and Hayashi*, trans. Ikuko Hirota, ed. Neehar Douglass (Twin Lakes, WI: Lotus Press, 2007), 68.

• • • • • • • •

abdomen (*hara*). Clients paid money for treatments, and there were internships available for students, which included volunteer hours in the clinic.[49]

Additional information about Hayashi's teachings comes from the son, Tadao Yamaguchi, of one of his students, Chiyoko Yamaguchi. Tadao currently teaches a form of reiki known as *Jikiden Reiki*, *jikiden* meaning "directly transmitted or passed down from one's teacher," and in his book, *Light on Reiki*, he describes seminars taught by Hayashi and attended by his mother, Chiyoko, and her older sister, Katsue. At the time, Hayashi would often travel around Japan to teach, and following an invitation by one of Tadao's relatives, he came to Ishikawa in 1935 to lead a seminar, which was attended by Tadao's aunt, Katsue; his mother, Chiyoko, attended her first seminar in 1938. Tadao writes, "The tuition fee for Reiki seminars in those days was 50 yen, when the average salaried workers were getting 47 yen a month," but Chiyoko's uncle felt it would be more worthwhile spending money for his niece to attend the seminar over lavish wedding arrangements: "This shows how seriously the family took Reiki."[50]

When she arrived for the seminar, Chiyoko remembers, many of the participants were wearing very formal attire, which lent a very serious atmosphere to the occasion. She was ushered into a room with rows of floor cushions (*zabuton*) and instructed where to sit. The coordinator explained that the lights would be turned off, and participants would be asked to sit in a kneeling posture (*seiza*) with their eyes closed, "taking care no pressure is put on the lower *tanden* (a spot three cm lower than the navel)."[51] They were to place their hands in prayer position (*gasshô*) and remain seated and quiet until the reiju was completed. After the introduction, Hayashi entered the room dressed in traditional Japanese attire, and Chiyoko was very impressed by his stature and bearing; she said he seemed to have a light shining all around him. Hayashi then led the group in reciting the five reiki principles, which were written on a scroll hanging in the room, a total of three times. Occasionally, Hayashi would also chant poetry from the Meiji Emperor (*gyôsei*). He would then give reiju to the group. This was followed by reiju given by other members of the *shihan* (teacher) degree, and Chiyoko estimates that there were three shihans present.

After the reiju, the group came together in a circle, hands touching, allowing reiki to circulate (this is called *reiki mawashi*; see page 233), during which time Hayashi would join in the circle or sit in the center, giving instructions. Over the course of the five-day seminar, students would receive repeated reiju, and Hayashi would give lectures and practical training. Students were required to practice on each other and occasionally on a guest who lived close to the venue and was suffering from an illness.

49. Stiene and Stiene, *The Reiki Sourcebook*, 82.
50. Yamaguchi, *Light on the Origins of Reiki*, 30.
51. Yamaguchi, *Light on the Origins of Reiki*, 31.

Hayashi Reiki Kenkyû Kai divided instruction into *shoden* and *okuden*, the first two courses, often taught together as a five-day seminar, and upon fulfillment of certain requirements, students could continue to the *shihan-kaku* (assistant teacher) and *shihan* (teacher) training.[52] The final two levels were originally less formal in structure and did not contain a set curriculum as they do today. There were also prerequisites to the shoden and okuden courses, known as *kyu* (degree). Tadao believes there were four levels of kyu, beginning with sixth kyu and ending with the highest, third kyu. These degrees were given when participants experienced a reiki session, but they were not yet permitted to practice reiki on others.[53]

Hayashi died on May 11, 1940, having taken his own life. Tadao writes that Hayashi traveled to Hawaii shortly before war broke out, which was especially risky for him as a former high-ranking naval officer, and upon his return to Japan, he was questioned by naval authorities. His refusal to give information was sure to lead to severe punishment, "which would have had a major effect on his family," so he instead chose what he felt was an honorable death.[54] According to one of his students, Hawayo Takata, Hayashi was concerned that he would be forced to fight in the war, killing many people, and this is why he chose to end his life.

Hawayo Takata (1900–1980)

In 1935, Hawayo Takata was lying on an operating table in Japan, having been told that surgery was required to remove a tumor and gallstones, among other physical issues. It was then that she heard a voice telling her to ask the surgeon for alternatives, that the operation was unnecessary. Based on the recommendation of the hospital's dietician, Takata soon found herself in Hayashi's reiki clinic. She could feel heat and vibrations emanating from the practitioners' hands as they gave her a treatment. When she returned for a follow-up the next day, she checked for machinery that might have been used to generate heat, but there was nothing.[55] Hayashi explained the basics of the treatment to her, but Takata was told that this technique was not taught to foreigners; while both of her parents were Japanese, she had been born and raised in Hawaii.

By all accounts, Takata was nothing if not persistent, and after only three weeks of treatments, she was feeling much better, which only stoked her curiosity and desire to learn. Eventually, Hayashi relented and she was allowed to study as an honorary member. She continued receiving treatments for six months, after which she moved in with the Hayashi family to spend another year studying and practicing. She would spend the mornings in the clinic as a practi-

---

52. Yamaguchi, *Light on the Origins of Reiki*, 139.
53. Yamaguchi, *Light on the Origins of Reiki*, 69.
54. Yamaguchi, *Light on the Origins of Reiki*, 69.
55. Stiene and Stiene, *The Reiki Sourcebook*, 166.

tioner and travel to do house calls in the afternoon, progressing to the okuden level at the end of this period.

In 1937, Takata finished her practitioner training and returned to Hawaii, and Hayashi and his daughter arrived a few weeks later, staying for six months in order to help her establish a practice in Honolulu. Before returning to Japan, Hayashi announced that Takata was now a Master of the Usui system. Hayashi used Mikao Usui's name on her certificate, rather than the name of his own organization, and scholar-practitioner Hiroshi Doi explains this was a way of showing respect to the original teachings (although Hayashi had, by this point, changed the teachings to a certain extent).[56]

In 1939, Takata built a healing practice with living quarters for her family in Hilo, and it was not long before it took off, becoming a huge success. Her treatments might have been a single session, lasting up to a couple of hours, or they might have been given on a recurring basis for as long as a year. She would sit cross-legged on the floor while giving treatments, starting at the head or the abdomen, and there is a story of her allegedly bringing someone back to life after five and a half hours of treatment at the solar plexus. It appears that she would charge clients who were able to pay and treat those who could not free of charge.

In January of 1940, Takata had a distressing dream about Hayashi, and in April of that year, she decided to return to Japan to see him, despite his family's assurances that all was well. When she arrived, she learned of Hayashi's decision to take his own life. Takata claims that Hayashi left her his practice and home in Tokyo, which she accepted, leaving it in the hands of Hayashi's wife, Chie, so she could return to the US. When she came back to Japan fourteen years later, she found the house divided into apartments at Chie's discretion to house refugees in the aftermath of World War II, and Takata officially gave the house and clinic to Chie and returned, once again, to the US.[57]

Takata spent the next thirty years working out of Honolulu, although she would also travel around the islands to teach, and in 1973 she began teaching on the mainland and in Canada as well. She didn't teach her first official master-teacher level student until she was seventy-six. She charged $100 for her level one training in 1975, increasing it to $125 in 1976, and $400 for the level two training. From 1976 to 1980, her master-level training was $10,000, and Takata explained that this high price tag generated the proper amount of respect for the teachings. As the Stienes write, she felt that "students would feel more responsible and have more respect for the system once they had paid their hard-earned money to receive it."[58] According to reiki teacher-scholar

56. Stiene and Stiene, *The Reiki Sourcebook*, 168.
57. Stiene and Stiene, *The Reiki Sourcebook*, 171.
58. Stiene and Stiene, *The Reiki Sourcebook*, 172.

· · · · · · · ·

Robert Fueston, the following people completed their master-teacher–level training under Takata (the date of certification is indicated in parentheses):

1. Virginia Samdahl (1976)
2. Ethel Lombardi (1976)
3. John Harvey Gray (October 1976)
4. Beth Gray (1976; official certificate received in 1979)
5. Dorothy Baba (1976)
6. Barbara Lincoln McCullough (1977)
7. Harry M. Kuboi (April 1977)
8. Fran Brown (January 1979)
9. Iris Ishikuro (1979)
10. Phyllis Lei Furumoto (April 1979)
11. Barbara Weber (September 1979)
12. Bethal Phaige (October 1979)
13. Barbara Brown (October 1979)
14. Wanja Twan (October 1979)
15. Ursula Baylow (October 1979)
16. Paul Mitchell (November 1979)
17. George Araki (1979)
18. Shinobu Saito (May 1980)
19. Patricia Bowling (September 1980)
20. Mary McFadyen (September 1980)
21. Rick Bockner (October 1980)

Fueston also includes Takata's sister, Kay Yamashita, on this list. While Takata does not appear to have considered her sister an official teacher, she told one of her students, John Harvey Gray, that Kay could replace her as a teacher if need be.[59]

Takata claimed that the system of reiki was an oral tradition, giving her permission to teach as she wished, and based on a comparison of notes taken by some of her students in different classes, it seems that her teachings frequently varied. While in Japan, she speaks of meeting with other practitioners, and she felt that their teachings were highly complex, requiring many years of training, closely tied to religious practices, and inappropriate for non-Japanese learners.

59. Stiene and Stiene, *The Reiki Sourcebook*, 174.

• • • • • • • •

To all her students Takata taught a simple version of the five precepts and hand positions, the latter of which has been the subject of controversy. It is believed that Usui did not originally teach hand positions, although later this evolved into five hand positions, all for the head, as shown in the *Reiki Ryôhô Hikkei*, a healing guide published by the Usui Reiki Ryôhô Gakkai. The symbols, too, seemed to have varied in Takata's teachings. Students were not permitted to keep copies of the symbols, and in 1982, during the first teacher-student meeting after her passing, each person drew the symbols that had been given to them by Takata and to their surprise they differed from one another in some respects. The group decided to standardize the symbols, although none were entirely sure if they were using the correct rendition or not. The group later became the Reiki Alliance, with Phyllis Lei Furumoto named grandmaster, which originally meant that she was responsible for training other master-teachers and was considered the "lineage bearer of the system of Reiki."[60] Eventually, all the teachers were permitted to train other teachers. Barbara Weber Ray was not present at the meeting to standardize symbols; she claimed to be Takata's successor and went on to create her own branch, the Radiance Technique.

The version of Mikao Usui's history as popularized by Takata in the 1970s is still quite persistent in many reiki circles today, in spite of new information, including the discovery of Usui's memorial stone and research conducted by various scholars and practitioners. It's unclear whether her stories were intended to be taken as factual or were more like parables, but these are a few of the lingering inaccuracies:

- That Usui was a Christian (or a Christian minister). There is no evidence that this was the case; Usui was a practicing Buddhist. This may have been her way to introduce the teachings to a Western audience, particularly in the political climate of World War II.

- That he attended certain universities, such as the University of Chicago or Doshisha University (Tokyo), even though these institutions have no record of him working or attending there.

- That he was a medical doctor (this may have been Takata's translation of the honorific *sensei*).[61]

The fact remains that Hawayo Takata played an integral role in bringing reiki to the West, and her treatments and teachings have impacted thousands of people. While it seems impossible to determine, as a whole, how much her teachings differed from Hayashi's, or from student to student, this does not, in my mind, lessen her immense contribution to the reiki community. Hawayo Takata passed away on December 11, 1980.

60. Stiene and Stiene, *The Reiki Sourcebook*, 188.
61. Stiene and Stiene, *The Reiki Sourcebook*, 180.

• • • • • • •

Reiki's Decline and Reemergence in Japan

Reiki teacher and researcher Masaki Nishina discusses the changing attitudes toward spiritual healing practices in Japan before and after World War II in his book *Reiki and Japan: A Cultural View of Western and Japanese Reiki*, and it's helpful to look at these shifts, as they shed light on reiki's diverging trajectories in Japan versus elsewhere in the world. Prior to the war, there were numerous alternative healing methods and traditional folk remedies in use. During the Meiji period, when the government sought to Westernize the country's healthcare system, there was an increase in out-of-pocket medical expenses, and a ban was instituted against any healing methods that relied solely on prayer and incantations without the use of medical treatments or prescribed drugs. In spite of the ban, the number of traditional Japanese midwives, acupuncturists, and Chinese herbal pharmacists increased between 1884 and 1926, while the number of Western-trained providers remained fairly constant, and Nishina credits this, in large part, to the rising medical costs and people's need to secure affordable healthcare.

This climate gave rise to many alternative therapies, and while they were new techniques, they were based on older Shintô, Buddhist, or Shugendō practices. Practitioners were known as *reijutsu-ka* (*rei* = "mysterious," *jutsu* = "technique," and *ka* = "professional"), and many books and magazines describing these techniques were published. In 1868, the government created National Shintô, standardizing religious practice and placing the emperor as a living god at the center of worship. In response, many people wanted to return to older forms of Shintô, while others created new movements based on older teachings, many of which included forms of hands-on healing techniques. Usui began teaching and practicing his system during a time when traditional and alternative therapies were on the rise, perhaps in reaction to the government's attempts at standardization and Westernization.[62]

Following the war, there was a marked decrease in these practices, however, and there may be several reasons for this shift. Following Allied occupation, attitudes toward traditional Japanese culture changed, and in particular, many things deemed "unscientific" were regarded with suspicion, including spiritual healing techniques and hands-on energy therapies. In 1947, the GHQ (General Headquarters of the Allied forces) issued a law banning folk and traditional therapies, with the exception of massage, acupuncture, moxibustion, and bone setting, categorizing them as "quasi-medical." It wasn't until 1960 that the Supreme Court ruled that only those "quasi-medical" therapies that were harmful to human health would remain illegal, and Nishina writes, "Since then, many therapies, now called 'alternative therapies' have been practiced in a

---

62. Masaki Nishina, *Reiki and Japan: A Cultural View of Western and Japanese Reiki*, ed. Amanda Jayne (self-published, CreateSpace, 2017), 27.

• • • • • • • •

grey area. Even today in Japan, if I were to refer to myself as a therapist, it wouldn't be accepted by society who would see me as a 'would-be' therapist."[63]

In the post-war period, the GHQ ordered the removal and exclusion of "undesirable personnel" from public office, the vast majority of which were army and navy personnel. Anything deemed to be military related was also banned, including martial arts, such as judo and karate, as well as *sado* (tea ceremony), *kabuki* (historical plays), and Shintô. As noted earlier, many of the Usui Reiki Ryôhô Gakkai's original members and leaders were connected to the Japanese navy. After the war, the society closed its doors to the public, and it is very difficult for non-members to access any information about the organization directly. One can become a member now only through formal introduction by an existing member; thus, their numbers have decreased to only a few hundred—quite a difference from the purported 7,000 members in 1930.

In the 1980s, Mieko Mitsui, a journalist living in New York who had been trained in Barbara Weber Ray's style of reiki, the Radiance Technique, came to Japan and began teaching Western reiki classes, sparking a resurgence in its popularity. She also translated Ray's book, *The Reiki Factor*, into Japanese, making information about the system, at least from a Western point of view, more accessible. Mitsui was only authorized to teach up to level two, however, so it was still difficult to find teachers in Japan, given that few people knew of the existence of the Gakkai at this point. Reiki teacher and researcher Frank Arjava Petter, who had been trained to the master-teacher level in the Reiki Alliance lineage, began teaching in 1993 in Hokkaido, offering instruction in all levels, and many of his students went on to create their own reiki schools. One of these students, a man named Toshitaka Mochizuki, published a book on Western reiki called *Iyashi no Te* ("healing hands"), thus contributing to reiki's renewed popularity in Japan.

One of the first students to receive an attunement from Mieko Mitsui was a man named Hiroshi Doi (see page 340), and in learning that he could not train to become a teacher with Mitsui, he began to research the origins of reiki, in the hopes of finding a successor of Usui still living in Japan. It was through this line of inquiry that he discovered the Gakkai and was permitted to join after being introduced by one of its members. He studied with Kimiko Koyama, the Gakkai's sixth president, and he "was amazed at how different it was from the Western reiki of Ms. Mitsui."[64] He eventually went on to form the system of *Gendai Reiki Hô*, with the aim of uniting Usui's original teachings with Western reiki in a way that resonates with modern users while still retaining its effectiveness.

63. Nishina, *Reiki and Japan*, 112.
64. Doi, *A Modern Reiki Method for Healing*, 40.

· · · · · · ·

Comparing Systems of Reiki

In the appendices, we'll look at the various branches of reiki created over the decades, but here, we'll look more broadly at some of the possible differences between Dento Reiki, or Usui's system of reiki as it was originally taught (keeping in mind that our information in this regard is incomplete), and Western reiki. The latter category, too, requires a caveat, because there are so many branches that fall under the Western reiki umbrella, making it difficult to apply any one statement to all.

One tenet that appears consistent among all traditional teachings is that reiki does not require concentration and effort, and indeed, intense concentration or the use of one's will to direct the energy is to be avoided. Masaki Nishina writes that the use of "personal intention, imagination and/or deliberate breath" renders the energy "no longer pure Reiki,"[65] and Hiroshi Doi says, "It is crucial to relax and place the hands without any intentions."[66] There are numerous Western reiki systems that incorporate visualizations, setting of intentions, and other techniques that run contrary to this principle. I use these techniques in my own practice and have not found that they "sully" the energy, but I also appreciate making the distinction between these techniques and more traditional reiki practices.

There is also a conflict between the Western belief that the ability to use reiki is "obtained" only after an attunement, or that this ability has to be granted or bestowed by an external agent of some kind, and the Japanese belief that reiki is innate. In some Western schools, the attunements given at different levels of training are said to activate more powerful (or otherwise distinct) levels of energy within the student, and some teachers even claim that attunements only last for a certain period of time, after which they "expire" and the student must receive another attunement to continue using reiki. In traditional reiki, only one form of attunement is used, *reiju*, and rather than being viewed as something that grants a mysterious reiki ability to the student, it is seen as a way of opening the person to the natural flow of this energy. Throughout life, based on myriad factors, our energy channels may become blocked and unable to channel as much energy as is needed to effectively administer a reiki treatment. While other methods of "declogging the pipes" are certainly available, a reiju is a quick and effective means for clearing our energy channels, after which your regular practice maintains this clarity and increases your ability to channel reiki effectively.

Finally, the use of symbols may differ in traditional versus Western reiki, again, depending on the branch of Western reiki in question. Some branches teach a heavy reliance on the power of the symbols, that certain symbols can only be used after a particular level of attunement, that

---

65. Nishina, *Reiki and Japan*, 165.

66. Doi, *A Modern Reiki Method for Healing*, 21.

· · · · · · · ·

symbols must be used in a special order if they are to work, or that reiki cannot flow without "activation" via the symbols. It seems that Usui used the symbols as teaching tools to help students who had difficulty in sensing particular vibrations of energy but that, with practice, the symbols would no longer be necessary. It also appears that the fourth symbol, sometimes known as the master symbol or *Dai Kômyô*, may have been introduced by Hawayo Takata; it does not seem to be part of Usui's original teachings. When asked about the master symbol, one of the teachers at the Gakkai, Fumio Ogawa, replied, "I have never seen that before."[67]

Now we've placed reiki in its historical context, and if you wish to learn more about reiki's development from Mikao Usui's time to the present, including the many new branches of schools and teachings that have arisen, please see the appendices. In the next chapter we'll get up close and personal with reiki as we discuss receiving a reiki treatment, including tips for making the most of your healing session.

67. Nishina, *Reiki and Japan*, 263.

CHAPTER 8

Receiving Reiki Treatments

In this chapter, we dive into the experience of receiving a reiki treatment. Reiki works to deliver precisely what we need in each moment, and, thus, a reiki treatment is a highly personal experience. That said, there are some basic things that you can expect from every treatment, as well as things you can do, as the recipient, to get the most from your experience, which we'll cover below.

Choosing a Reiki Practitioner

There is, it seems, endless variation in energy work practices, which can make it tricky to establish any sort of universal criteria for choosing the right practitioner, but here are some useful points to consider:

- What is their training?
- What is their general healing philosophy? For reiki practitioners in particular, how do they feel reiki works to create or support healing?
- What is the format of a typical session?
- How much do sessions cost?
- Do they offer an initial no-obligation session or do they require a multiple-session commitment?
- What is expected of you, the client?
- What results might someone with your issues and goals reasonably expect?
- Do they have prior experience working with clients experiencing similar issues?
- Are reviews available from past or current clients?

· · · · · · · ·

I wouldn't advise working with practitioners who claim to provide the sole route to healing, for example, by requiring you to work only with them, or who recommend that you stop allopathic treatments. Energy work is meant to be a complement to any necessary medical protocols. In some cases, you and your healthcare team may decide that it's okay for you to cease allopathic treatment, but this is not a decision to be made by the energy practitioner. It's always good to work with a practitioner on a trial basis before signing up for any lengthy or expensive packages, since even the most experienced, highly recommended practitioners aren't the best fit for everyone. You should feel comfortable asking the practitioner questions and receive direct answers. Ultimately, trust your intuition!

A Typical Reiki Session

While your experience will vary from practitioner to practitioner, it's reasonable to expect all or most of the following from your treatment experience. When you first arrive for your session, there will be time to go over your health history, current issues, and goals for the session. The practitioner will give you an overview of the session format so you know what to expect and leave space for you to ask any questions you might have. You should feel safe and comfortable in the treatment room. Some practitioners will ask that you remove any jewelry or metal objects, but you should never be required to undress for a reiki session. As a massage therapist, I combine bodywork and reiki; thus, my clients are often undressed and under the massage drape, but for a reiki-only session, I never ask my clients to undress. Reiki can penetrate clothing just fine, so be wary of practitioners who claim otherwise. Hopefully this goes without saying, but reiki is entirely non-sexual in nature. There is no need for the practitioner to touch your private areas under any circumstances, nor should they make comments of a sexual nature. Even if you are experiencing health issues related, for example, to your reproductive system, reiki can affect these areas without direct contact. Practitioners should hover above areas of privacy or work via adjacent areas.

The treatment will be performed with you sitting in a chair or lying on the treatment table. If you're on a table, you may have the option to use a sheet, blanket, and/or bolsters. Many clients close their eyes to bring their focus inward, but if you are uncomfortable doing so, you may leave your eyes open. Throughout the session, the practitioner will either place their hands on your body (excepting areas of privacy) over clothing or linens or hover their hands above your body. Some practitioners follow a sequence of set hand positions, while others follow their intuition.

To get the most benefit, I recommend setting the intention to receive whatever it is you most need in this moment, in accordance with your highest good. During the treatment, you may experience a variety of sensations, which can vary from session to session and from one area of the body to another. Some examples include temperature (hot or cold), tingling or mild "itching," and pulsing or vibration. Sometimes you might not feel much at all, and this is not cause for alarm. When I am receiving reiki, either from myself or another practitioner, there are times when my energetic awareness ebbs and flows, yet I still receive the full benefit of the treatment. While it can be useful to be aware of the possible sensations you might feel so you're not alarmed during your treatment, ideally you will go into each session without expecting a particular experience. Reiki initiates healing in the way that is best suited to your highest good in each unique moment, and preconceived ideas of what you "should" be experiencing can get in the way of receiving what is most needed.

After Your Session

Be sure to drink plenty of water (unless you have a medical condition for which this isn't advised) to assist in moving energy through the body and flushing out unneeded energy. While it's common to feel calm and relaxed after a session, it's also possible to feel some discomfort. Reiki treatments can initially intensify or exaggerate any issues undergoing healing. If you were to undertake a physical detoxification process, there is often a period during which you feel worse before getting better, which can be caused by, for example, the die-off of harmful bacteria, which can release toxins into your system, or a release of toxins stored in body tissues. In a similar fashion, reiki can trigger the release of stored toxic energies (and, indeed, this can take the form of physical substances, which are also energy) that must be flushed out of your system.

I have noticed another aspect to this process, and that is heightened awareness. After a treatment, you may become more aware of an issue that, previously, was operating largely in the unconscious. For example, after a session you might see an unhealthy pattern that has been playing out in your significant relationship, and following the treatment, it might be very uncomfortable to continue engaging in this pattern. This necessitates learning a new way to respond in the relationship, such as setting clear boundaries or being more open about your feelings. The treatment provides a window of opportunity when our self-awareness is sharpened and our energy is primed to move in a new direction, but in large part, it is up to us to make the shift. If we go back to business as usual, we will reroute our energy to its former pattern. Thus, after a session, I like to spend some time journaling about any insights that arose and any changes that reiki has inspired, coming up with concrete ways to support these shifts in my body, mind, and soul.

Benefits of Receiving Reiki

Reiki supports healing on all levels, and it does so in a way that is specific to what the recipient most needs in the moment; therefore, specific results are impossible to predict. Most people enjoy a sense of calm and relaxation during the treatment, and these effects can linger for hours or days, particularly if the recipient consciously uses this opportunity to cultivate and prolong this state of being. One of my teachers explained that reiki works on the most current, surface-level issues first, followed by progressively addressing deeper and deeper layers, uncovering

· · · · · · · ·

and healing the roots of current dis-ease that may extend far into your past. I think there's a great deal of merit to this idea, although I don't necessarily agree that reiki will always follow this format.

What I can say with confidence is reiki works best when we actively partner with this energy, rather than treating it like a magick pill that absolves us of responsibility for our well-being. There's a mix of surrender and sacred duty involved: we must open to receive whatever it is we most need in the moment, surrendering the ego's plans and preferences, while simultaneously acting on the guidance we receive. Reiki will illuminate where our soul expression is hampered, where our energy has been rerouted through confining or convoluted channels, and it will support us in freeing this energy via more authentic expression and remembrance of our True Self, but it is up to us to embody this change. Reiki can inspire and support us, but it cannot force our hand. We must make different choices, moment-by-moment, day-by-day. I have found that when I take actions that are aligned with my True Self, there is a powerful momentum aiding and guiding me, like I'm riding divine flow rather than paddling upstream. Reiki will support us, often in ways that seem downright miraculous, but reiki works through us, not for us.

How Often to Receive Reiki

I'm a big fan of giving myself reiki treatments daily, here and there throughout the day. Perhaps I'll do a little jôshin kokyû hô (see page 230) in the morning and give myself reiki while I wait for my tea to steep, followed by mini reiki sessions whenever I have some time on my hands. If I'm reading or watching a movie, I'll place my hands on my belly or any area that feels in need of a little TLC and let reiki flow. Can you do this even if you haven't been attuned? I believe that you can, that every human being has the ability to transmit healing energy through their body, especially the hands. Others would disagree, though. In the end, follow your heart, and if you feel inspired to take a class and receive an attunement, go for it!

In terms of receiving reiki treatments from another practitioner, the recommended frequency varies. If this is your first treatment, I recommend doing two to three treatments no more than a month apart, ideally only one or two weeks apart, to gain the most benefit. If you are working with a more serious health issue, you might find that scheduling your first three treatments a week apart is best. As discussed earlier, reiki can temporarily intensify symptoms, and regular treatment helps to mitigate this. For general stress relief and relaxation, once a week to once a month works great. As a reiki master, I still enjoy getting treatments from fellow practitioners, as they will sometimes be drawn to areas that exist in one of my energetic blind spots. In calling my attention to these areas, they help me remember more of my True Self, so regardless of your level of experience with reiki, know that you can always learn from others.

In the next chapter, we'll look at the various options for studying reiki and how to choose the right program and teacher for you.

. . . .

CHAPTER 9

Studying Reiki

Like many facets of the practice, reiki instruction has evolved over the years, and students now have a choice between more traditionally structured classes and a wide range of alternative teachings. In this chapter, we'll look at how reiki was taught in Usui's time (as best as we can gather from available documentation) and the modifications made by reiki teacher Hiroshi Doi, who sought to blend traditional Japanese reiki and Western developments in his system of Gendai Reiki. We'll also cover average course costs and how to select the right teacher. For more information on non-traditional systems, see the appendix.

Levels of Training

Here we look at the three levels of study in Usui's traditional system, as well as the four-level format created by Hiroshi Doi, which blends characteristics of Eastern and Western reiki.

Usui System

In the original system as taught by Usui, there are three levels of training: *shoden*, *okuden*, and *shinpiden*, and as students progress through these levels, they are assigned a proficiency number, from six (the lowest) to one (the highest). It is said that Usui rated himself at proficiency level two, acknowledging that one should always leave room for self-development.[68] The proficiency levels could be considered as an energy ranking system with which teachers could determine when a student was ready to learn new techniques, receive "new energies," and progress in their studies.[69]

68. Stiene and Stiene, *The Reiki Sourcebook*, 136.
69. Stiene and Stiene, *The Reiki Sourcebook*, 309.

- **Level One, Shoden:** Upon receiving their *shoden* (level one) initiation, a student was given the proficiency level of six, called *roku-to*, and they were required to practice for some length of time, presumably determined by the teacher who monitored their progress. They were taught *byôsen reikan hô*, a scanning technique in which the practitioner glides their hands over the body, intuitively sensing where imbalance or illness lies, and upon mastery of this technique, they would progress to proficiency level five, or *go-to*. After further practice, the student was instructed in *reiji-hô*, whereby the hands are guided intuitively to areas of the body in need of treatment, and the student would reach the fourth proficiency level, known as *yon-to*. When they had fully mastered this technique, they would progress to the third proficiency, or *san-to*, and would be eligible to progress to *okuden* (level two) training.

- **Level Two, Okuden:** The *Reiki Ryôhô no Shiori*, a brochure published by the Gakkai, describes this second ranking as "Mastering Secret/Mystery teachings to become a healer."[70] In the question and answer portion of the *Reiki Ryôhô Hikkei*, Usui explains that "Okuden includes *Hatsureiho*, patting with hands method, stroking with hands method, pressing with hands method, telesthetic method and propensity method. I will teach people who have learned shoden and who are good students, good conduct and enthusiasts."[71]

  Okuden training was divided into two stages: *okuden-zenki* and *okuden-koki*, the latter of which would be completed over a lengthy period of time. During this level, the student would receive three separate attunements to the energies of focus, harmony, and connection.

- **Level Three, Shinpiden:** During the third level, *shinpiden*, the student would receive an additional attunement and learn how to give the attunements to others. After demonstrating proficiency in these techniques and a commitment to meditation and energetic practices, the student would become an assistant teacher (*shihan-kaku*), eventually progressing to *shihan*, with the ability to teach their own students. The remaining two proficiency rankings, two and one, were not associated with a specific level of training, and the *Reiki Ryôhô no Shiori* states that only Usui himself achieved ranking two, and one is described as "noble status."[72]

70. *Reiki Ryôhô no Shiori*, ed. by Kazuwa Toyokazu (Tokyo, Japan: Usui Reiki Ryôhô Gakkai, 1974), 7.

71. Rick Rivard, *Reiki Ryoho Hikkei*, last modified July 21, 2011, http://www.threshold.ca/reiki/Usui_Reiki_Hikkei.html.

72. Rick Rivard, *Reiki Ryoho Hikkei*, last modified July 21, 2011, http://www.threshold.ca/reiki/Usui_Reiki_Hikkei.html.

• • • • • • • •

Hiroshi Doi's Gendai Reiki System

Hiroshi Doi's Gendai Reiki system divides the learning material into four levels.

- **Level One:** In level one, you receive an attunement, which is performed three times to open the energetic pathways, allowing you to use reiki immediately. Doi describes the attunement as "set[ting] up the conditions to connect with Reiki energy and becom[ing] a pathway for it by following a particular procedure."[73] Students are given an overview of reiki, including the history and basic philosophy; they are taught the basics of healing (hand positions, aura cleansing, etc.), using reiki for healing on self and others, the basics of conducting a reiki session, reiki healing for animals and plants, how to use energy to purify places and charge or infuse objects, various healing techniques, and *giho* (methods) for self-purification and self-growth.

- **Level Two:** In level two, three attunements are given, one for each symbol and *kotodama* (the mantra or sound associated with each symbol), which Doi says will "allow you to harness Reiki energy with more potentiality," while also using reiki in different ways, such as sending it to the past or the future or to distant places.[74] This level focuses on healing with the symbols and kotodama with detailed instruction for each symbol, traditional Japanese *giho* (methods), and additional techniques for self-purification and self-growth.

- **Level Three:** The third level once again uses three attunements, this time in association with the fourth or master symbol. Teachings include detailed instruction on fourth symbol usage, how to connect to the higher self or higher dimensions, how to deepen your meditation practice, Usui's philosophies, making use of reiki in daily life to achieve spiritual awakening, and further techniques for self-purification and self-growth.

- **Level Four:** Finally, level four is for reiki masters who wish to teach, and the training includes learning the theory of and how to perform attunements, how to behave and live as a reiki master, what to teach in each level, further instruction for all four symbols, *reiju* (what Doi refers to as "Japanese attunement"), and how to perform the "integrated attunement with all four symbols for a new Reiki Master."[75]

With so many branches of reiki now in existence, the curriculum varies widely from school to school, ranging from a more traditional three-level system to seven levels, one for each chakra, or more. When looking for a suitable program, it's helpful to start by determining which features are important to you.

---

73. Doi, *A Modern Reiki Method for Healing,* 25.
74. Doi, *A Modern Reiki Method for Healing,* 26.
75. Doi, *A Modern Reiki Method for Healing,* 28.

How to Choose a Teacher

Do you want a teacher with a clearly mapped lineage or certain qualifications? Are there certain populations that you wish to practice with, such as conducting sessions in a healthcare environment or working with animals? Are you looking for more traditional teachings or are you curious to try different "flavors" of reiki, such as Karuna Reiki or Shamanic Reiki (see appendix B)? If your interests are more specialized, this will likely narrow your search, as there are a smaller number of teachers specializing in, for example, Shamanic Reiki than the more traditional branches.

Other considerations include in-person or online instruction; cost; class size and level of individualized instruction (if any); post-instruction support and community; length of the training (this can vary from a couple of hours to multiple days stretched out over months); and, if you intend to continue your studies, the minimum amount of time and practice requirements in order to progress from one level to the next (some programs smush all levels into a weekend; others require a month or more in between).

In terms of course cost, this can vary a great deal among teachers and schools, but a higher price tag does not necessarily equate to a higher level of instruction. As of this writing, a fairly typical cost for a level one or two course is between $100 and $400. Some teachers charge more for master-level courses, anywhere from $200 to $1,000 (or more!). The Reiki Alliance's website lists the following prices for courses, stating that "each step of the Usui System path has a specific monetary fee": $150 for level one, $500 for level two, and $10,000 for level three.[76]

There are also teachers who feel it is unethical to charge anything for reiki instruction, and while I can understand arguments around not wanting to create a financial barrier to spiritual energy, personally, I feel this is conflating two things: the energy itself and the teacher or practitioner's time. It seems unethical (and misguided) to set oneself up as the sole source of this spiritual energy and charge people for access. We all have access to reiki; it is (I believe) an innate part of existence that no one need pay to use. However, a teacher's time is a finite resource, and as a teacher myself who has real-world bills to pay, it would be impractical and unsustainable for me to work for free. Do we need to charge the moon and stars for our courses? Probably not, but from my perspective, it is completely reasonable to be compensated for one's time and skill as a teacher or practitioner.

As a general rule, I advise steering clear of teachers who claim to teach the only "real" form of reiki or otherwise suggest that their teachings are the sole route to healing, enlightenment, and so on. In addition, avoid teachers who claim that their attunements expire after a certain amount of time. I look for teachers who are transparent about their background and aren't try-

---

76. "Usui Shiki Ryoho," The Reiki Alliance, accessed March 22, 2019, http://www.reikialliance.com/en /article/usui-shiki-ryoho.

ing to manufacture an impressive lineage, are knowledgeable about their subject material, and have an attitude of, if not humility, *humanness* to them. If a teacher is very invested in cultivating an untouchable guru persona, this is usually a red flag for me. Finally, I tend to avoid programs that require excessive secrecy. Certainly, respecting proprietary materials and the privacy of fellow students makes sense, but if secrecy is mandated in a cult-like fashion, this sort of learning environment doesn't appeal to me. In the end, you'll have to be the judge! Do whatever research you can about the teacher or organization; speak to past or current students and the teacher, if possible; and use your intuition.

CHAPTER 10

❧

Reiki Attunements

What is a reiki attunement, and are they necessary in order to practice reiki? Not everyone in the reiki community agrees on the answers to these questions, so in this chapter, we'll look at various opinions so you can decide for yourself.

First off, what is an attunement? Many teachers describe this as the process of opening the student up to become a channel for reiki. Some assert that you aren't able to channel reiki at all prior to an attunement, while others believe that your ability to channel reiki was always present and simply becomes more powerful following the attunement. A common metaphor is that of a plumbing pipe or a river. The pathway can become obstructed, allowing for very little to no water flow, and an attunement is akin to declogging the pipe or un-damming the river.

The more traditional teachings seem to share the idea that we are all channels for reiki, regardless of whether or not we have been attuned, but our ability might be so limited, due to numerous factors, such as lifestyle or mental outlook, that we can't channel sufficient energy for effective healing, either of ourselves or of others. Thus, an attunement helps increase this ability, opening us up to a greater flow of reiki. These teachings also share the idea that one must practice consistently to maintain the openness of this conduit and to gradually increase the overall amount of energy one is able to contain and channel. Practice could include using the various reiki techniques, which we'll get to in chapter 14, regular meditation, and living in accordance with the reiki precepts (you'll learn about these in chapter 13).

Another belief is that successive attunements can be used to open the student up to different types of energy, and we might think of this as a radio that is programmed to pick up more than one station. For example, some teachings assert that one attunement opens the student to

• • • • • • • •

reiki energy as a whole, with additional attunements giving them the ability to use certain symbols or perform attunements for others. Another variation on this idea is that different attunements work on different levels of being, such as physical, emotional, and so on. Other teachings, however, assert that reiki works on whichever level is most appropriate for the student in that moment, which is not for the teacher to decide.

In my previous book, *Living Reiki*, I proposed that an attunement is, in part, a ritualized way of granting reiki permission to work more powerfully in your life. This is not to say that reiki isn't present in your life beforehand, but the attunement could release conscious and unconscious beliefs and other limitations that prevent reiki from operating most effectively. Another way of saying this is reiki helps us remember our True Self, and an attunement is a powerful dose of remembrance.

I believe that reiki contains and conveys divine information, including what I call your blueprint of original wholeness, a template of who you *really* are before the mind steps in and creates limitations and layers of the persona, thereby obscuring your True Self. An attunement is akin to downloading a fresh copy of this blueprint and seeing yourself through the eyes of the Divine. After the experience, you have the opportunity to live more in alignment with this holistic self-image, honoring the True Self through your choices, thoughts, and actions instead of submitting to the mind's fears and false beliefs.

Distance Attunements

Some teachers give attunements distantly, sometimes requiring the name and location of the student in order to "send" the energy to the appropriate place. I have received a reiki treatment from a practitioner who was attuned distantly, and it was just as effective as treatments given by practitioners attuned in person, so I feel both methods are valid. Due to time zone differences, you might receive an attunement during a time when you are normally asleep. Many teachers assert that this is completely fine, that there's no need to set an alarm to wake up; the attunement will work just the same (and I would agree). That said, with the abundance of attunement options out there nowadays, not all of them are created equal, so just as with in-person courses, use your smarts and your intuition to determine whether a potential long-distance teacher feels right for you.

Another form of distant attunement is one obtained from books. For example, Chris Comish has a book entitled *45 Free Reiki Attunements* that states, "The attunements are received by all who read this book regardless of name of recipient, location of recipient, or time zone of recipient. The attunements are received instantly the moment the recipient reads the words in this book."[77] The attunements are presented in a specific order, and Comish recommends starting with the Usui attunements before progressing to what he describes as more advanced systems, such as Golden Ray Empowerment and Shamballa Multi-Dimensional Healing. Given that the attunements are presented without any accompanying teachings, aside from a one- to three-paragraph summary of each system, this method doesn't seem to do justice to the modalities in question, which I imagine would be more beneficial in the context of more in-depth study.

Receiving an Attunement

The process of receiving an attunement varies quite a bit from teacher to teacher. Some teachers prepare the physical space, perhaps by cleansing it with reiki and/or other tools, like sage or bells. Others might light a candle and display a photo of Usui or a scroll with the five precepts. Students are often given instructions beforehand—for example, "place your hands in *gasshô* and close your eyes." My teacher took a small group of us into a separate room where we were seated in a row of chairs. We closed our eyes, and she performed a series of movements and breaths in front of and behind us, occasionally tapping us on the shoulder to cue a small movement on our part. For my final level, I was the only one in the class, so my attunement was one-on-one but was otherwise carried out in the same fashion. It was said that Usui did not use any particular ritual when performing an attunement (which he would have called a *reiju*), and it was enough for him to simply touch or be near the student for this energetic process to take place.

Attunements typically take only a few minutes, during which time the recipient may experience mild or deep relaxation, physical sensations, or imagery, although if you don't experience any of those things, this alone isn't reason to suspect that the attunement didn't "work." I received a reiki treatment from a friend who felt nothing out of the ordinary during their attunement, and they were channeling reiki just fine. Many traditional teachers advise not to get overly attached to the "bells and whistles" one might be expecting during the attunement and simply allow the experience to unfold, setting the intention to receive whatever is needed at this time.

Before receiving the attunement, the teacher might advise a variety of preparatory practices, such as a light fast, saltwater bath, or meditation, but other teachers simply ask you to show up as you are. Either method works. For me, I like to mark the occasion and prepare as I might for any special ritual, which, for me, looks like a hot saltwater bath, meditation and journaling, and a short tarot reading. I also recommend drinking plenty of water, as I have found energy work (whether giving or receiving) to be more effective and less likely to leave me feeling out of whack when I'm properly hydrated. After my first attunement, my teacher asked that we give ourselves reiki treatments for twenty-one days, mirroring Usui's experience on Kurama-yama,

---

77. Chris Comish, *45 Free Reiki Attunements* (self-published, Lulu.com, 2010), 3.

• • • • • • • •

and I highly recommend it not only as a wonderful experience but a great way to build the habit of using reiki on a regular basis.

Ultimately, the choice to receive an attunement lies with you. Unless it is prohibitively costly or otherwise unavailable to you, my recommendation is to explore using reiki prior to an attunement, and then receive an attunement to see if and how the energy changes for you. While an attunement may not be necessary to channel reiki, in my opinion, it can be a lovely experience that is well worth seeking out.

CHAPTER 11

Hand Positions for Healing

There are certain hand positions that are typically used in the practice of reiki, and in this chapter, we'll look at basic positions for the head and for full-body treatment given to yourself or administered on another person.

Originally, it seems that Usui only taught five head positions, and the rest of the body either wasn't treated directly or hand placement was intuited.[78] Treatment of the head focuses on calming the mind, because once the mind is at peace, the rest of the body will more naturally follow. The crown is also seen as our connection to spirit, thus focusing on this area enhances one's connection to spiritual energy, which, again, will have a beneficial effect on the entire body.

78. Stiene and Stiene, *The Reiki Sourcebook*, 79.

Five Head Positions

1. **Zentô Bu** (Forehead): Standing behind the seated recipient, lightly place or hover your hands over the eyes, fingertips together and pointing inward. You can also perform this on yourself by simply placing your hands over your eyes.

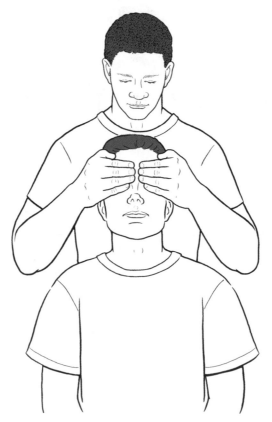

Figure 9: Zentô bu

2. Sokutô Bu (Both Temples): Hover hands on either side of the temples.

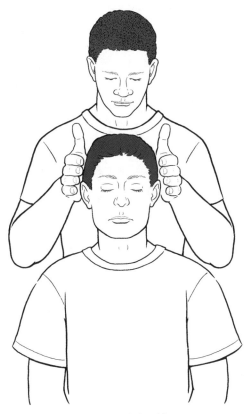

Figure 10: Sokutô bu

3. Kôtô Bu (Back of Head and Forehead): Standing to the side of the seated recipient, hover one hand in front of the forehead and one hand behind the head.

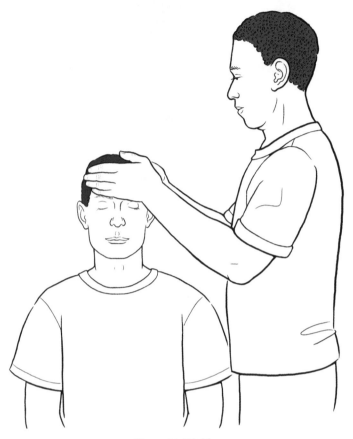

Figure 11: Kôtô bu

4. Enzui Bu (Sides of Neck): Hover hands on either side of the neck, just above the shoulders.

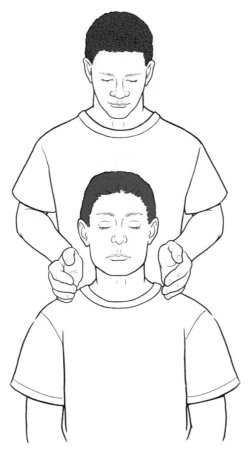

Figure 12: Enzui bu

• • • • • • •

5. **Tôchô Bu (Crown)**: Standing behind the seated recipient, fingers together, hover the hands over the crown, then curl the fingertips downward, pointing at the crown. You can do this for yourself by hovering your hands above your crown or resting your hands on the top of your head.

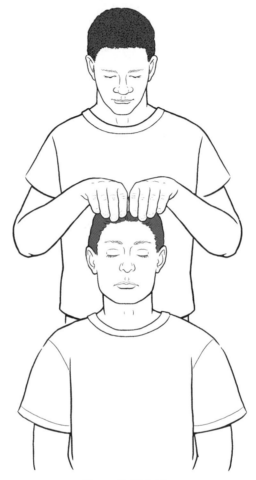

Figure 13: Tôchô bu

It is advised to hold each position for as long as you can feel energy flowing from your hands into the recipient, which might be anywhere from a few minutes to half an hour (or longer in some cases). We'll talk more about energetic sensations during a treatment when we learn the technique of *byôsen* in chapter 14.

• • • • • • • •

Two primary sources for traditional hand positions are the *Reiki Ryôhô Hikkei*, the healing guide portion of the fiftieth anniversary materials published by the Usui Reiki Ryôhô Gakkai, and the *Ryôhô Shishin*, the treatment manual published by Hayashi's clinic, the Hayashi Reiki Kenkyukai. Both the *Reiki Ryôhô Hikkei* and the *Ryôhô Shishin* contain sections of healing protocols for various disorders, divided by area or system of the body, such as digestive system diseases, gynecological disorders, and circulatory diseases. In the *Reiki Ryôhô Hikkei*, nearly all the protocols involve treatment of the head, in addition to other areas, such as specific organs. In contrast to the *Ryôhô Shishin*, the *Hikkei* also includes treatments aimed at specific spinal vertebrae, and Tadao Yamaguchi writes, "Chiropractic theory was first introduced to Japan around the time Usui Sensei was teaching Reiki, so he may have been inspired and adapted its concepts."[79] The *Shishin* is heavily focused on specific organs, which might be a reflection of Hayashi's medical training.

The Gakkai's manual indicates that only one hand should be used for administering treatment, and you should decide at the start which hand you will be using throughout, with the exception of paired structures, such as the kidneys or ears, which can be treated with both hands. The manual states that "it is best to touch the patient's skin when you treat," but contact over clothing is fine, as the energy can penetrate the fabric.[80] Touch isn't necessary when the client does not wish to be touched or an infectious condition is present.

In many modern-day reiki books, there is a standard series of hand positions for whole body reiki treatments. In my research, I was unable to find the source of this sequence, but it is so commonly used (and it's effective, in my experience) that it merits inclusion here, and I've presented two versions: one for self-treatment and one for treating others.

79. Yamaguchi, *Light on the Origins of Reiki*, 128.
80. Yamaguchi, *Light on the Origins of Reiki*, 37.

• • • • • • • •

The Basic Twelve Positions for Self-Healing

1. **Front of the Face:** Place both hands over your face with your fingertips resting on the forehead so the palms are cupped over your eyes.

Figure 14: Front of the face

2. **Sides of the Face:** Place both hands on either side of your face, fingertips resting on the temple, palms curving over the jaw. Alternate position: Bring the fingertips together along the midline at the top of the skull. Your palms will fold along the sides of your head, above your ears.

Figure 15: Sides of the face

3. **Back of the Head:** Bring your palms to the back of your head, forming a triangle with your hands—index fingertips and thumb tips touching. Your palms will be cradling the base of your skull. Alternate position (and one I especially like): Place one hand over your forehead, fingers parallel to your eyebrows and the other hand on the back of your head, opposite the front hand.

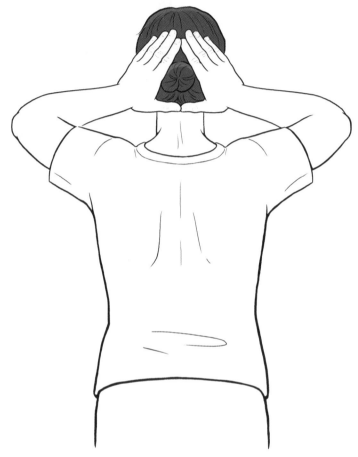

Figure 16: Back of the head

. . . .

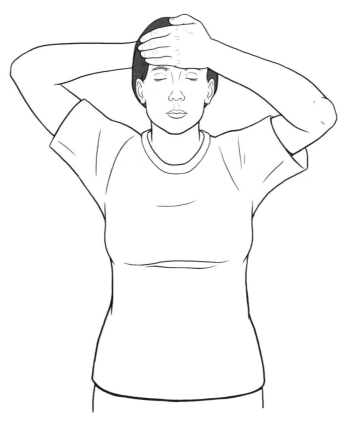

Figure 17: Back of the head, alternate

4. **Throat:** Bring the heels of your hands together and bring them close to your throat, fingers wrapping gently around either side of your neck. No need to strangle yourself; a light, gentle clasp is what you're aiming for.

Figure 18: Throat

5. Heart: Place your palms over your chest, one higher than the other.

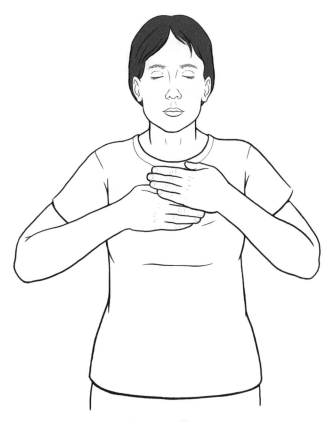

Figure 19: Heart

• • • • • • • •

6. Upper Abdomen: Place your hands, fingertips touching and horizontal, right under the breasts.

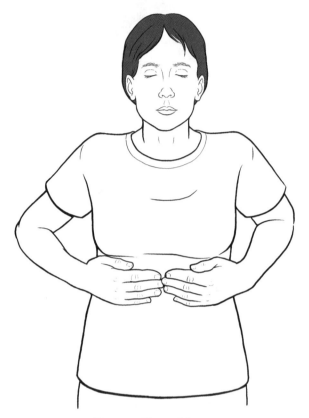

Figure 20: Upper abdomen

· · · · · · · ·

7. Middle Abdomen: Move your hands just below position 6.

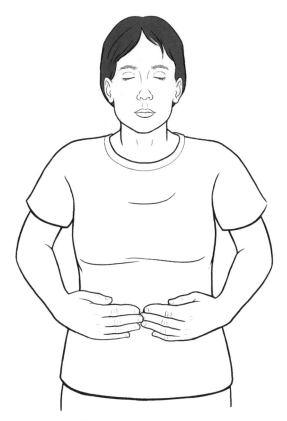

Figure 21: Middle abdomen

• • • • • • • •

8. **Lower Abdomen/Tanden:** Move your hands lower on the abdomen, just under the navel. Alternate position (and another that I'm quite fond of): Place one hand over the center of your chest at heart level and the other hand just below your navel.

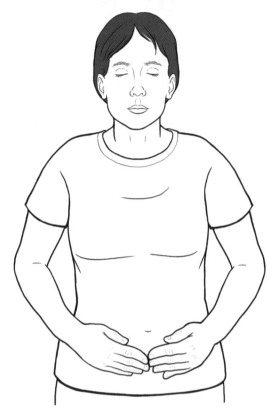

Figure 22: Lower abdomen/tanden

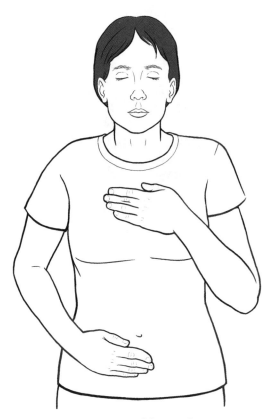

Figure 23: Lower abdomen, alternate

9. Upper Back: Reaching over your shoulders, place your hands on your upper back. Depending on your shoulder mobility, your fingertips will rest somewhat higher or lower between your shoulder blades.

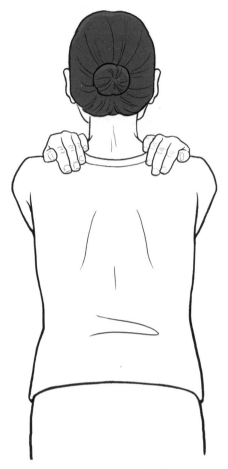

Figure 24: Upper back

10. **Middle Back:** This can be a bit difficult to reach, depending on shoulder mobility, so keep in mind that reiki will go wherever it is needed, even if your hands can't reach. If comfortable, bring your hands back and around your sides, placing them on your mid-back. Sometimes it helps to lean forward a bit, and you can also do one hand at a time.

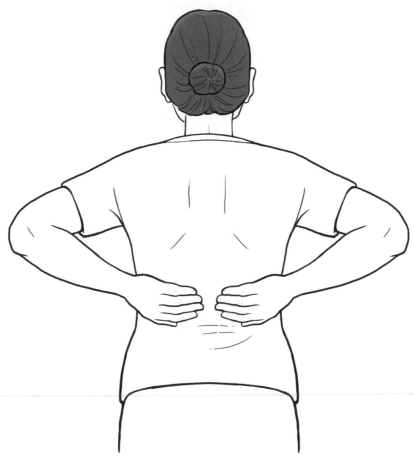

Figure 25: Middle back

11. **Lower Back:** Bring your arms around and back, placing your hands on your lower back. Your fingertips will brush the tops of your hips. As with position 10, feel free to do one hand at a time if that's more comfortable.

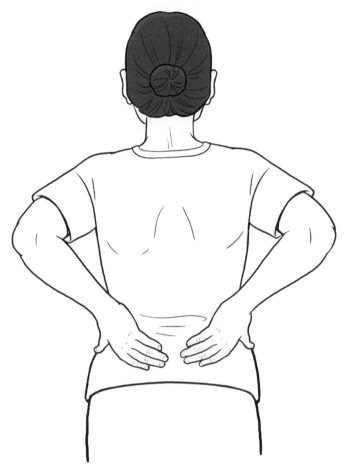

Figure 26: Lower back

12. **Sacrum:** The sacrum is a bone at the base of your spine. The tip of the sacrum is commonly known as the tailbone. Reach around your back and place your hands over your sacrum. It's usually most comfortable to angle the fingers down, palms angled up and out, forming a V shape.

Figure 27: Sacrum

The Basic Hand Positions for Treating Others

If this is new to you, before administering treatments for others, please read chapter 18, which outlines how to conduct a reiki session in more detail. These instructions assume that the client is lying face up on a treatment table to start. Cover the table with a single-use disposable or washable linen and offer them a sheet or blanket. You can also place a bolster or rolled-up blanket underneath the knees to relieve tension in the low back.

1. **Front of the Face:** Place both hands over the person's face with your palms gently cupping over the eyes and your fingertips resting on their cheekbones. I like to place a folded, clean tissue over the eyes to prevent the clammy feel of skin-to-skin contact on the face. You can also hover over this area without touching.

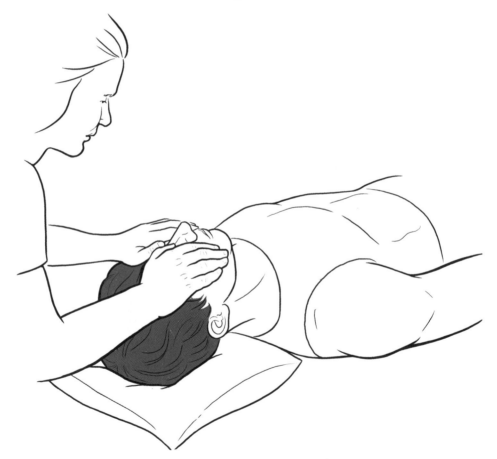

Figure 28: Client, face

• • • • • • • •

2. **Temples:** Place both hands on either side of the head, fingertips over the temples, palms curving over the sides of the skull, possibly meeting at the crown of the head, depending on the size of your hands and the recipient's head.

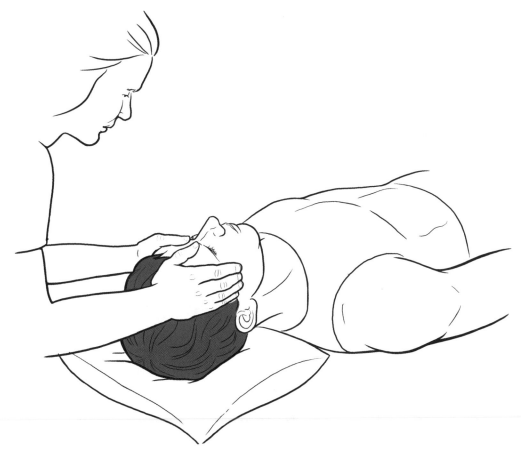

Figure 29: Client, temples

3. **Ears:** Hover your hands in a cupped position over the person's ears. I prefer to hover along the sides of the head as opposed to covering the ears, as the latter can feel constricting, but feel free to experiment and check in with the recipient's preference.

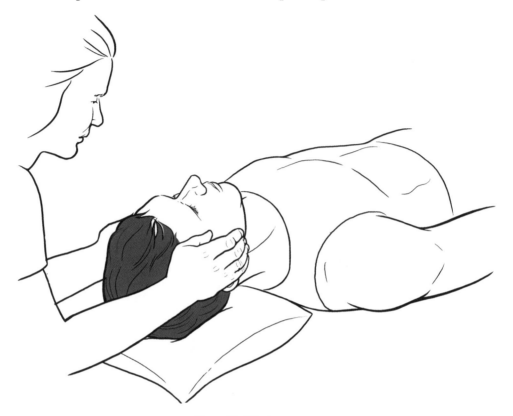

Figure 30: Client, ears

4. **Back of the Head:** Place your hands on either side of the person's head with the backs of your hands contacting the treatment table. Gently rock their head to one side, enough to allow you to slide the opposite palm under their head, and repeat with the other hand so you are cradling the back of their skull in both hands. Make sure you aren't wearing jewelry on your hands or wrists that could dig into their scalp.

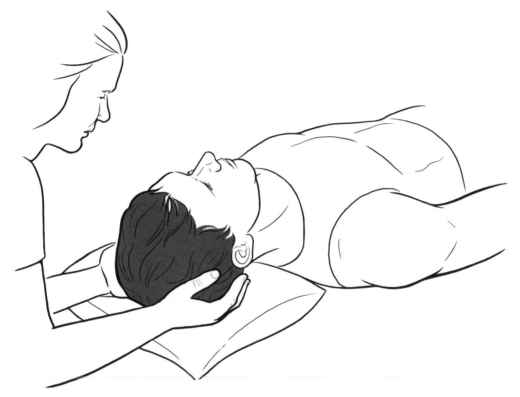

Figure 31: Client, back of the head

5. **Throat:** Two versions for this one, depending on the recipient's preference and comfort. You can lightly place your fingers over the front of the throat on both sides. Your fingertips will meet in the center in line with the sternum (breastbone). Be very aware of the amount of pressure you are applying as a little can feel constricting in this sensitive area. A variation that I prefer is to place the pinky-edge of the hands on the clavicle (collarbone) so your fingertips meet at the sternum and your palms are facing the underside of the person's chin. You are able to send energy to the throat region without applying pressure with the palms to the throat.

Figure 32: Client, throat

• • • • • • • • •

6. **Heart:** Hover your hands over the heart region. You can overlap your hands in the air so that the palm of one hand partially covers the fingers of the other or you can stack them on top of each other. Hopefully this goes without saying, but do not touch female clients' breasts.

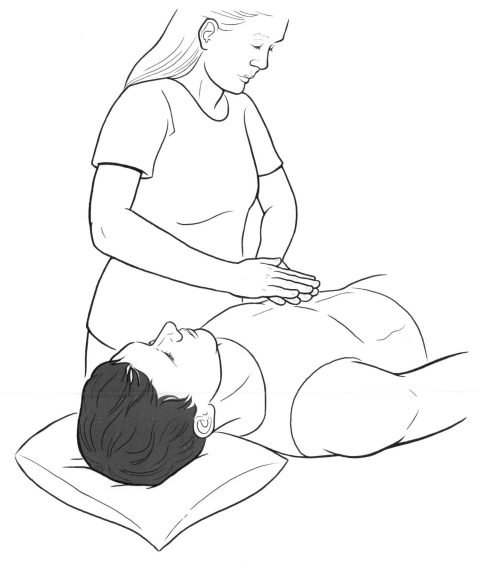

Figure 33: Client, heart

7. **Ribs:** Working on one side of the body at a time, place your hands side by side (i.e., one hand closer to the recipient's head, the other hand closer to the hips) over their ribs. You can move to the other side of the table to treat the opposite side of the body or simply move your hands if you are tall enough to do so without straining or overreaching.

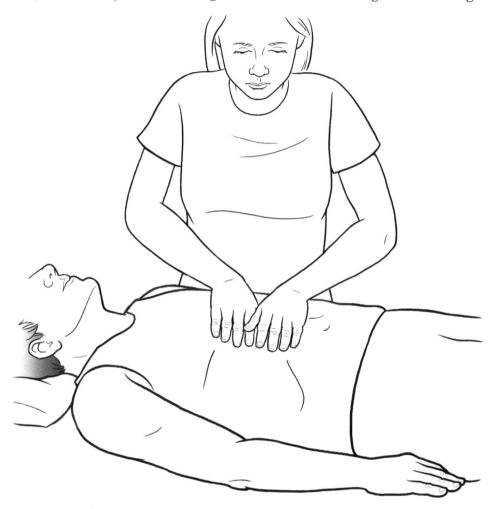

Figure 34: Client, ribs

8. Lower Abdomen/Tanden: Place both hands in line with each other, just above the navel for the lower abdomen. Move your hands right below the navel for the tanden.

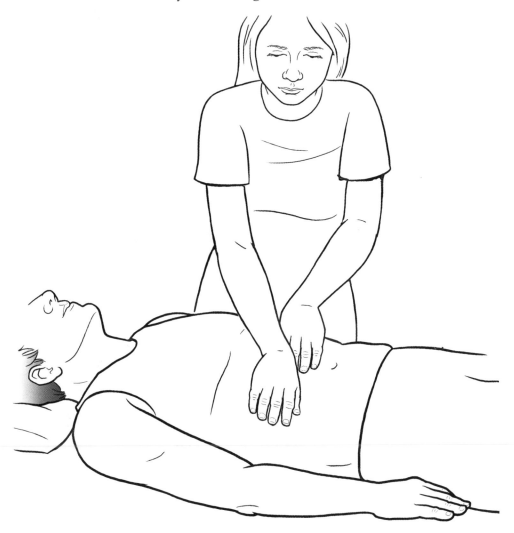

Figures 35A and 35B: Client, lower abdomen/tanden

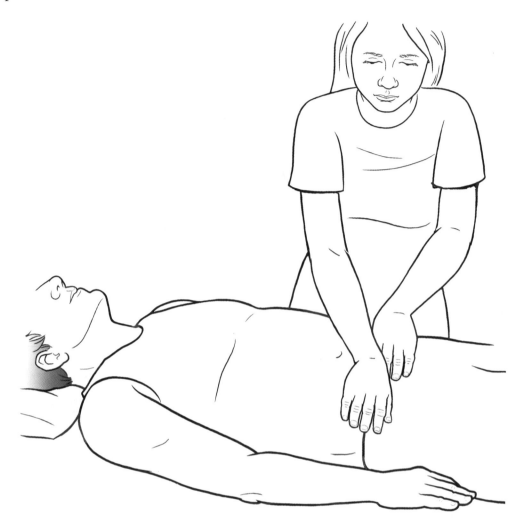

9. Hips: Place your hands on the sides of the hips (where a side seam would run if the recipient were wearing jeans).

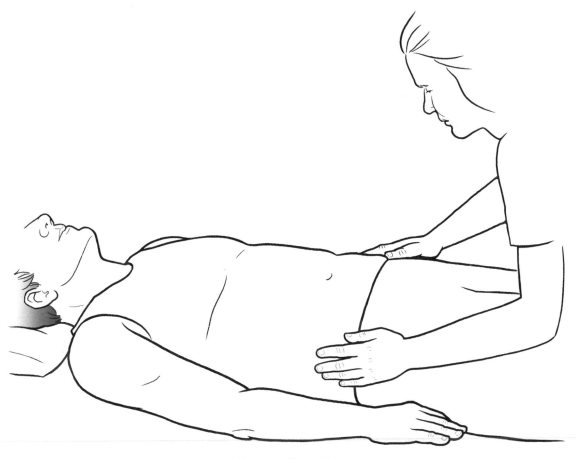

Figure 36: Client, hips

· · · · · · · ·

10. **Thighs:** Move progressively from the upper thighs to just above the knees, using both hands on the same leg and repeating on the opposite leg or placing your hands on both legs simultaneously if this doesn't cause you to overreach and introduce strain into your body.

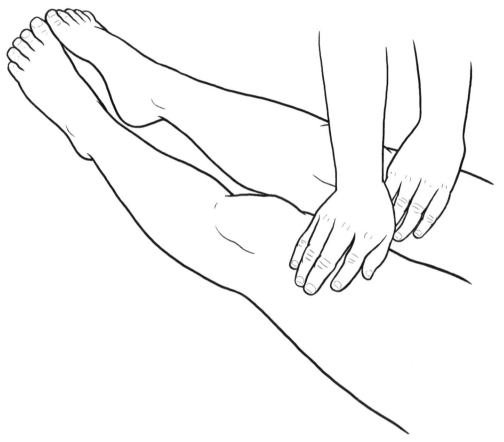

Figure 37: Client, thighs

11. **Knees, Lower Leg:** Using the same hand placement options as for the thighs, move from the knees to the ankles.

12. **Feet:** Gently grasp the ankle with both hands and repeat on the opposite ankle.

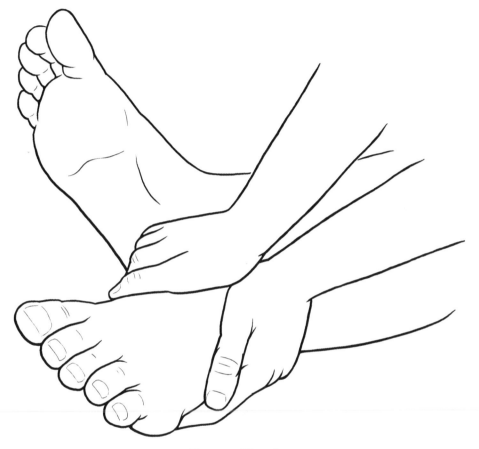

Figure 38: Client, feet

If using, remove the bolster from beneath the knees, and raise the face cradle of the treatment table. The recipient will roll over to their stomach, placing their face in the cradle. (Face cradles should be covered with disposable paper or reusable, washable fabric covers with a fresh cover used for each person.) Check to see if the cradle needs to be adjusted for comfort. The bolster can be placed under the recipient's ankles in this position.

· · · · · · · ·

13. Upper Back: Use the same hand position as described for the heart area, this time placing your hands just above the scapulae (shoulder blades).

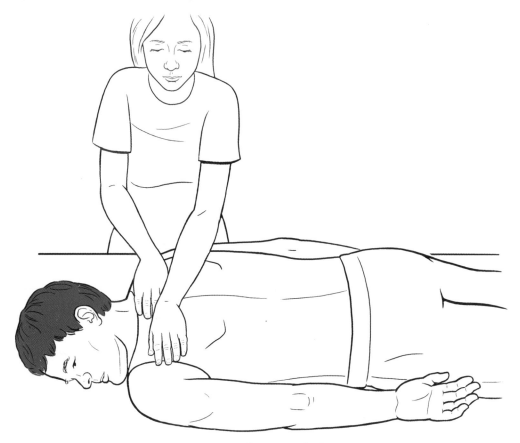

Figure 39: Client, upper back

• • • • • • • •

14. Shoulder Blades: Move down the back, placing your hands over the shoulder blades.

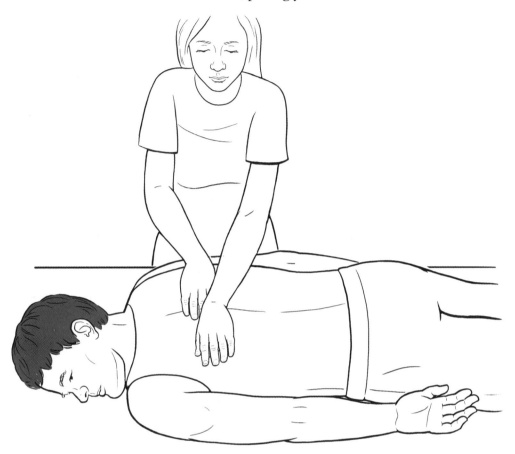

Figure 40: Client, shoulder blades

15. Middle Back: Move down the back, covering each section from below the shoulder blades to the hips.

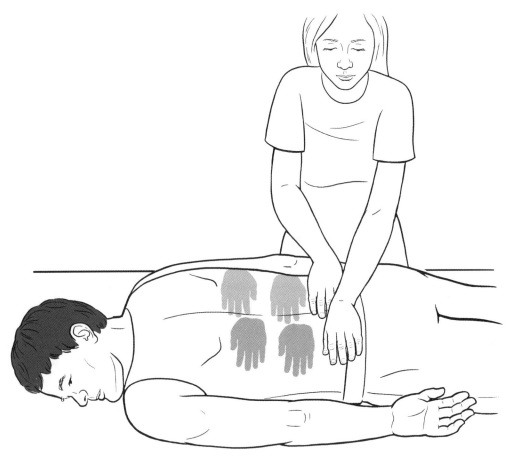

Figure 41: Client, back

16. **Sacrum:** The sacrum is a bone at the base of your spine. The tip of the sacrum is commonly known as the tailbone. Place your hands at the uppermost part of the sacrum, right above the top of the gluteal cleft so you're not handling their glutes.

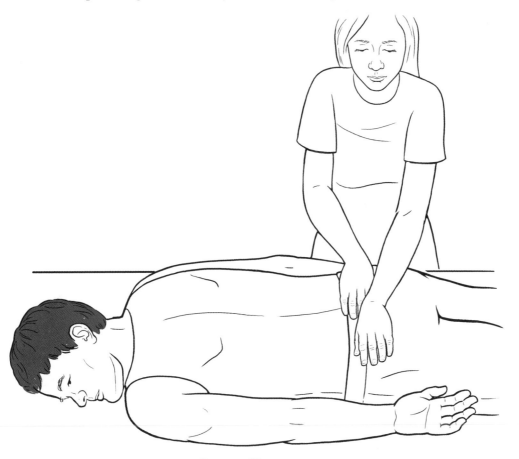

Figure 42: Client, sacrum

17. **Knees:** Place your palms over the backs of the knees. This is an area where you need to be sensitive of your pressure. There is neurovasculature that can be compressed if you are bearing down on the backs of the knees.

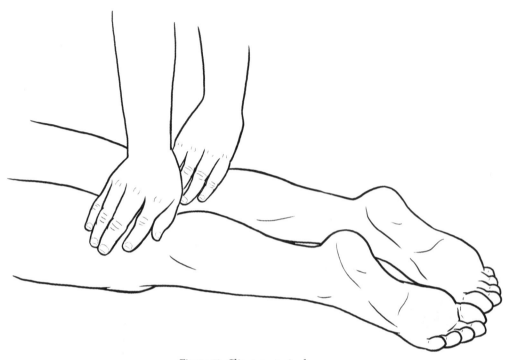

Figure 43: Client, posterior knees

18. Ankles: Move to the foot of the table and gently wrap your hands around the backs of the ankles.

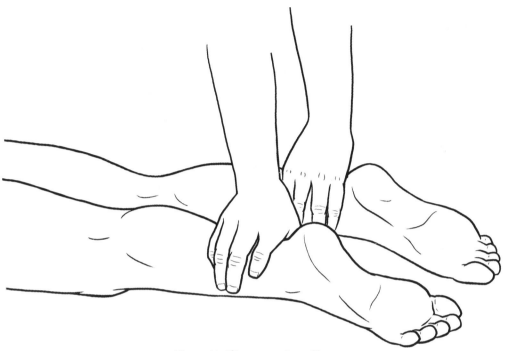

Figure 44: Client, posterior ankles

• • • • • • • •

19. Feet: Place your hands over the soles of the feet, from the toes to the middle of the foot, depending on the size of your hands.

Figure 45: Client, soles of feet

To conclude the treatment, gently sweep your hands over the person's aura, usually about a foot to a foot and a half above their skin, starting at the crown of the head and ending at the feet. This constitutes one sweep. Walk back up to the head of the table and repeat with a second sweep, and conclude with a third aura sweep. Remove the bolster from beneath the ankles to make it easier for them to get off the table, and provide assistance or a stepping stool if necessary. Offer them a cup of water and the restroom if needed. You can use *kenyoku hô* (page 229) on yourself to completely end the session, and if you made contact with the clothing or skin, wash your hands between clients.

Ketsueki Kôkan Hô

In Jikiden Reiki, a treatment concludes with a light massage or *ketsueki kôkan hô*. Some areas require a license to touch, so check local regulations before including this in your treatments. This technique is done with the recipient lying face down on the treatment table.

1. If you incorporate symbols into your reiki practice, you can use Symbol One here (see page 153 for more details), drawing the symbol on either side of the base of the skull with your finger. It is said that this intensifies the flow of reiki in the head, but this technique works quite well without the symbol, too.

2. Using your index and middle finger, quickly and lightly sweep your fingers down the back, one finger on either side of the spine, repeating about twenty times.

3. Find the sacrum at the base of the spine, and draw Symbol One on either side to send reiki to both the upper and the lower body. You can also forego the symbol and simply place your hands over the sacrum, allowing reiki to flow.

4. Mentally divide the upper body into five or six bands. Starting in the uppermost band, place your palms on either side of the spine and sweep down to the sides of the body, like you're brushing something off the person's back. Repeat for the remaining bands, down to the hips. Repeat this three or four times.

5. Rub the lower back with light palm pressure, moving your hands back and forth about ten times.

6. Starting at the hip, sweep your hand along the outside of the leg, all the way down to the ankle, and repeat three or four times. Do the same on the other leg.

7. Sweep your hand from the bottom of the glutes to the ankle along the back of the leg, repeating three or four times. Do the same on the other leg.

8. Sweep your hand from the inner thigh (avoiding areas of privacy) to the inner ankle, and repeat three or four times. Do the same on the other leg.

9. Apply gentle compression on the belly of the hamstrings with your left hand, and clasp just above the ankle with the right hand. Use your body weight to gently traction (pull) the leg. Do the same on the other leg.

10. Pat all over the back, from the shoulders down to the glutes, and repeat three or four times.

11. Pat down the outside of one leg, then the back of that leg, and the inside of the leg, repeating three or four times. Repeat on the other leg.

Now that you know the basic hand positions for reiki treatments, it's time to learn another foundational aspect of reiki practice, symbols and mantras, which we'll cover in the next chapter.

· · · · · · · ·

CHAPTER 12

Symbols and Mantras

One of the foundational elements of the reiki system, in addition to hands-on healing techniques, is the symbols and mantras, and in this chapter, we'll look at both traditional and non-traditional symbols and the many different ways you can incorporate them into your reiki practice.

Secrecy and Reiki Symbols

As with many aspects of the system, there is a fair amount of controversy surrounding the symbols, starting with whether or not they should be shared with the public. The main reason for keeping the symbols private is to honor the tradition that they only be shown to students, specifically students who have reached level two of their training, which is when the first three symbols are typically taught (the fourth symbol, if it is taught at all, is reserved for the master level). It is seen as a matter of respect to keep the symbols secret.

I'll admit that as a lover of the mystery school model of teaching, I like the idea of special symbols reserved only for initiates—and perhaps if we lived in a different, internet-free age, this privacy could have been maintained—but the reiki cat is well and truly out of the bag at this point (and running freely about the neighborhood). Some teachers maintain that even if someone sees the symbols outside of a level two training, they wouldn't be able to use them anyway, because the second-degree attunement serves to activate the symbols. Having learned of this controversy only after taking my second degree, alas, I can't run a personal experiment to determine if I sense a difference in using the symbols before and after, but my belief regarding the symbols mirrors my belief around attunements: we aren't somehow barred from accessing these energies without the "right" instruction or ritualized processes, but our experience of them is very likely enhanced following instruction and attunement.

Symbols in Early Reiki Teachings

As discussed in a previous chapter, it appears that Usui did not use the symbols in his early teachings, but they were added later (likely around 1922) to assist students with less experience in sensing energies. We do not see the symbols in the *Reiki Ryôhô Hikkei*, and it is said that the students copied the symbols from their teachers.[81] Rather than a one-size-fits-all approach, students would be given symbols and mantras based on their level of ability to help them experience and internalize the teachings. This is akin to tailoring directions to your house based on the recipient: a more visual person might prefer a map or description of landmarks, while someone else would find an ordered list of street names easier to navigate. From this perspective, it follows that one mustn't get overly attached to the signposts. They're useful tools, but they're not the sole means of finding our way, nor are they the way itself.

Hiroshi Doi, founder of the Gendai Reiki system discussed in chapter 7, writes that the system he learned at the Gakkai included the symbols (called *ho* or *hi-ho*) but not the mantras, which Doi refers to as *kotodamas*.[82] Kotodama means "words carrying spirit" and can be thought of as the sacred sound and power that resides in a word. A similar term is *jumon*, which is sometimes used interchangeably with mantra. Jumon is "a sound that invokes a specific energetic vibration," and both kotodama and jumon are concepts found in the indigenous Japanese religion of Shintô.[83] They are seen as ways to interact with elements of the world in a very deep way, by tuning in to their inherent vibrations. For example, by deeply listening to and attuning with the sound of a burbling creek, you can come to know the creek more than you could simply by looking at it, wading into the water, or reading a book about creeks. In a similar fashion, the mantras in reiki can help us attain a deeper, more profound understanding of the energy, giving us a primal, embodied understanding that goes beyond purely mental concepts and ideas.

Using the Mantras

Many teachings suggest chanting each mantra three times while drawing or visualizing the corresponding symbol, but you can also chant the mantras without the symbols. I like to chant until I feel the sound really resonating in my body and continue chanting for as long as this resonance feels right—sometimes for only five or six rounds, other times as long as ten minutes or more.

81. Stiene and Stiene, *The Reiki Sourcebook*, 84.
82. Doi, *A Modern Reiki Method for Healing*, 61.
83. Stiene and Stiene, *The Reiki Sourcebook*, 86.

· · · · · · · ·

Reiki Symbols

In the West, the symbols are often given the name of the associated mantras, even though the symbols and the mantras are distinct. In Japan, the symbols are numbered and simply called Symbol One, Symbol Two, and so on, and we will be following the same convention here.

Symbol One

The first symbol is sometimes called the Power Symbol, and it is said to focus and amplify energy. It's associated with earth energy, and thus has a grounding effect, bringing energies back into balance with the natural rhythm of the earth.[84] This symbol is said to stimulate the *hara*, the energetic center in the lower belly, which also enhances the sensation of being grounded. This spiral symbol has parallels in other cultures, where variations of the symbol are often used to denote the movement of energy.[85]

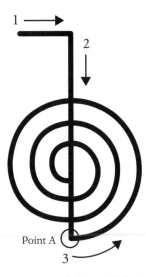

Figure 46: Symbol One, Choku Rei

This symbol can be used in a number of ways, most of which center on the theme of focusing reiki in a particular area. For example, you can draw the symbol with your finger over a body part, in a physical space (such as your desk before sitting down to work), and over food and drinks to concentrate reiki and its healing effects. Gendai Reiki founder Hiroshi Doi considers it to be useful in the area of business and money given its earth associations, and he suggests drawing the symbol over bills; over your wallet, cash, or credit cards; or before engaging in business activities. He also recommends Symbol One for purification of self, space, or objects. Some

---

84. Doi, *A Modern Reiki Method for Healing*, 62.

85. Stiene and Stiene, *The Reiki Sourcebook*, 95.

teachers feel that Symbol One is necessary to activate or "anchor" Symbols One and Two and that they cannot be used without it, but I have not found that to be the case in my own practice.

Non-traditional Use

The symbol doubled, with the one on the left reflected so that the top lines of both symbols are facing inward, creating a gate-like structure, is said to be a powerful tool for manifestation. See also the Kriya symbol (see page 167) in the Karuna Reiki section.

Mantra: Choku Rei

The mantra associated with Symbol One is *Choku Rei*, pronounced CHO-koo-ray, and the symbol is used in *misogi*, a form of purification in Shintô practice. "In this context, *choku* means 'straight' which conveys the idea of 'honest.'"[86] In my own experience with the mantra, I find it useful in removing all but the essential elements of a situation, allowing me to focus on what is most important, which is, in a way, a form of purification. In both the *Oomoto* and *Byakkô Shinkôkai* religions, the mantra literally means "Direct Spirit." It is seen as a part of the divine that resides within each of us. It is also translated to "imperial order or command" or "supreme spiritual emptiness (void)."[87] I internalize these meanings as the realization of one's divine nature (in other words, recognition of the Direct Spirit) removes the illusion of separateness and temporary form, giving rise to a supreme "emptiness" in which all is one. Connecting this to the energetic spiral of Symbol One, when illusion falls away, this allows one to see the great spiral of energy moving through all things.

Symbol Two

This symbol is sometimes referred to as the mental-emotional symbol in modern teachings, while traditionally it was said to have the energetic quality of harmony. It is associated with the moon, yin energy, and the element of water, and Doi relates these concepts through the tides, which are caused by the gravitational force of the moon, which, in turn, is said to affect the water within our bodies. While the first symbol helps us find balance by synchronizing us with the energetic rhythm of the earth, the second symbol harmonizes our energy with the rhythm of the moon. The moon is often associated with the emotions and intuition; thus, this symbol is said to bring healing on an emotional level and strengthen our intuition.

Use this symbol to relieve physical or mental tension, to release blocked emotions and clear up confusion, before meeting people or to heal relationships, to initiate forgiveness of self and others, to receive spiritual guidance, and to release negative habits. You can follow Symbol Two with Symbol One, as the second symbol is believed to have a certain fragility, subtlety, or gentle-

86. Stiene and Stiene, *The Reiki Sourcebook*, 93.
87. Stiene and Stiene, *The Reiki Sourcebook*, 95.

ness to it that must be anchored by the first symbol.[88] I have not found this to be strictly necessary, but experiment and do what feels right to you. It is also associated with the solar plexus and heart chakras and is said to be quite healing to these energetic centers.

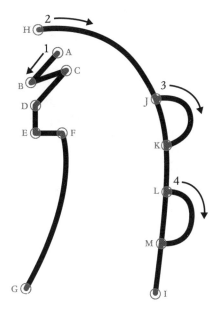

Figure 47: Symbol Two, Sei Heki

Non-traditional Use

This symbol, doubled and drawn upside-down, is said to balance the left and right hemispheres of the brain.

Mantra: Sei Heki

The mantra associated with the second symbol is *Sei Heki*, pronounced say-hay-KEY. Reiki master Penelope Quest equates it with the meaning "to make things straight…to restore balance," and Frans Stiene says it is "our inclination to remember our True Self."[89] The two meanings make sense when you consider that remembering one's True Self will restore balance, and this also speaks to healing on an emotional-mental level, because so many of the disturbances in this area stem from forgetting our true nature. When we become overidentified with the limited self-perception of the ego, this can generate all manner of imbalances, often stemming from the false core belief that we're unworthy or somehow not enough. When we remember our True Self, we have a deeply felt sense of our innate worth, which heals the otherwise punishing drive

88. Doi, *A Modern Reiki Method for Healing*, 65.

89. Penelope Quest, *Reiki for Life: The Complete Guide to Reiki Practice for Levels 1, 2 & 3* (New York: TarcherPerigee, 2016), 178; Frans Stiene, *The Inner Heart of Reiki: Rediscovering Your True Self* (Winchester, UK: Ayni Books, 2015), 71.

• • • • • • • •

to prove ourselves, perhaps by overworking, mistreating our bodies, competing in relationships, or spending the majority of our time on *shoulds* and *have tos* over doing what truly nourishes and inspires us.

Working with the mantra on a regular basis is a means of continually recalibrating our energy with that of divine harmony, supporting us in meeting life's diverse challenges with more equanimity. Over time, this boosts our mental and emotional resilience, as we witness our increasing ability to respond mindfully instead of reacting thoughtlessly. From this place, we become less concerned with expending vast amounts of energy trying to control life, and instead, we trust that whatever comes our way, we will have the creativity, strength, and capacity to deal with it.

Symbol Three

The third symbol is sometimes called the Distance Symbol and can be used to send reiki to other times and places. This symbol is associated with the sun, transcendent consciousness, and the meaning "I become one with God."[90] It is described as a "bridge between worlds," uniting the above and below, inner and outer, heaven and earth, and transcending any separations between time and space.[91] Rather than thinking of reiki as being sent like a letter or even a beam of light, I see this symbol as a tool for recognizing (or remembering) that separation is an illusion, that everything is one; thus, in a sense, there is no "here" nor "there." Reiki doesn't need to be "sent" anywhere, because it is already there. You might think of Symbol Three as a way of tuning in to the reality of oneness before, for example, doing a healing for someone who is not physically present, thereby dissolving any false perceptions that you aren't connected to this person simply because of geographical distance. Like the other two symbols, Symbol Three is another signpost pointing us toward the underlying nature of reality: oneness. This symbol is said to be especially useful in healing the fifth and sixth chakras, as they are related to our ability to communicate and connect. Some teachings state that it cannot be used on its own and must be paired with Symbol One and sometimes Symbol Two. I have not found this to be necessary in my personal practice, but experiment to see what works best for you.

Frans Stiene offers another translation of Symbol Three, "I am right mind," which he equates with the realization that distance and separation are an illusion.[92] One aspect of a right mindfulness practice is witnessing our tendency to label things: This is good. That's bad. Friend versus foe. Right versus wrong. "When we have a direct experience of Right Mindfulness, we begin to stop labeling things. We just see things as they are, and we don't get carried away by our dualis-

90. Stiene, *The Inner Heart of Reiki*, 66.
91. Stiene, *The Inner Heart of Reiki*, 179.
92. Stiene, *The Inner Heart of Reiki*, 77.

· · · · · · ·

tic thinking."[93] This transcendence of opposites leads to healing, in large part because it allows us to see our fullness of self rather than scooting under the rug any parts within us that don't conform to our ideals. These rejected aspects are denied the light of consciousness, like a plant hidden from the life-giving rays of the sun, and they become stagnant—caught, as it were, in a time loop where they cannot grow and change. When we invite these parts home by healing the dualistic belief that we can be either good or bad, these stagnant areas are transformed. It is in this capacity that I relate to another one of Symbol Three's associations: that of healing the past and purifying karma.

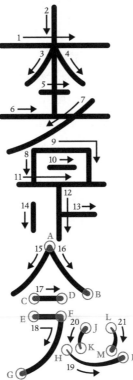

Figure 48: Symbol Three, Hon Sha Ze Sho Nen

To use Symbol Three, Doi recommends drawing the symbol in the air once while repeating the mantra *Hon Sha Ze Sho Nen*, three times. You can do this on an object or a photo of someone to whom you wish to "send" reiki (or a slip of paper with their name written on it), and then hover your hands over the object or photo and allow reiki to flow. You can also give yourself "distance" reiki by drawing the symbol, chanting the mantra three times, and choosing three positions on your body. With your hands on the first position, say, "Head," and give reiki. With your hands on the second position, say, "Front," and finish with the third position, saying,

93. Stiene, *The Inner Heart of Reiki*, 79.

• • • • • • • •

"Back."[94] This allows three positions to stand in for a full-body treatment, which is wonderful when you're short on time or when your flexibility or reach prevents you from using the standard hand positions.

Non-traditional Use

Drawing Symbol Three twice ("doubling" the symbol) is said to heal future lives.

Mantra: Hon Sha Ze Sho Nen

The mantra associated with the third symbol is *Hon Sha Ze Sho Nen*, pronounced HONE-sha-zay-sho-nen. Stiene gives the following translations:

Hon: True, book, origin, real, to find the origin in

Sha: Person, someone, the one (who/which), he/she who is

Ze: Right, correct, just so, this, justice, perfectly, it is this

Sho: Correct, true, straight, the basis of correct knowledge, righteous

Nen: Thought, feeling, mindfulness, mind, memory, meditative wisdom, patience, forbearance[95]

I encourage you to meditate on these translations, combining them in different ways like a divine word jumble to see what messages arise for you. One meaning that resonates with me is "meditating on the nature of the True Self allows us to reclaim our original wisdom." In other words, Hon Sha Ze Sho Nen acts as yet another signpost, guiding us back to our True Self. And another: "Our original self, our True Self, is perfect, just as it is, and meditating on this truth gives rise to wisdom." What meaning resonates with you?

Symbol Four

Sometimes referred to as the Master Symbol, this symbol may or may not have been part of Usui's teachings; as with many aspects of reiki, its origins are surrounded in controversy. According to Frans Stiene, Hiroshi Doi knew of a student who learned this symbol from Usui, and both Chûjirô Hayashi and Hawayo Takata knew and taught this symbol as well.[96] Stiene surmises that not all students were taught this symbol based on their level of readiness, which is reasonable given that we know Usui adapted many of his other teachings to fit the experience level and aptitude of individual students. Masaki Nishina asserts that this symbol was not a part of Usui's original teachings and claims it is a "Western technique developed in the Western community by

94. Doi, *A Modern Reiki Method for Healing*, 67.

95. Stiene, *The Inner Heart of Reiki*, 77.

96. Stiene, *The Inner Heart of Reiki*, 93.

somebody who knew a little about the Japanese language," and he offers that it might have been Takata who developed it for her master-level students.[97]

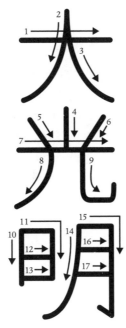

Figure 49a: Symbol Four, Dai Kômyô

This symbol is not exclusive to the system of reiki, and it can be found in temples throughout Japan. It is used in the *Mikkyô* teachings of Tendai Buddhism to help one merge with the "Light Wisdom of the original Buddha nature," and it is also found in *Shugendō, Sekai Kyûsei Kyô, Kurama Ko Yo,* and various martial arts.[98] This symbol is associated with the universe and God, and with the union of the sun and the moon. It can be used in conjunction with any of the other symbols to make them "finer and more harmonious" and can be used first to achieve this effect.[99] This symbol can be used for purification, for example, by drawing the symbol before meditation, breathing exercises, or practices such as qigong, and it will surround your endeavors with light, making it a great symbol to use before doing just about *anything*: going to work, giving a presentation, making an important decision, creating art, and so on. Use the fourth symbol if you are having trouble with something and you seek higher guidance. You might draw the symbol before bed, asking for guidance on a particular issue, and giving yourself reiki until you fall asleep. When you wake up, redraw the symbol and reaffirm the intention that your every thought, word, and deed are divinely guided before going about your day.

97. Stiene, *The Inner Heart of Reiki,* 188.
98. Stiene, *The Inner Heart of Reiki,* 103.
99. Doi, *A Modern Reiki Method for Healing,* 75.

Mantra: Dai Kômyô

The mantra associated with the fourth symbol is *Dai Kômyô*, pronounced die-CO-myo. It is said to be useful in healing the seventh (crown) chakra and connecting to higher sources of guidance, and it is often translated as "great bright light." The kanji for *dai* represents, in certain esoteric traditions, the five elements: earth, water, fire, air, and space (or void), and for me, this speaks to the unifying effect of this mantra. When we see ourselves in the "great bright light" of divine consciousness, we see all our parts, all our internal elements, as one unified whole—in other words, we see our True Self. Similar to Symbol Three, this mantra is another signpost or tool that helps us shed the layers of illusion created by the mind, illusions that cause us to label parts of ourselves as unacceptable, creating self-rejection, suffering, and dis-ease. The light of Dai Kômyô can trigger remembrance of our own inner light, dispelling the shadows of ignorance that have led us to forget our True Self.

This mantra can be used for purification—for example, a Mikkyo practice involves chanting the mantra "to overcome inner obstructions such as worry, fear, or attachments," and some practitioners use it to clear self and space prior to giving a reiki treatment or *reiju*.[100] This mantra is also associated with the quality of empowerment, which can range from using it to "supercharge" any of the symbols to a deeper form of empowerment arising from remembering one's True Self. One practice I particularly love is chanting Dai Kômyô every morning for a twenty-one-day period. When you're in need of a serious reset or simply wish to go deeper with the mantra, I highly recommend giving this a try. You might be surprised at the insights that arise and the shift in your baseline energy!

Symbol Four Alternate: Dai Kômyô (Tibetan Version)

This is an alternate, non-traditional version of Symbol Four, also known as Dumo or the Tibetan Master Symbol. It is said to be more intuitive for Westerners to work with, and Maya Cointreau writes, "Many feel that it has a gentler way of healing, yet gets to the root of dis-ease more quickly and is more powerful."[101]

---

100. Stiene, *The Inner Heart of Reiki*, 98.
101. Maya Cointreau, *The Practical Reiki Symbol Primer* (self-published, CreateSpace, 2015), 18.

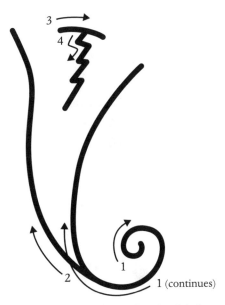

Figure 49b: Symbol Four Alternate, Dai Kômyô (Tibetan version)

New Reiki Symbols

Throughout reiki's journey from Japan to the rest of the world, different practitioners have adapted the practices in a variety of ways, and some of those adaptations have introduced new reiki symbols, sourced either from previously existing spiritual traditions or through meditation and channeling. Traditional practitioners assert that these symbols are not part of reiki, but it's up to each practitioner to decide what works for them. If you feel so called, experiment with the new symbols to see if they enhance your reiki practice. You can also explore using sacred symbols from other traditions, such as the Egyptian ankh, the Celtic triskele, or Norse runes, to see how they affect your energetic experience. Some practitioners feel that non-traditional symbols are potentially harmful, and if this is a concern for you, set the intention that your explorations unfold in accordance with the highest good, harming none.

Figure 50: Ankh

Figure 51: Celtic triskele

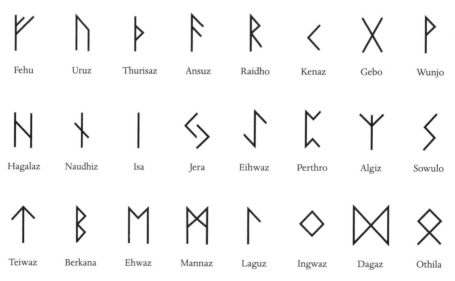

Figure 52: Elder Futhark runes

Karuna Reiki Symbols

The following symbols are found in the Karuna system of reiki, covered in appendix B.

Gnosa

The word *gnosis* is Greek for "knowledge," and the word is commonly used to refer to knowledge of esoteric or spiritual matters. This symbol helps to clear away preconceived notions and false beliefs, creating space for deeper understanding to arise. Thus, it is very useful when learning new things, be they physical skills, mental information, emotional understandings, or spiritual truths. *Gnosa* can heal communication, and, by extension, the nervous system, which is one of the body's central communication systems. Gnosa is pronounced NO-sa.

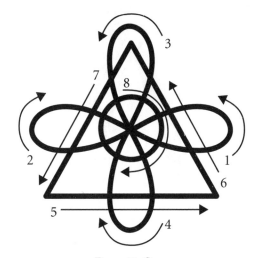

Figure 53: Gnosa

Halu

After the practitioner uses Zonar (see page 174) to prepare the recipient for deep healing, Halu is used to find areas that are holding on to unhealthy patterns, which Laurelle Shanti Gaia perceives as tangled energetic shapes and strands. When the energy of Halu reaches these obstructions, "the tangles appear to relax and unravel."[102] This symbol is also used to identify and heal our shadow aspects, which are those parts of ourselves that we repress or deny, and they can include not only unhealthy facets but also hidden gifts and awareness. Thus, this symbol is a powerful tool for fostering self-acceptance. Visually, this symbol looks like Zonar with a pyramid added, and this addition is said to be one of the mechanisms by which Halu amplifies the energy of Zonar.

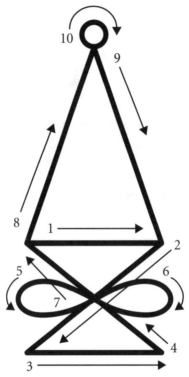

Figure 54: Halu

---

102. Laurelle Shanti Gaia, *The Book on Karuna Reiki: Advanced Healing Energy for Our Evolving World* (Hartsel, CO: Infinite Light Healing Studies Center, 2001), 65.

· · · · · · · ·

Harth

This symbol represents universal compassion, and Laurelle Shanti Gaia sees this symbol as the heart of Karuna Reiki. She explains that we cannot truly have compassion for another being until we have compassion for ourselves, and work in this area can support healing in our relationships. While it might sound contrary to the concept of oneness, part of this healing often involves setting clear boundaries, and this parallels the work of researcher Brené Brown, who asserts that we cannot truly have compassion for others without healthy boundaries, because the person who allows the world to treat them like a doormat is usually cradling a simmering pot of resentment.[103] Shanti Gaia offers a unique way to use Harth for relationship healing by choosing a crystal or other object to represent the energy of the relationship. Use the traditional Usui Symbol Three, Symbol Two, and then Harth before sending reiki to the relationship via the crystal.[104]

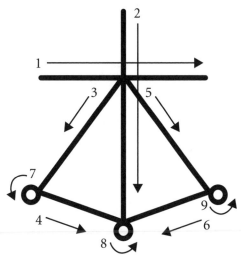

Figure 55: Harth

103. Brené Brown, *The Gifts of Imperfection* (Center City, MN: Hazelden, 2010), 19.
104. Gaia, *The Book on Karuna Reiki*, 67.

Iava

Another symbol from Karuna Reiki, Iava (pronounced EE-ah-vah) helps us connect to and heal with the earth, nature spirits, and devas. This symbol helps us see that we are active creators of our reality, and if we embrace this truth, we will find empowerment through this symbol. It can help heal codependent relationships through the establishment of healthy boundaries while simultaneously experiencing the interconnectedness of all beings. The first three spirals are said to represent the energy of the triple goddess, sometimes referred to as the maiden, mother, and crone aspects, and the four loops on the right-hand side represent the elements of earth, air, fire, and water.

Figure 56: Iava

Kriya

This is a double traditional Symbol One, which is said to supercharge the manifestation process, and it is related to the Kundalini yoga practice of *kriya*, which is used to create change on all levels of your being in order to bring about a specific desired outcome, such as aura purification, liver detoxification, or elevated energy levels. You might think of them as spiritual protocols to achieve a particular end goal. The Kriya symbol is associated with the earth element, and it is a powerful tool for grounding, which is also related to manifestation, as this can be viewed as the process of taking our desires and grounding them in tangible reality. When drawing with your fingers, you can create both right and left symbols simultaneously. If drawing on paper or if doing both is difficult, I like to start with the right-hand symbol and then draw the one on the left, but use whichever order feels best to you.

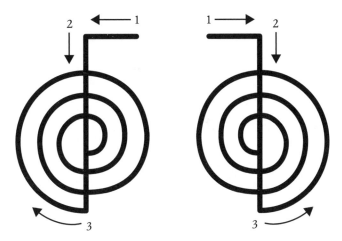

Figure 57: Kriya

Motor Zanon

Some sources claim this symbol has Tibetan or Sanskrit origins, and it is taught in Seichim Reiki and Karuna Reiki, with some traditions referring to it as the Antiviral Symbol for its ability to attach to and remove viruses. To use Motor Zanon, first draw the traditional Symbol One once and chant the Choku Rei mantra three times. Then draw Motor Zanon once, chanting "Motor" three times, then finish by drawing Symbol One and chanting Choku Rei three more times. Christopher Penczak recommends visualizing the symbol entering the recipient's body where the corkscrew shape will spin, "attracting viral particles, filling the funnel shape. Use your intuition to know when to take it out." [105] To remove the symbol, chant Choku Rei three times, then "Zanon" three times, finishing with three intonations of Choku Rei as you visualize drawing the symbol out of the body. When you're done, purify the energy by using Halu or simply visualizing it dissolving in pure, white light.

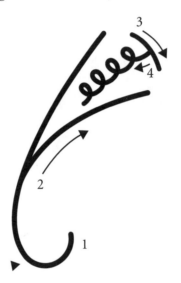

Figure 58: Motor Zanon

105. Christopher Penczak, *Magick of Reiki: Focused Energy for Healing, Ritual & Spiritual Development* (St. Paul, MN: Llewellyn Publications, 2004), 136.

Om

This ancient Sanskrit symbol has been adopted by Karuna Reiki, and it represents the oneness of all creation, hence it can be used to initiate a powerful feeling of integration, harmony, and unity with all beings. The dot symbolizes the detachment of the true essence from its creation, so this symbol can also be used to support healthy detachment—for example, if we find ourselves stressing over a particular outcome and attempting to control and micromanage situations and people.

Figure 59: Om

Raku

The Raku symbol is also known as the Fire Serpent or Completion Symbol. It can be used during treatments and attunements to align the energy through the chakras and remove obstructions, while some practitioners claim it activates kundalini. Used at the end of a session, Raku aids in settling the body and bringing a sense of grounding and completion.

Figure 60: Raku

Rama

This symbol is the final symbol in level one of Karuna Reiki, and it is a powerful tool for harmonizing the upper and lower chakras, bringing healing to the entire energy system. Rama calls all of a person's energy back into their body for integration, similar to the shamanic concept of soul retrieval, in which the soul, in whole or in part, has been separated from the body, often due to trauma, and must be brought home. This symbol has a strong grounding force and can be used at the end of a session to bring the recipient fully back to the here and now. You can use this symbol to navigate abrupt change, such as changing time zones when traveling or unexpected life events.[106] The five loops of the symbol represent the five elements, and the two intersecting lines represent polar creative energies; some associate this symbol with Archangel Michael.

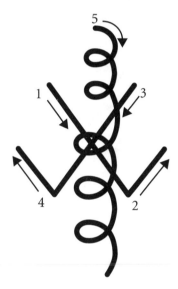

Figure 61: Rama

106. Penczak, *Magick of Reiki*, 70.

Shanti

This is a Karuna Reiki symbol that brings peace of mind, and it is named after the Sanskrit word for peace or tranquility. Shanti can support us in releasing attachment to things outside of our control, finding calm in the present moment. It can heal insomnia, chronic fatigue, and fear, and it is said to open the chakras and bring about clear psychic insights when we meditate on the symbol entering the third eye chakra.

Figure 62: Shanti

Tibetan Fire Serpent

This Karuna Reiki symbol is sometimes referred to as Raku or the Fire Dragon, and it is said to represent kundalini energy coiling through the seven chakras. It can be used to balance the energy system and to prepare oneself for reiki sessions and attunements. Depending on the manner in which it's used, some practitioners assert that it can both ground energy through the lower chakras or raise energy in the upper chakras, and it may map the energy pattern experienced during an attunement.

Figure 63: Tibetan Fire Serpent

Zonar

A level one symbol in Karuna Reiki, Zonar is said to pave the way for deeper healing, and it addresses multidimensional issues, such as those rooted in past lives. It can release negative emotions, such as fear, hate, and shame, that are trapped at a deep cellular level, and it is associated by some with Archangel Gabriel, who is connected to healing. Reiki master Laurelle Shanti Gaia uses Zonar at the start of a treatment, as she feels it acts as a "spiritual anesthetic," preparing the recipient to receive reiki into their subtle and physical bodies with little to no discomfort.[107]

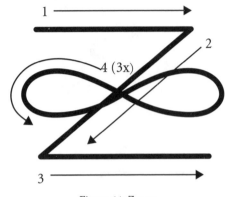

Figure 64: Zonar

107. Gaia, *The Book on Karuna Reiki*, 64.

Seichim Symbols

The following five symbols are found in the Seichim system of reiki, covered in appendix B.

Cho Ku Ret

This is the power symbol of the Seichim tradition, and it transforms the spiral energy at the heart of the traditional Symbol One into an infinity symbol. Cho Ku Ret can be used to heal not only people, animals, and plants, but also "non-cellular beings," such as crystals and machines. It is sometimes referred to as the Inanimate Object Power Symbol or Zara, and similar to Symbol One, it is used to focus and direct energy to the healing subject.

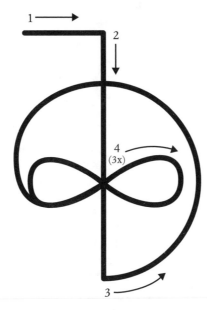

Figure 65: Cho Ku Ret

Angel Wings

This symbol is associated with realizing one's full potential, what some refer to as the individual's angelic divinity, so it can be shared for the benefit of all beings. This symbol helps us connect with angelic beings and higher spirit guides, and it can be used to draw protection from those realms. The first diagram depicts the traditional way of drawing the symbol, and the second is a method I have found to be effective in my personal practice. I use the latter when tracing the symbol in the air—use both index fingers and begin at the left and right starting points, bringing your fingers to meet at the top.

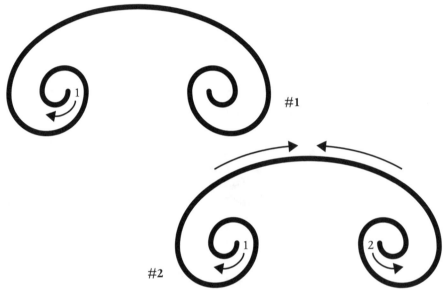

Figure 66: Angel Wings

Male Female

This symbol balances forces of polarity and helps us see opposing points of view. It can also heal the effects of societal gender constructs and open us up to a more expansive perspective and sense of self. It also goes by the names of Everlasting Flower, Yin-Yang Balance, and Everlasting Flower of Enlightenment.

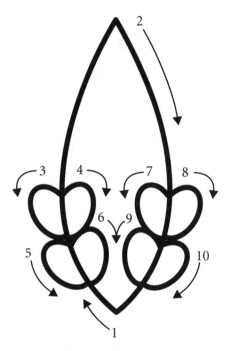

Figure 67: Male Female

High-Low-God

Another symbol from Seichim Reiki, this is said to align the higher and lower self with the divine, integrating your entire being with love and light. It initiates powerful change in your life, illuminating any aspects that are not in alignment with your highest good so you can bring awareness and healing to them.

Figure 68: High-Low-God

Eeeftchay

Sometimes spelled *Ift Chei*, this Seichim symbol represents "endless inner sight" and is used to shed light on any issue, bringing clarity and understanding. You can draw the symbol over individual chakras to illuminate issues related to that energy center, and when drawn over the third eye, Eeeftchay activates natural psychic faculties.

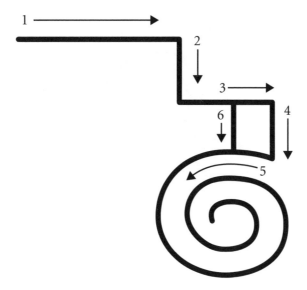

Figure 69: Eeeftchay

Otherkin Symbols

The following symbols were channeled by Corey Thorn, a practitioner of the Otherkin and Opensource Reiki traditions.[108] Drawing instructions aren't given, as the symbols are meant to be drawn intuitively, as each practitioner sees fit.

Akinara

This symbol is associated with enlightenment.

Figure 70: Akinara

Go She Ki

This symbol can be drawn on areas of inflammation and joint pain or over the entire body to heal general inflammation. It is said to be useful in treating carpal tunnel syndrome.[109]

Figure 71: Go She Ki

108. Jarandhel Dreaminger, "Corey Thorn's Reiki Symbols," WanderingPaths, accessed April 27, 2019, http://wanderingpaths.dreamhart.org/reiki/coreysymbols.html.

109. Cointreau, *The Practical Reiki Symbol Primer*, 37.

• • • • • • • •

Ho Ta Li

This symbol is said to gather and store energy, and when the symbol is added to one's personal protection shield, the stored energy will remain until it is triggered by another person's negativity. The energy will then work to counteract this negativity with positive energy.

Figure 72: Ho Ta Li

Kainar

This symbol is said to be grounding and centering.

Figure 73: Kainar

Kita No Kaze

Also known as the North Wind symbol, *Kita No Kaze* helps you tap into the element of air, bringing a breath of fresh air to your energy field, helping to clear away stagnation and introducing change.[110]

Figure 74: Kita No Kaze

Koshalin

This symbol opens the chakras in preparation for an attunement.

Figure 75: Koshalin

---

110. Cointreau, *The Practical Reiki Symbol Primer*, 64.

Kyu So Na

This symbol protects against harmful mental influencing, such as brainwashing, and can heal the mental and emotional damage wrought by external forces.

Figure 76: Kyu So Na

Sei Rea Ko

This symbol can be used to induce rain or to break up cloud formations. It is associated with the energy of the storm master as the bringer, destroyer, and controller.

Figure 77: Sei Rea Ko

Shimatsu

This symbol clears negative energy surrounding a person, including negative thoughts and feelings, and it can be used as a protective shield against these energies.

Figure 78: Shimatsu

Shonen-Fe

This symbol can be used on its own or in conjunction with Tinara for powerful relaxation. It works on the central nervous system, and can reduce or heal nerve damage while promoting deep relaxation. It may also be useful in lessening the severity and occurrence of epileptic seizures.

Figure 79: Shonen-Fe

• • • • • • • •

So La Kyu

This symbol is said to be useful in the treatment of cancer.

Figure 80: So La Kyu

Tinara

This symbol is used to promote relaxation and relieve stress. It can be drawn on the hands before giving massage or placing the hands on an area of the body experiencing muscle tension or cramps.

Figure 81: Tinara

Toh Rai Sin

This symbol is useful in healing the environment, be it a physical place or a mental-emotional environment, and it is effective for both individual and group healing.

Figure 82: Toh Rai Sin

Tsuriai

This symbol is used to balance and center, especially when one feels thrown out of whack due to external pressures. Each of the four elements are contained within the symbol: earth by the house-like upper structure, air by the bottom left symbol, water by the bottom middle, and fire by the bottom right. It might be possible to evoke specific elements by drawing specific parts of the symbol.

Figure 83: Tsuriai

Christopher Penczak Symbols

The following symbols were channeled by witchcraft teacher and reiki practitioner Christopher Penczak and can be found in his book *Magick of Reiki*.

Al Luma

During a healing session, this can be used to connect the recipient with higher sources of guidance, including spirit guides. Christopher Penczak's guides call this symbol a "cosmic ark," as it helps users journey inward, connect with spirit guides, and otherwise release expectations and flow with the experience as it unfolds.[111]

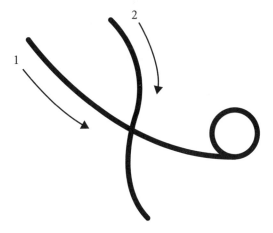

Figure 84: Al Luma

---

111. Penczak, *Magick of Reiki*, 236.

Antibacterial

Penczak channeled this symbol after asking reiki for guidance in healing an infection, and as the name suggests, it is useful in fighting bacterial infections.

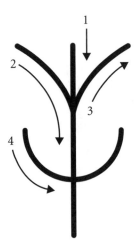

Figure 85: Antibacterial

Antipoison

Penczak received this symbol while working with Shamballa energy, seeking an effective way to deal with poisons and toxins, such as venomous insect bites.

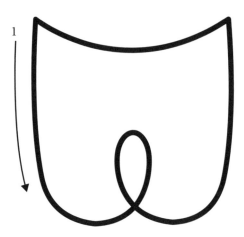

Figure 86: Antipoison

At Mata

This symbol is used to "cross over into a new threshold of healing,"[112] and it can remove emotional blocks that are obscuring deeper truths.

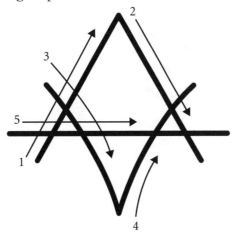

Figure 87: At Mata

---

112. Penczak, *Magick of Reiki*, 241.

Chakra Symbols

The following symbols are given without instructions for drawing them, so use your intuition to develop a method that works best for you.

Crown

Third eye

Throat

Heart

Solar plexus

Navel

Root

Figure 88: Chakra symbols

Dagu

This symbol is used to balance overabundant masculine energy and provide healing for those who are overly aggressive, hyperlogical, and goal-oriented, while making it easier to honor emotions, intuition, and non-linear process. It is useful for activating the energy of the spiritual warrior archetype.

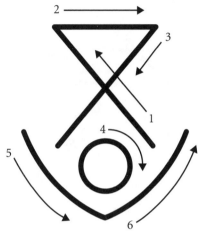

Figure 89: Dagu

Dai Koko Mi

Penczak received the guidance that this symbol was only to be used in the context of healing initiations to cleanse and open the chakras. The seven outer strokes represent the seven primary chakras.

Figure 90: Dai Koko Mi

Dazu

This symbol is used to heal on the devic, or nature spirit, level, and it is best used while out in nature. It can be used on plants when harvesting them for healing or magickal purposes, and it is effective in healing ecological disturbances and destruction wrought by humans.

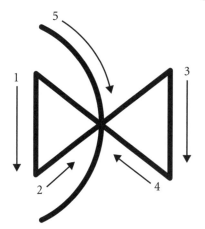

Figure 91: Dazu

Harmony

This symbol balances the flow and polarity of the energy in the body and aura, and it's useful at the end of a session to seal and protect, much like the traditional Usui Symbol One.

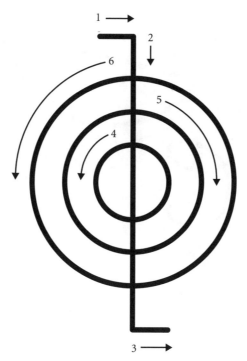

Figure 92: Harmony

Kir Mall

This symbol is useful in alleviating pain and discomfort. The four loops represent the four elements, so this symbol can be used to bring about internal elemental balance.

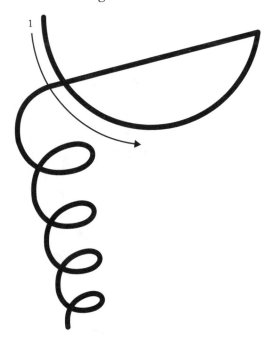

Figure 93: Kir Mall

Kundalini Balance

This symbol clears the energetic channels through the chakras, preparing one for a smoother flow of kundalini energy, and it can act to raise one's consciousness in daily life.

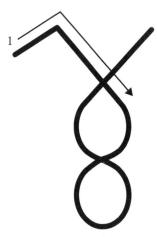

Figure 94: Kundalini Balance

Live Li

This symbol is similar to Motor Zanon, and it can be used to remove unwanted energy of any kind. You can "push" it into the body, where it will form a "three-dimensional tetrahedron with a mouth-like opening," which breaks up and devours harmful or unwanted energies.[113] Chant "Live Li" three times when pushing the symbol into the body, and repeat to call the symbol out of the body.

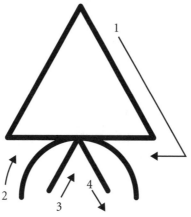

Figure 95: Live Li

Ra Ta Rio

This symbol integrates polar energies, harmonizing opposites and helping one integrate shadow material.

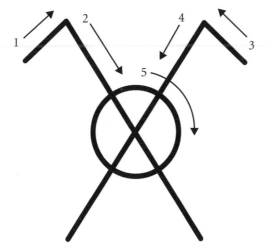

Figure 96: Ra Ta Rio

113. Penczak, *Magick of Reiki*, 241.

Um Mal

This symbol brings balance and harmony to the physical and spiritual selves and can help one live in more alignment with their spiritual values. It also helps one access deeper emotions and fears so they can be healed.

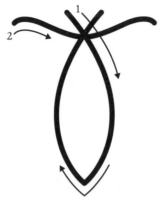

Figure 97: Um Mal

Why Ti

This symbol brings in and helps integrate new energies within the body, while introducing balance to the entire chakra system. It can help one be more open to change.

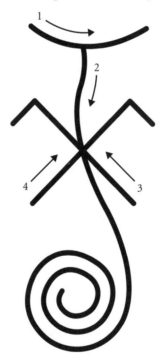

Figure 98: Why Ti

Zen Lu Ma

This symbol can be used to remove deeply entrenched mental and emotional blocks, or physical pain. The symbol will spin and enter the body to clear away obstructions.

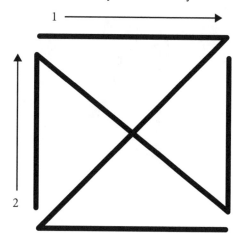

Figure 99: Zen Lu Ma

Reikifire Ministry Symbols

The Reikifire Ministry lists a set of fifteen symbols channeled by the late Rajeev Wagle, founder of the Wagle Reiki system.[114] There are no instructions, so you will need to use your intuition and experiment when drawing them.

Biru Kai

To increase or create love.

Figure 100: Biru Kai

114. Reikifire Ministry, "Wagle Reiki Symbols Index," Reiki Spirit, last modified January 4, 2005, http://reikispirit.net/church/sym.lib.wagle.html.

Chi Hai

To ensure success in new ventures.

Figure 101: Chi Hai

Furu Pyo Sho

To aid meditation.

Figure 102: Furu Pyo Sho

Hang Seng Dor

To remove blockages and challenges; can be placed on walls.

Figure 103: Hang Seng Dor

Jai Jin

To aid self-expression.

Figure 104: Jai Jin

Jin So Gen

To create peace in relationships.

Figure 105: Jin So Gen

Kat Sei Chen

To alleviate depression.

Figure 106: Kat Sei Chen

· · · · · · ·

Ki Yin Chi

To increase prosperity; can be placed on walls.

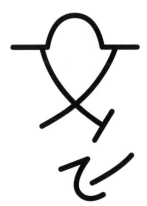

Figure 107: Ki Yin Chi

Michi Ka Ro

To harmonize.

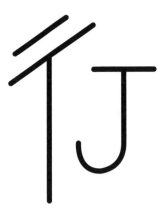

Figure 108: Michi Ka Ro

Mil Qu Zoo
To alleviate scarcity.

Figure 109: Mil Qu Zoo

Samye Meldru
Peace.

Figure 110: Samye Meldru

Senz Tan
To achieve victory.

Figure 111: Senz Tan

Tse Ne Dong
To promote happiness and ease.

Figure 112: Tse Ne Dong

Yoshi Te

To heal relationships.

Figure 113: Yoshi Te

Zen Kai Jo

To increase abundance; can be placed on walls.

Figure 114: Zen Kai Jo

Shamballa Symbols

According to founder John Armitage (a.k.a. Hari Das Baba), there are 1,024 symbols in the Shamballa system, channeled through a being Armitage refers to as Germain, who was said to be a high priest of Atlantis. Here are two commonly used symbols in the Shamballa tradition.

Mer Ka Fa Ka Lish Ma

This symbol represents the power of the divine Mother, and it contains the Egyptian ankh, a symbol of life, and the Greek caduceus, the healing staff carried by the god Hermes. This symbol is said to heal at a genetic level, to balance the chakras, connect with goddess energy, and heal the earth.

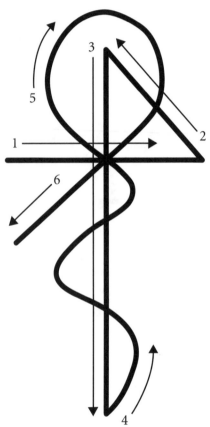

Figure 115: Mer Ka Fa Ka Lish Ma

Palm Di Ko Mio

As the name suggests, this symbol is used to activate the palm chakras, as well as move energy throughout the entire chakra system. It is sometimes referred to as the Palm Master Symbol. It is seen on some statues of Buddha, associating it with higher healing abilities. Cointreau writes that it can also be used on the brow to "decalcify and activate the pineal gland."[115]

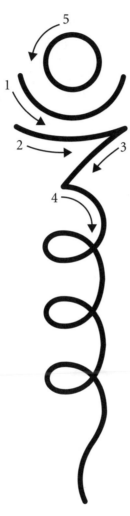

Figure 116: Palm Di Ko Mio

115. Cointreau, *The Practical Reiki Symbol Primer*, 155.

Tera Mai Symbols

These symbols are part of Kathleen Milner's Tera Mai healing system, covered in appendix B.

Hosanna

This symbol can be drawn in two different ways, either to send out clearing energy (first version) or to focus on a specific issue for healing (second version), and it is used in the Tera Mai tradition to evoke energies from higher realms. It is said to aid in the creation of harmonious relationships and clearing of emotional issues, and some practitioners draw it on either side of the traditional Symbol One.

Figure 117: Hosanna

Om Benza Satto Hung

This is a purifying symbol that can be used in meditation and during treatment to draw up harmful energies so they may be transformed. In the Tera Mai tradition, it can be used to remove unwanted energies and reverse the effects of attunements to other traditions when they are deemed to be of human and not divine invention.

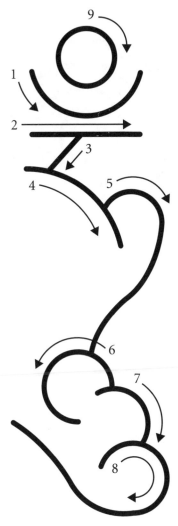

Figure 118: Om Benza Satto Hung

Other Reiki Symbols

Dai Zon

This is a shamanic symbol channeled by Lyn Roberts-Herrick, and it can be used to start and end a session. Some practitioners use Dai Zon by spiraling in toward the recipient's heart center, moving inward through all of the chakras. The direction can be reversed to close the session. It means "from my heart to your heart," and is pronounced DIE-don.[116]

Figure 119: Dai Zon

116. Penczak, *Magick of Reiki*,141.

Johre

Pronounced JO-rey, this symbol is said to mean "white light," and it will help in the release of unneeded or harmful energy, opens the chakras, and connects one to spirit guides.[117]

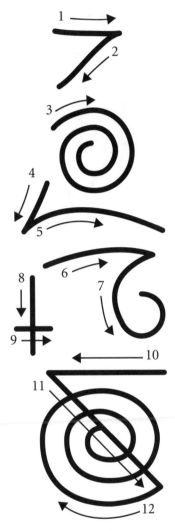

Figure 120: Johre

117. Penczak, *Magick of Reiki*, 138.

Len So My

This symbol represents pure, unconditional love and is associated with Earth Angels. It can surround you in the nurturing, protective energy of love while helping you to remain grounded and secure. This is an excellent symbol for healing feelings of abandonment and neglect.

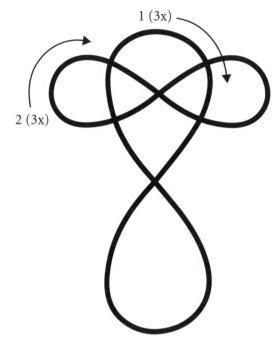

Figure 121: Len So My

Lon Say

This symbol is used to dispel negativity and heal infections. Christopher Penczak recommends using this symbol down the entire body, beginning at the crown of the head, focusing the spiral in the chest area, and drawing the wavy lines over the abdominal region.[118]

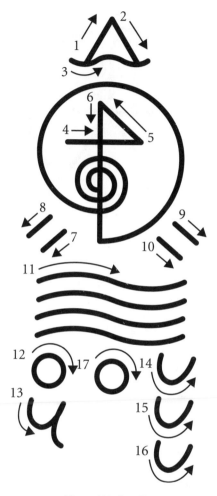

Figure 122: Lon Say

118. Penczak, *Magick of Reiki*, 149.

Tam A Ra Sha

This symbol is used to bring balance to your entire being, and it is also useful for calming energetic upheaval and pain in the body. It is said to clear the chakras and meridians, allowing energy to flow more freely to all parts of the system.

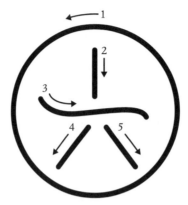

Figure 123: Tam A Ra Sha

There are more reiki symbols than what can be included here, with new ones being created or channeled, no doubt, as this book goes to press, and in your own practice, you, too, may receive symbols that can be used to enhance your healing work.

Using the Reiki Symbols

There are two basic ways of using the symbols: drawing them and visualizing them, and these methods can, of course, be combined. When drawing the symbols, you can do this with your finger or whole hand in the air, above the body or an object, in a chosen space, with the tip of the tongue inside the mouth, or by literally drawing them with pen on paper. Visualizing the symbol can be done in many ways, such as picturing the symbol in your mind's eye, projecting your mental image of the symbol onto a body part or other physical location, or onto a distant recipient or place. While many teachers advise not drawing the symbols and displaying them publicly, you could draw them in your journal to bring healing to an event or issue. In magickal practice, the symbols can be carved into candles, used in sigil magick, or drawn on paper for spells.

Animals

While some animals may allow you to give reiki with direct touch, this is more difficult with others. By using Symbol Three, you can connect to the animal from a distance, and using Symbol One will amplify the energy transmission. See page 279 for additional techniques.

Distance Techniques

Certain symbols are associated with the ability to channel reiki to locations and recipients who are not physically present. See chapter 14 for more information.

Food and Drink

You can trace the symbols over your food, draw the symbols into the condensation of a drinking glass, or draw the symbols into the cooking pot with a spoon. You can also give reiki to individual ingredients before making a recipe. Use the symbols to enhance the benefits of medications, vitamins, and other supplements.

Healing Issues or Challenging Situations

Write out the situation you desire to heal on a piece of paper, then hold it between your hands, setting the intention that reiki will flow into the situation, healing it on every level. Draw Symbol Three over the paper and intend that reiki connect with the situation, and repeat this process with Symbol Two, then Symbol One. Hold the paper, giving reiki for five to ten minutes, and when the energy flow tapers off, draw Symbol One once more, chanting the associated mantra three times. If you intend to repeat this exercise, place the paper somewhere safe, perhaps on an altar if you have one. If you are ending the process here, I like to burn the paper and put the ashes into the earth.

I have used this process in combination with tarot readings about a particular issue. After I perform the reading, gathering any necessary insights about the situation, I treat the layout with the same process as described with the piece of paper above (without burning my cards at the end, of course!). When done, I "reset" the cards by hovering my hands over the layout and giving reiki with the intention that the cards are cleansed on all levels, followed by making a horizontal chopping motion with my hand, three times over the cards.

Inanimate Objects

In magickal traditions, charging an object with reiki is akin to creating a talisman or an amulet. While the terms are often used interchangeably, some traditions specify that a talisman is used to attract energy or amplify existing energies, while amulets ward you from unwanted energies and influences. You can trace a symbol over the object (most commonly, Symbol One, although experiment and see if different symbols work best with certain objects), and then hold it in your hands to "fill it" with reiki. You can also use symbols over malfunctioning objects, like your car or computer, or preventatively, when the machine is working just fine.

A similar technique involves empowering objects with reiki, which serves the dual purpose of enhancing the object's functioning while also setting it up as a reiki transmitter of sorts. For example, if you empower a clock, you can get a nice little reiki boost every time you look at it to check the time. The process is simple: draw Symbol One over the object, chanting the mantra three times, and holding the intention of filling the object with reiki so that it will emanate healing energy. You can do this with anything in your life, such as phones and other devices, shower heads, mirrors, clothing, beauty products, kitchen appliances, your favorite pen, bedding, furniture, your journal, and the list goes on!

Past-Life Healing

Choose a comfy spot where you won't be disturbed, and draw Symbol One on all four sides of you, above you, and below you, intending that you are protected from harm on all levels throughout this experience. I like to chant the mantra as I do this, feeling the sound clearing the space of any unwanted energy. Feel reiki surrounding you, and take a few breaths to calm and center yourself, hands in gasshô. If you work with any spirit guides (see chapter 16) that feel appropriate for this work, you can call on them to help you in this past-life healing. Draw Symbol Four, chanting its mantra three times, and intend that this experience unfold in accordance with the highest good.

Draw Symbol Three and chant its mantra three times. Envision the symbol creating a bridge of reiki, and intend that it connects you to the past life most in need of healing right now. There are two options for this step:

1. Travel this bridge in your mind's eye, entering this past life as an observer, exploring, asking questions, and emanating reiki from your entire being, healing everything you encounter. This method adds techniques of journey meditation.
2. Send reiki through this bridge, healing this past life without entering it. This is a slight variation on a standard distance treatment.

Continue giving reiki for as long as feels necessary, then return along the same bridge if using option one, coming back into your body and present time. With both options, see the bridge in front of you, and draw Symbol One over it, intending that the bridge is dissolving, no longer connecting you to this past life. Draw Symbol One on both palms, then clap three times, completely releasing any remaining links to that life. If you worked with spirit guides, thank them now. Perform kenyoku hô and end with hands in gasshô, giving thanks.

Plants

You can use Symbol Three to connect to plants at a distance (try this when you're away on vacation and your plants need a little love) or use Symbol One to amplify the transmission of reiki while you place your hands on or over the plant. This can also be done for seeds prior to planting, to the watering can, and to any organic soil amendments.

Protection

Penelope Quest provides two methods for using Symbol One in a protective fashion that I find quite effective.[119] For the first method, draw a large version of Symbol One in front of you, chant the mantra three times, and step into the symbol, imagining it surrounding you while focusing on the intention that you are protected from harm on all levels. The second method involves drawing Symbol One in front of you, on both sides, and visualizing drawing it behind you. Chant the mantra three times as you intend that it forms a protective shield all around you. If you like, you can draw the symbol over your head and under your feet, too.

You can use a similar method to create a protective barrier around your house, car, and so on. Draw Symbol One over the object and imagine it expanding to cover it completely, on all sides. If the object isn't physically present, you can use Symbol Three first to create a connection before surrounding it with protective energy using Symbol One. I like to refresh this barrier on a regular basis. I might do this once a month under normal circumstances, but if I'm traveling, for example, I'll refresh the shield on my car more frequently or do the same distantly on my house while I'm away.

Psychic Activation

I have found that simply using reiki on a regular basis fine-tunes my intuition and activates psychic senses, but you can also use the following process to enhance these abilities. Draw Symbol One and Symbol Two on the palm of each hand. Place one palm over your forehead and the other hand behind your head. Intend that reiki flow into your third eye chakra, activating your psychic abilities in the manner that is correct and good for you, and allow reiki to flow.

You can also prepare a tea of mugwort, lemon balm, and anise seed, charging each of the herbs with reiki using Symbol One and Symbol Two. Brew the tea and draw the symbols over the cup, intending to activate your psychic abilities in a manner that is correct and good for you. With hands in gasshô, focus on this intention while bringing awareness to your third eye. Drink some of the tea, and with each breath, let reiki flow into you, gathering at your third eye. Continue until the process feels complete, then finish with hands in gasshô, giving thanks.

If you find yourself overwhelmed by psychic input, use the techniques in the protection section, setting the intention that only helpful energies are permitted into your field and all other energies are deflected with love.

Purifying a Space

Draw a large version of a symbol into the space. Symbol One is often used here, although there are non-traditional symbols that work well, too, such as Hang Seng Dor and Kita No Kaze. Some

---

119. Quest, *Reiki for Life*, 219.

practitioners advise drawing the symbol in each corner of the room, on each wall, on the ceiling, and on the floor, and I like to combine this with chanting one of the mantras, as the sound is a powerful aid in the cleansing process. You can also pair the symbols with other energetic cleansing techniques, such as smudging with sage or sweetgrass. Light the plant matter, blow out the flame, and disperse the smoke around the space. Leave a window open to allow unwanted energies a means of exit. You can also spray a dilution of sage or palo santo essential oil or Florida water around the room.

Purifying Yourself

Many of the techniques in chapters 14 and 15 serve to purify your body and energy field, and here is an additional method. Draw a large Symbol One over the front of your body with your finger as follows: Start the horizontal bar at the top in front of your crown, then bring the vertical line down to your hara. With your finger pointing at the floor, draw the three spirals, imagining each one surrounding your body. Throughout this process, intend that reiki is cleansing you on all levels, and chant the associated mantra three times (I like to use the chant while tracing the three spirals).

Travel

Holding the intention that reiki protect you (and any traveling companions) throughout your trip, use the symbols to give reiki to your mode of transportation (car, plane, etc.) or to your destination (visualizing it in your mind or using a photo). You could use Symbol Three, followed by Symbol One, or any combination of symbols that feels best to you. Objects such as jewelry or clothing can also be charged with reiki in the same manner and worn during your travels. I really like this technique from Penelope Quest: "Draw the Distant Symbol, saying its mantra to yourself three times, and imagine it forming a bridge of light connecting you with your destination.… Imagine a Power Symbol traveling ahead, clearing the way for you along the bridge of light formed by the Distant Symbol."[120]

In this chapter, you learned about the traditional and non-traditional reiki symbols, as well as myriad uses for them. In the next chapter, we'll cover another aspect of reiki practice: the five precepts and other philosophical teachings.

120. Quest, *Reiki for Life*, 220.

CHAPTER 13

⁓

The Five Precepts and Other Reiki Teachings

Usui's original teachings included five major elements, a number of which we've covered thus far: hands-on healing, symbols and mantras, attunements (or reiju), healing techniques (see chapter 14), and what are known as the five precepts, or *gokai*, which we'll cover in this chapter. Usui's Memorial Stone recommends that the "Five Precepts be chanted and kept in mind mornings and evening."[121] One of his students, Suzuki-san, said that Usui was teaching the precepts as early as 1915, while Hiroshi Doi writes that they were made an official part of the teachings in 1922 with the creation of the Gakkai. The precepts may have originated even earlier, from Japanese Buddhist teachings from the ninth century.

The Five Precepts

Just for today …

Do not anger.

Do not worry.

Be grateful.

Do your duties fully.

Be kind to others.

---

121. Stiene and Stiene, *The Reiki Sourcebook*, 68.

Just for Today

I find this line to be equal parts illuminating and reassuring. There's an acknowledgment of the vital importance of the present moment, the moment in which we will have the greatest impact, while also giving a nod to our human fallibility. Rather than admonishing us to *always* be grateful or *never* get angry, "just for today" suggests that we will be most successful in our endeavors if we focus on the next step, not the next ten thousand. It also contains the invitation of a fresh slate, each and every day. If things go sideways on Monday and we find ourselves snapping at our partner, waiting impatiently in line for our morning latte, and taking our safe, comfortable home for granted, well, there's always Tuesday. And Wednesday. Just for today encourages us to reset our intentions and do our very best, which might look different from day to day. We learn from and take responsibility for the moments when perhaps we could have responded differently without weighing ourselves down with shame and the heavy concept of a "ruined track record." Just for today awaits us every morning, every moment, reminding us that we have the power to choose, and we can use each and every decision to illuminate our True Self, regardless of what we chose yesterday or five minutes ago.

Do Not Anger

There are a number of ways one could embody this precept, including the most obvious: try not to be angry. For me, this is a tad bit unrealistic (and that's putting it mildly, depending on the day), but I do find it incredibly useful to examine the things that trigger my anger, because they typically have something to do with a story my ego is creating. The most common theme these stories share is expectation and a sense of deserving. For example, if I expect to be able to drive to work in fifteen minutes but it takes twenty-five, my ego is quite skilled at creating a story about this, resulting in anger. The anger isn't an automatic part of the experience, though, as much as it might seem to be at times. It's a choice. If I'm not in any particular hurry, the weather is nice and my windows are down, and there's a good song on the radio, that extra ten minutes might slide by unnoticed or even be relished; it all depends on the story I tell myself.

This precept invites us to look at those stories and to remember that we have a say in their telling. When we're overidentified with the ego, we can take its chatterings as fact, but when we use the five precepts and other mindfulness tools to witness these ego tales, we can play an active role in writing ones that foster curiosity for what *is* rather than outrage at what *isn't*, acceptance of the things that aren't under our control, and a more informed response to the things that are.

Do Not Worry

If I had to pick a favorite, this precept would be a top contender, because there truly is no value whatsoever in worrying. Worry can be sneaky, though, and fool us into thinking that we're doing something about the issue at hand—after all, we stayed up all night worrying about it, didn't we? So much energy can be thrown into worrying, leaving us with precious little left to actually address the situation that has us all tied up in knots. Worry and fear are bedfellows, and we are most likely to get caught in a worry loop when we allow the mind to spin out worst-case scenarios, living in these mental constructs as if they're really happening. And, indeed, when we visualize something, this process impacts our brain in strikingly similar ways to actually doing that thing, so mentally playing out our fears spikes our stress levels, which in turn has a negative impact on our blood pressure, immune system, ability to concentrate, and so much more.

The moral of the story? Don't waste your valuable time, energy, and health worrying. I find it helpful to write down what I'm worried about and then list the aspects of the situation that I can address. Of those, I circle the ones that I actually intend to do something about, and I get to work. Nine times out of ten, the action steps are so much easier than the worried mind would have us believe, and taking practical steps to address the issue gets our energy moving, clears away the cobwebs of confusion, and often leaves us with a sense of renewed purpose. All the things on the list that I either don't intend to address or couldn't even if I wanted to become fodder for releasing in whatever way feels best. I might burn the piece of paper and send the worries up in smoke, speak them into a heavy stone and plunk it into moving water, or whatever method feels intuitively right. The point is to acknowledge that you are letting these thoughts go rather than constantly toying with the idea that maybe, *just* maybe, you'll do something about them, driving yourself to distraction. Let 'em go, and just for today … don't worry.

Be Grateful

It's easy to get caught up in cataloguing all the things that aren't going the way we'd like, from the minute to the monumental, but if we pause for a moment and really appreciate how truly amazing it is to be alive—remembering that our time here is, in the grand scheme of things, preciously brief—we shift our mental soundtrack. Gratitude helps us see what's working and expand on those things. It uncovers previously hidden options and creative solutions more effectively than complaining ever will, and it magnetizes support and assistance from those around us. Chronic dissatisfaction, on the other hand, primes us to home in on what's not working, and as much as we rail against these things, we also create attachments to them, writing ourselves into the role of the victim or the rebel without a cause. To maintain this familiar (if ill-fitting) identity, we unconsciously need things to keep sucking—we need something to complain about, to pit ourselves against, or we don't know who we are and how to act. Gratitude frees us from this trap and allows us, one grateful observation at a time, to forge a new path, one that is an expression of our True Self. Just for today, what can you be grateful for? What in this moment

• • • • • • • •

brings a little smile to your face or a sense of calm? Focus on these things, no matter how small they might seem, and watch them expand.

Do Your Duties Fully

Often translated as "work hard," this precept invites us to bring our full self to everything we do. When we phone it in, we cultivate a sense of apathy and listlessness, and it's hard to make inspired choices in this state of mind. I like to think that this precept also invites us to get curious about the areas in which we're only delivering a fraction of our full effort and explore why that might be. Is this something we truly want to be doing? If not, why are we doing it? The answer to this frequently involves a heavy helping of *shoulds* and *have tos*, but I encourage you to look deeper. Why do you "have" to do this? What do you fear would happen if you didn't? How might you respond if that fear were realized?

The ego's stories can be quite convincing, and if we don't take the time to question them, they become our life credo, regardless of how much they run contrary to who we truly want to be. The ego deals in certainties, and it doesn't care much whether these certainties are actually true or not, just so long as we can be *certain* about them. To balance this tendency, we must question, question, and question some more. If the ego churns out a thought like "I'll never be able to leave this job" or "I can't tell her how I feel," get curious! Become the Sherlock Holmes of your own mind and ask, Why? What if? What then? I wonder if … Could we? And then …? When we give ourselves permission to question the *shoulds* and *musts*, we start to release the things in our life that don't light us up, that only drum up lackluster efforts, that separate us from "doing our duties fully." When we reclaim our right to choose what those duties are rather than wallowing in resentment, we transform our actions into devotions, and every moment becomes an opportunity to be of service by expressing our True Self.

Be Kind to Others

Like all the precepts, we can't go wrong by simply taking this at face value: treat others with kindness. But we are also rewarded by meditating on alternate layers of meaning, such as how you treat others is a mirror of how you treat yourself. Some aspects of our self-image are closer to the surface and easier to spot, and the same is true of select snippets from our mental soundtrack—some thoughts are loud and attention getting, while others are more subtle and sneaky. It's these harder-to-put-your-finger-on thoughts and beliefs that we can explore through this precept.

Looking at what we think and how we treat others offers a powerful glimpse of our inner realms. For example, if we find ourselves frequently judging people, we can bet that a harsh self-critic is lurking within. On days when I find myself quick to judge, this is an invitation to look at where I am not being as kind to myself as I could. When I amp up the self-care and self-love, this heals judgmental tendencies better than white-knuckle willing myself to "just be nice." If you find yourself annoyed by your coworker's habit of dominating the conversation, getting curious could lead to any number of insights, such as a desire to speak up more in conversation rather than playing the resentful audience member. Admiring your friend's ability to say no with grace could highlight a need to practice better boundary setting in your own life. The more we witness and work with this inner material, treating ourselves with compassionate curiosity, the more we will be naturally, authentically kind to others.

The version of the precepts from the *Reiki Ryôhô no Shiori*, a booklet published by the Gakkai, is as follows:

The secret art of inviting happiness

The miraculous medicine of all diseases

Just for today,

Do not get angry

Do not worry

Be filled with gratitude

Devote yourself to your work.

Be kind to people.

Every morning and evening, join your hands in prayer.

Pray these words to your heart and chant these words out loud[122]

The Precepts and *Kamiza*

Tadao Yamaguchi shares his mother's experience in one of Chûjirô Hayashi's seminars, where a scroll containing the five precepts was hanging in a corner of the room, and the workshop began with Hayashi chanting the precepts three times as the participants followed along.[123] This seems to follow the same format Usui used when teaching. In Jikiden Reiki, this tradition is honored with modern-day seminar participants chanting the gokai in Japanese, and a replica of Hayashi's scroll with the handwritten precepts is hung in the room in a precisely chosen location based on energy flow within the space.

The highest energy location is called *kamiza* and the lowest, *shimoza*. Like a river that flows from elevated areas to lower ones, the energy in a room flows from kamiza to shimoza, thus by placing the scroll in the high-energy spot, its energy flows with ease to the rest of the room. Yamaguchi writes that the kamiza spot is often the corner that is furthest from the room's entrance, and he advises keeping this area neat and tidy.[124] This principle can be used when setting up your treatment

---

122. *Reiki Ryôhô no Shiori,* 8.
123. Yamaguchi, *Light on the Origins of Reiki,* 33.
124. Yamaguchi, *Light on the Origins of Reiki,* 109.

• • • • • • •

221

space, too, with the recipient's head pointing toward the kamiza, which assists the natural flow of energy from the head to the rest of the body.

Poetry (Waka)

Another aspect of Reiki teachings is poetry (*waka*), specifically that written by the Meiji Emperor, and Usui included 125 of these poems in his teachings. Poetry created by an emperor is referred to specifically as *gyôsei*. In Shintô and Shugendō traditions, waka was seen to embody magickal powers and function as a sort of spell, and the contemplation and recitation of poetry was common in Japan during Usui's time. He advised his students to recite the emperor's poetry as a personal development practice, which would serve to enhance both their meditation and their energetic abilities.[125] In the *Reiki Ryôhô no Shiori*, recitation of gyôsei is said to clear the mind of thoughts in preparation for receiving spiritual energy. They were included in the teachings because "Master Usui, the founder of our association, respected the emperor's virtue like the way a child respects his parents, and chose 125 songs from his poems as a basic guidance for his study of Reiki Therapy."[126]

Waka contains thirty-one syllables: five in the first line, seven in the second, five in the third, and seven in the fourth and fifth lines. Each poem is given a title: for example, "The Wave," "Fallen Flowers on the Water," and "A Gemstone."

Working with the Waka

In addition to reciting and meditating on the poems, I like to borrow a Benedictine practice called *lectio divina* to deepen my understanding. While this practice can be used with any written materials, if you're interested in working with the waka, in *The Spirit of Reiki*, Frank Arjava Petter includes all 125 gyôsei, translated by his mother-in-law from an older form of Japanese into modern Japanese, and then by himself and his then-wife, Chetna Kobayashi, into English (see recommended resources). While the practice of *lectio divina* varies somewhat by source, I use the following four-step process.[127] Choose a poem to work with (you can do this intentionally or open to a random page) and take a few minutes to calm and center yourself. Read the poem and start by exploring it on a narrative level. What's happening in this poem in a literal sense? Look at the who, what, when, where, and why. You can discuss with a partner or group, journal your thoughts, or simply muse silently to yourself. Second, reread the poem and look at it allegorically. What associations does this poem recall for you? Does it remind you of another work of art, such as a book, painting, or movie? Does it trigger a personal memory? Fill in the blank:

125. Stiene and Stiene, *The Reiki Sourcebook*, 75.
126. *Reiki Ryôhô no Shiori*, 11.
127. "Spiritual Practice Resources," Harry Potter and the Sacred Text, accessed June 2, 2019, http://www.harrypottersacredtext.com/spiritual-practice-resources.

"This poem makes me think of _____." Third, reread the poem and contemplate how it relates to your own life. Does it invite you to see an aspect of yourself or a situation in a different way? In what ways does the poem resonate with you, and in what ways does it seem unrelated to your experience? And fourth, read the poem one more time and reflect on an action that this piece inspires you to take. Perhaps you feel called to pay more attention to a certain aspect of your life, shift a specific behavior to align more with your values, or reach out to someone you know. When the experience feels complete, find a way to mark the end of the process, such as placing your hands in *gasshô* and taking a small bow.

The Three Pillars

Frank Arjava Petter describes the foundational aspects of reiki as the three pillars: *gasshô* (two hands coming together), *reiji* (indication of spirit), and *chiryô* (treatment).[128] Here, we'll look at the first two elements, gasshô and reiji, and in the next chapter we'll explore various healing techniques, or chiryô.

The word *gasshô* means "two hands coming together," commonly referred to as "prayer hands." This is associated with a meditation technique, *gasshô meiso*, which is a wonderful practice to calm and clear the mind and increase your energy.

EXERCISE: Gasshô Meditation

Find a comfortable place to sit where you won't be disturbed, and bring your hands into gasshô at heart level. If your arms get tired at any point, you can rest them in your lap, still in gasshô. Close your eyes or leave them open with a soft, unfocused gaze. Bring your awareness to your breath, inhaling through the nose and exhaling through the mouth. On the inhale, lightly touch the tip of your tongue to the roof of the mouth, just behind the teeth, and on the exhale, let the tongue relax. Bring your attention to the point where your middle fingers touch; you might even feel the wind of the breath here. If your mind starts to wander, gently press the middle finger pads together to retrain your focus on this area. Continue the meditation for up to thirty minutes.

Petter lists the esoteric Buddhist associations for the fingers and fingertips, which are being united in gasshô.[129] Each corresponds to an element and a quality:

Thumb: The void and discernment

Index: Air and operation

Middle: Fire and perception

128. Lübeck, Petter, and Rand, *The Spirit of Reiki*, 145.
129. Lübeck, Petter, and Rand, *The Spirit of Reiki*, 148.

· · · · · · · ·

Ring: Water and reception

Pinky: Earth and form

By bringing our attention to the middle finger, we burn away distractions with the element of fire, stoked by the air of our breath, and sharpen our perception.

The technique of *reiji* helps us connect with higher guidance, and it strengthens our intuition. The word means "indication of spirit," and in her diary, Takata described it as the "utmost secret in the energy science."[130] This is a great technique to use before a reiki treatment, as it will heighten your ability to sense byôsen, guiding the placement of your hands.

EXERCISE: Reiji-hô

Sit or stand comfortably and close your eyes. Bring your hands in gasshô in front of your heart and set the intent to open to the flow of reiki. With your hands still in gasshô, move them up to the center of your forehead. Then, open your eyes and let your hands move to an area of the body in need of treatment, remaining there until you get a sense that it's time to move on. Continue treating different areas of the body as you feel guided until the session is complete. Bring your hands back into gasshô and give thanks.

The Five Objects of Reiki

According to Kimiko Koyama, the sixth president of the Gakkai, there are five objects of Reiki Ryôhô:[131]

1. *Tai* (body), *Ken* (health)
2. *En* (relation, connection, fate, karma, love), *Bi* (beauty)
3. *Kokoro* (heart and mind), *Makoto* (sincerity, authenticity)
4. *Sai* (talent), *Chikara* (power)
5. *Tsutome* (duty), *Do* (work)

I use the objects as a focus for meditation, and while insights differ each time I work with them, here are some of my current thoughts for each object:

1. Listing this as the first object seems significant to me, as a healthy body provides a solid foundation for personal growth. While certainly not impossible, it's more difficult to pursue spiritual practices when our health is in shambles, as we're often consumed with simply getting through the day. By tending to our body like a sacred temple, we create more ease and

130. Lübeck, Petter, and Rand, *The Spirit of Reiki*, 150.
131. Lübeck, Petter, and Rand, *The Spirit of Reiki*, 97.

expansion on the physical plane, thereby liberating energy for deeper mental, emotional, and spiritual explorations. This creates a self-perpetuating cycle: the more we explore and heal these non-physical levels of our being, the more health we experience in the body.

2. This object brings to mind a concept I learned through the work of C. G. Jung, something called *amor fati,* or "love of one's fate." Through dedicated spiritual practice, we begin to see the threads woven throughout our life experiences; we see the patterns of karma (cause and effect) more clearly and understand how and why we are here in this present moment. Like glimpsing a method to the madness, we see beauty in the chaos and feel a deep appreciation for everything that happened in precisely the way it did to shape who we are today. Rather than getting hung up on "Why me?" and "If only this hadn't happened," we release the notion of regret and see the gems hidden in every challenge—we fall in love with our fate.

3. When we suppress our True Self, we create turmoil in the mind and in the heart. By constantly biting back our words, swallowing our feelings, and stuffing down our needs and desires, we create obstructions in our energy field, which can eventually manifest on the physical plane. Living in alignment with our values liberates this blocked energy, leaving us better able to respond to each moment with curiosity and full presence, because we're not mentally running possible responses through a complicated algorithm of how we think we *should* feel, think, and act. This isn't to say we throw civility and kindness out the window—quite the contrary. When we respect ourselves by honoring our authentic nature— by speaking truthfully, by being vulnerable enough to share how we really feel, by expressing our needs instead of simmering with resentment—we naturally extend this respect to others.

4. This object feels related to the concept of a "Zone of Genius," introduced by Dr. Gay Hendricks in his book, *The Big Leap*.[132] When we embrace and cultivate our talents, we inhabit our zone of genius, which we can think of as the polar opposite of chilling out in our comfort zone. The zone of genius requires us to really bring our A game, but it returns the favor by gifting us with an energetic power that seems to snowball our efforts far beyond their initial effect. When we're operating in our genius zone, rather than sticking with safe and manageable pursuits, the feeling is almost palpable; it's electric and carries a self-sustaining momentum that we can only dream of in our comfort zone. Have you ever talked to someone about their life's passion? Their voice takes on a fiery energy, they stand taller and with an openness to their posture, like they're ready to take on the world, and the

132. Gay Hendricks, *The Big Leap: Conquer Your Hidden Fear and Take Life to the Next Level* (New York: HarperOne, 2010).

energy can be downright contagious. This is precisely the sort of power that comes to mind when I meditate on this object.

5. This object reminds me of the reiki precept "do your duties fully," an invitation to bring our full attention and presence to each moment, and through this deep engagement, we create meaning in our life. I'm reminded of a passage from Abraham H. Maslow's *Religions, Values, and Peak Experiences:* "The great lesson from the true mystics, from the Zen monks … is that the sacred is in the ordinary, that it is to be found in one's daily life. … To be looking everywhere for miracles is to me a sure sign of ignorance that everything is miraculous."[133] By bringing awareness to the details of our day—one might even call it a sense of devotion—we turn our duties into the great work of crafting a life of meaning.

Now that we've explored the philosophy of reiki, it's time to round out our practice with hands-on healing techniques, the focus of the next chapter.

---

133. Abraham H. Maslow, *Religions, Values and Peak-Experiences* (New York: Penguin Compass, 1994), 4, Kobo.

• • • • • • • •

CHAPTER 14

❦

Traditional Reiki Techniques

The reiki system is, at its heart, a healing tradition, and it offers numerous techniques for initiating healing in ourselves and in others. Like the symbols and mantras, these healing techniques, or chiryô, range from traditional practices that were a part of Usui's original teachings to newer methods developed within the many offshoots of Usui's system. In this chapter, we'll cover techniques that can be traced back to Usui himself or methods that are taught by Japanese branches of reiki that claim to be working in a traditional manner, and in the next chapter, we'll cover non-traditional reiki techniques.

The following four techniques are from the booklet *Reiki Ryôhô no Shiori*, and they can be easily incorporated into a treatment session.

EXERCISE: Sensing Imbalances (Byôsen Reikan Hô)

Byôsen is described as "disease radiation," and it refers to the energetic sensation given off by areas of imbalance. To scan the body for byôsen, center yourself by bringing your hands in gasshô, palms together at heart center, eyes closed, focusing on your breath for a few cycles. Open your eyes and hover your hands a few inches above the body, slowly scanning until you feel a sensation in your hands that might include tingling, pulsing, heat or cold, itchiness, and so on. Place your hands on that part of the body and remain until the sensation has passed. Move onto the next area of imbalance. When finished, bring your palms together at your heart and give thanks.

EXERCISE: Detoxification (Dokukudashi)

Place your hands on the stomach, three fingers' width below the navel, and set the intention, "I am getting rid of poison." Maintain your concentration on this intention and remain in this position for thirty minutes. (Yes, this is a long time! You might want to pull up a chair.) This treatment can be repeated a few times for more severe cases.

EXERCISE: Blood Exchange (Koketsuhô)

This is a strengthening technique and is well suited for those who are chronically ill or recovering from a major illness or injury. It is recommended to repeat this treatment anywhere from two weeks to six months, depending on the severity of the condition. The *Reiki Ryôhô no Shiori* gives two variations:

- **Upper Body Blood Exchange:** Making direct skin contact, place the palms on either side of the spine at the top of the back and sweep the hands out to the sides. Repeat down the entire length of the back. Repeat fifteen to twenty times. Then, place two fingers on either side of the spine, and sweep down from the back of the neck to the hips, pressing on either side at the bottom, just above the hip bones. Repeat this about fifteen times.

- **Whole Body Blood Exchange:** Complete a reiki treatment on the head, lungs, heart, stomach, and intestines. Place the palms on either side of the spine at the top of the back and sweep the hands out to the sides. Repeat down the entire length of the back. Repeat fifteen to twenty times. Then, place two fingers on either side of the spine, and sweep down from the back of the neck to the hips, pressing on either side of the spine at the bottom, just above the hip bones. Repeat this fifteen times. Place the hands a couple of inches above the neck. Hold your breath as you sweep your hands down the length of the back to the tailbone. When you reach the tailbone, separate the hands and sweep them down the legs to the feet. Rub and sweep both arms, starting at the shoulder and moving to the tips of the fingers, repeating a few times. Sweep down the backs of the thighs to the toes to finish.

EXERCISE: Transferring Will Power (Nentatsu)

This technique allows you to send your thoughts to the recipient, and you begin by focusing your awareness "on your front hairline," concentrating on what you want to send to the receiver.[134] For example, you might send the thought "the illness will be cured," and you can also send the five precepts. Maintain this concentration for a few minutes. You can repeat this technique in subsequent sessions for very ill patients. The *Reiki Ryôhô no Shiori* explains that because reiki is a spiritual therapy, the results are largely dependent on the recipient's mental state. If someone is in a headspace that isn't conducive to healing, you can give them a boost by sending your thoughts with this technique.

---

134. *Reiki Ryôhô no Shiori*, 40.

EXERCISE: Hatsurei Hô

There are two methods for this technique. The first is taught by Hiroshi Doi. The second is from a 1933 book by one of Usui's students, a healer named Kaiji Tomita. Both are suitable for generating a more powerful flow of spiritual energy through the body.

Method One

Sit in *seiza* (kneeling, sitting back on your heels with an upright spine), hands in gasshô at your heart center. Close your eyes, and recite some of the waka (see page 222) or other meaningful text of your choosing to clear your mind.

Perform *kenyoku hô* (instructions follow)

Perform *jôshin kokyû hô* (instructions follow).

Perform *seishin toitsu* (instructions follow).

Recite the five precepts.

Give thanks with hands in gasshô (palms together at heart center).

Method Two

Sit in seiza and concentrate on uniting the body and the mind. Place your hands in gasshô without creating tension in the arms and shoulders with the aim of gathering and concentrating energy from the heart center into the hands. Relax your shoulders and lightly clasp your hands. Perform *jôshin kokyû hô,* which is designed to purify the mind. Silently recite waka or the text of your choice, allowing the words to resonate deep within you, until you feel one with its meaning. At this point, your hands should be feeling warmer with an electric-like tingling sensation. Repeat this process for five consecutive days, starting with a thirty-minute practice and gradually increasing to an hour.

EXERCISE: Dry Bathing (Kenyoku Hô)

This technique is great for purifying your energy field, like wiping the energetic slate clean, and I like to use it between client sessions. It's also useful anytime you feel like you need to "shake things off," perhaps if you're in a funk or otherwise stuck in an unproductive mental loop.

1. While seated or standing, place your right palm near your left shoulder, just over the outer edge of the collarbone (clavicle). Brush this hand over your skin, diagonally across your chest to your right hip.

2. Repeat on the opposite side, placing your left palm on right collarbone, swiping it diagonally to your left hip.

3. Repeat steps one and two.

4. Use your right hand to stroke your left wrist, over your open left palm and off the ends of your fingertips.

5. Use your left hand to stroke your right wrist, over your open right palm and off the ends of your fingertips.

6. If desired repeat steps 4 and 5.

EXERCISE: Breathing Method to Focus the Mind (Jôshin Kokyû Hô)

This exercise is not recommended for people who are pregnant or have high blood pressure. If you feel light-headed at any point, stop immediately and return to normal breathing.

Inhale through your nose and envision drawing reiki into your body through the nose. You might feel the reiki entering as tingling, heat, vibration, or waves, or you can visualize it as white light. Envision pulling the breath and the reiki down to your hara (slightly below the navel) with this inhale. On the exhale, visualize the reiki streaming out through your entire body, radiating into your surroundings. With each successive inhale, focus your awareness on reiki drawing down into your hara, followed by reiki expanding and permeating your entire body and streaming outward on the exhale. Continue for anywhere from five minutes to half an hour.

EXERCISE: Concentration or Unified Mind Technique (Seishin Toitsu)

Some sources refer to this technique as jôshin kokyû hô, and as mentioned above, it is not recommended for people who are pregnant or have high blood pressure. If you feel light-headed at any point, stop immediately and return to normal breathing.

With your hands in prayer position at heart center, focus your awareness on the hara (slightly below the navel). On the inhale, draw energy in from your hands, down into the hara. On the exhale, reverse the process, visualizing energy moving from the hara, down the arms, and out through the hands. Repeat these inhales and exhales anywhere from five to thirty minutes.

EXERCISE: Staring or Eye-Focus Method (Gyôshi Hô)

Reiki is said to emanate from the entire body but most strongly from the hands, eyes, and breath. This technique uses the eyes to focus healing energy and is especially useful when direct contact with the recipient is not possible. Gaze at the area of the body where you wish to give reiki, and intend that reiki flow from your eyes to the recipient's body. You can move to other areas or conclude the treatment once you have a sense that this particular area has received all the reiki that it needs right now.

EXERCISE: Navel Healing Technique (Heso Chiryô Hô)

Due to its focus on the umbilicus, this technique is said to heal your relationship to the mother—either in a biological or archetypal sense—while also strengthening the kidneys. Place your middle finger in the navel and apply slight pressure until you feel an energetic pulse (not a blood pulse). Allow reiki to flow until you feel a harmony between the energetic pulse and reiki. This can be done on yourself or clients (with their permission, of course, as not everyone will be comfortable with touch in this sensitive area).

EXERCISE: Breathing Method (Koki Hô)

This technique is useful for sending reiki to areas without touch, and it can be used on its own or as part of a longer session. With hands in gasshô at your heart, calm and center your mind. Inhale through your nose, focusing on drawing the breath into your hara. Hold the energy in this area while you trace Symbol One in your closed mouth with the tongue, then blow the breath onto the area to be treated. You can also visualize Symbol One as you exhale. (Make sure your breath is fresh, especially if you smoke, before using this technique with clients.)

EXERCISE: Stroking Treatment (Nadete Chiryô Hô)

While performing this technique, maintain the intention to clear the energy of the meridians and the organs, and carry out the stroke with the palm of your hand. The Stienes explain that *nadete chiryô hô* originates in Traditional Chinese Medicine, which gives the following emotion-organ associations:

Heart: Hurt, pain, joy, excitement, shock

Stomach: Sadness, worry

Liver: Anger

Spleen: Depression, frustration, resentment, pensiveness

Kidneys: Fear[135]

To treat the front of the body, start in the middle of the chest at the heart, sweeping your palm over the area (when working with female clients, I will hover over this area and sweep a few inches above the body), then sweep down to the stomach (left upper quadrant of the abdomen), over the liver (right upper quadrant), and travel all the way down the outside of the right leg, flicking energy off the toes in one continuous sweep. Begin again at the heart, sweeping down over the stomach and spleen (left upper quadrant), and down the outside of the left leg, once more flicking energy off at the toes. Return to the heart, and sweep over the shoulder and down the arm, flicking energy off the fingers. Repeat on the opposite arm.

Place the index and middle finger of both hands in between the brows, fingertips touching, and hold for twenty seconds. Sweep the fingers out to the temples, and hold for twenty seconds.

135. Stiene and Stiene, *The Reiki Sourcebook,* 262.

Sweep over the ears and flick the energy off. Place the index and middle fingers on either side of the nose, just below the eyes, and hold for twenty seconds. Sweep out to the ears and flick off the energy.

To treat the back of the body, start at the base of the neck and sweep down the spine to the tailbone, clearing the heart, kidneys, and spine meridians.

Exercise: Hand Pressure Method (Oshite Chiryô Hô)

This technique is useful on areas that feel tense and stiff. Apply pressure to the area with fingertips, a soft fist, or palm, and send reiki into the area. You could combine this method with trigger point methodology by applying firm pressure to the area for at least thirty seconds. (A license to touch may be required to do this, depending on local laws.)

Exercise: Purifying Inanimate Objects (Jakikiri Jôka Hô)

This method is only suitable for inanimate objects, such as crystals, jewelry, your house, car, and so on and is not recommended for use on people, animals, or plants.

Hold the object in your non-dominant hand and place your dominant hand about four inches above the object. Focus on your hara and make three horizontal chopping motions with your hand, stopping abruptly after the third chop. Give the object reiki for a few minutes. If the object is too large to hold, like your house, for example, draw Symbol Three in front of it, chanting the mantra three times, then perform the technique, visualizing your hand moving over the object.

Exercise: Tanden Chiryô Hô

This technique is good for energizing and strengthening willpower. Place one palm over the hara (slightly below the belly button) and the other hand on the back, behind the hara. Send reiki until your hands naturally lift off by themselves.

An alternate method, used to purify and clear the body, is to place one palm over the hara and one palm on the forehead, joining earth and heaven energy. Hold this position for about five minutes, then move the forehead hand and place it over the lower hand, so both hands are resting on the hara. Hold for about twenty minutes, then bring hands into gasshô and give thanks.

Exercise: Patting with Hands (Uchite Chiryô Hô)

Like nadete chiryô hô, this technique comes from Traditional Chinese Medicine, and it can be done with the palm or back of the hand, the side of the hand (like a "karate chop" motion, only much gentler!), or the fingers. Create the motion at the wrist without using the force of the entire arm. While you work, hold the intent to clear the energy of the meridians or organs.

For the upper (above the hips) front of the body, pat with the back of the hand. Start at the heart and pat down in a straight line (avoiding breast tissue) to the hara, being mindful not to use too much force over the abdomen. Begin again at the heart, this time moving out to the shoulder and down the inside of the arm, repeating on the other arm. Starting just above the hip bone, pat down the outside of the leg until you reach the knee, then switch to the inside of the leg, moving down to the feet and finishing by flicking the energy off the toes. Repeat on the other leg. On the back of the body, pat from the base of the neck along the spine, all the way down to the tailbone to clear the meridians.

EXERCISE: Reiki Exercise (Reiki Undô)

Undô means "exercise," and this technique was introduced to the Gakkai by Kimiko Koyama, a former president of the Gakkai.[136] It can be found in other cultures, such as *qigong* in China, *subud* in Indonesia, and *latihan* in India.

Find a safe place where you can roll around on the floor unharmed. Begin with hands in gasshô and say, "Reiki exercise start!" Take in a deep, rich inhale and let it out completely, releasing your body as you do so, allowing movement to arise naturally in the body. You may need to take in a few rounds of deeper breaths before the body relaxes enough to start moving spontaneously. It can take practice to let go of inhibitions and let the body move organically, so continue practicing on a daily basis. If sounds arise, let them. If feelings come up, give yourself space to experience them.

EXERCISE: Concentrated Spiritual Energy (Shûchû Reiki)

This is a group exercise that can be performed at a reiki share, class, and so on. One person is the recipient and lies down on the treatment table. The practitioners place their hands on the body, covering the main sections and any areas of imbalance. Give reiki and then finish with hands in gasshô to give thanks.

EXERCISE: Creating a Current of Energy (Reiki Mawashi)

Another group exercise, this allows participants to feel the energy flow, increasing their energetic sensitivity. Sit together in a circle and start with hands in gasshô, eyes closed, and give thanks. Then, each person places their hands out to the side with the left palm up and the right palm down. Each person's left hand will be under the right hand of the person to their left, and each person's right hand will be above the left hand of the person on their right. The hands are hovering, not touching. The teacher begins by sending energy to the right, and it travels around the circle, growing in intensity. Then, everyone swaps the orientation of their hands, right palms facing up, left palms facing down, and the teacher sends energy again, this time to the left. Finish with hands in gasshô, giving thanks.

---

136. Lübeck, Petter, and Rand, *The Spirit of Reiki*, 175.

EXERCISE: Distance Treatment Method (Enkaku Chiryô Hô)

According to traditional teachings, this method is not about "sending" reiki to another person or place; it is about becoming one—or more accurately, realizing that you are already one—with the recipient. You can use a photograph of the recipient, writing their name, age, and location on the back, or you can write this information on a piece of paper if you don't have a photo. You can also simply visualize the person between your hands. Begin in gasshô and set the intention to perform enkaku chiryô hô. Hold your hands over the photo or visualize the recipient and feel the connection. Maintaining focus on the recipient, draw Symbol Three, then Two, then One while chanting the accompanying mantras. Continue focusing on the recipient for as long as you feel the energy flowing, then end by bringing hands into gasshô and giving thanks.

In the next chapter, we'll look at additional reiki techniques that come from a variety of non-traditional sources.

CHAPTER 15

❧

Non-traditional Reiki Techniques

Since its original inception, reiki practice has been supplemented by practitioners around the world, who have added their own original techniques or practices borrowed from other healing traditions. In this chapter, we look at a variety of techniques that vary in origin. Some derive from Japanese traditions, such as those taught by Chûjirô Hayashi or Hiroshi Doi's system of Gendai Reiki, while others originated in the West.

Breathing Techniques

EXERCISE: Hui Yin Breath

Hui Yin is an acupuncture point, the first point on the Conception Vessel meridian. It's considered to be a yin point, and two other lines converge with the Conception Vessel here: the Governing meridian and the Penetrating meridian. To connect to this point, inhale and contract the perineum, the area between the anus and genitals, placing the tip of your tongue on the roof of your mouth, just behind the front teeth. Hold the breath for a few counts and release. Inhale again and repeat the contraction.

EXERCISE: Breath of the Fire Dragon

Begin with a few rounds of the Hui Yin Breath to calm and center yourself. Continuing this breathing pattern, when you inhale and contract, visualize breathing blue light into your kidneys, and release white light on the exhale. Do this three times. Visualize a white mist around the crown of your head, and breathe in all the way down to the Hui Yin point at the perineum. Hold your breath here, and allow the energy to rise up your spine. When it reaches your brain it will turn white, blue, purple, and gold. Visualize each of the traditional symbols once, chanting their mantras three times, and breathe the energy of the symbols out.

• • • • • • • •

EXERCISE: Chakra Kassei Kokyû Hô

Sit comfortably, spine upright, hands in gasshô. Calm and center yourself. Raise your arms to the sky, hands shoulder width apart, palms facing each other, and connect to reiki. Feel the flow of energy down through your arms and into your head. Place your hands, palms facing up, on your knees. With each inhale, feel energy entering your crown chakra and move it down through the entire body. Relax on each exhale.

You can work with each of the chakras individually from top to bottom, bringing energy down through the crown, or you can follow this basic pattern: Breathe in through your root chakra and bring the energy up to your heart. Pause, then breathe out through the heart center. Breathe in through the heart, bring energy up to the crown, and exhale through the crown. Breathe in energy through the crown, bring it down to the heart center, and exhale through the heart. Finally, breathe in through the heart, bring the energy down to the root chakra, and exhale here. Repeat for a few rounds, then bring your hands into gasshô and give thanks.

EXERCISE: Hadô Kokyû Hô

This technique is designed to boost the immune system, detoxify the body, and raise energy levels while simultaneously promoting a sense of calm. Bring your hands in gasshô, close your eyes, and center your mind. Rest your hands on your knees, palms facing up. Take a deep breath in, then let it out with a "haaa" sound, like you're trying to fog up a bathroom mirror. With practice, the exhale will lengthen, with the final aim of releasing the breath for roughly forty seconds (quite a long time!). At the bottom, release any tension in your abdomen to initiate the next inhale. Repeat for a few rounds, or longer if you have more practice and you can do so without becoming light-headed. End with hands in gasshô, giving thanks.

EXERCISE: Saibo Kassei Kokyû Hô

Sit comfortably, spine upright, hands in gasshô. Calm and center yourself. Raise your arms to the sky, hands shoulder width apart, palms facing each other and connect to reiki. When you feel the connection, move your hands down to rest briefly on top of your head, then bring them to your knees, palms facing up. Begin to mentally scan your body, and when you reach an area where you sense an imbalance, breathe in, and on the exhale send reiki to that area. Talk to the area, asking for insights and expressing your appreciation for what it has taught you and for the balance that is currently unfolding. With practice, you can simply say thank you to the imbalanced areas, and it will carry all of these sentiments of gratitude without your needing to voice them. When finished, bring your hands into gasshô and give thanks.

EXERCISE: Sekizui Jôka Ibuki Hô

Some Japanese traditions believe that our karma is recorded in our spine, and this technique is designed to clear the energy within the spinal cord (*sekizui*), bringing balance to the entire body. Sit comfortably, spine upright, hands in gasshô. Calm and center yourself. Raise your arms to the sky, hands shoulder width apart, palms facing each other and connect to reiki. When you feel the connection, move your hands down to rest briefly on top of your head, then bring them to your knees, palms facing up. Imagine that your spine is a river of energy running from crown to tailbone, and practice the hadô breath: Take a deep breath in, then let it out with a "haaa" sound, like you're trying to fog up a bathroom mirror. Gradually lengthen the exhales, up to forty seconds. As you do this, imagine the breathing clearing and purifying the river of the spine until this process feels complete. Then, imagine water entering at your tailbone and rising up the third eye. On the exhale, the water flows down and out through the tailbone. Repeat this seven times. End with hands in gasshô and give thanks.

EXERCISE: Violet Breath

Imagine a white mist around you and draw in the Hui Yin point at the perineum (like you're trying to halt the flow of urine), placing your tongue on the roof of your mouth, just behind the front teeth. Imagine a white light entering your crown, moving through the tongue, and out of the mouth, traveling down the front of the body, all the way to the Hui Yin point. From there, it travels back up the spine and into the center of the head. Visualize the white mist filling your head. Then, the mist turns blue, then indigo as it rotates clockwise. The mist turns violet, and within this violet mist, visualize a golden Dumo symbol (see page 160). If you are using this technique as part of an attunement, at this point you would blow the breath into the student's crown chakra, visualizing the symbol entering their head while you chant the mantra three times.

Chakra Techniques

EXERCISE: Chakra Balancing

This version of the technique doesn't treat the crown chakra directly, with the understanding that this chakra will naturally come into balance once the rest of the chakras are harmonized. You can perform this for another person, adapting the instructions to hover over any areas of privacy.

Lie down on your back, and place one hand over the third eye and one hand over the root chakra. Stay in this position until you receive the cue to move on, then place one hand over the throat chakra and the other over the navel chakra. Stay in position until the energy flow tapers off, then finish with one hand on the heart and the other on the solar plexus, staying there until the process feels complete.

• • • • • • •

EXERCISE: Reiki Boost

This technique opens and balances the chakras, allowing for a more harmonious flow of energy in the body, making it a wonderful preparation for an attunement. The client will be standing with the side of their body facing you. Hold your hands, palms down, over their crown chakra for a few minutes. Hover your palms, one over the third eye, the other on the back of the head, holding for a few minutes. Repeat this process at each chakra with one hand on the front of the body, the other at the back for the throat, heart, solar plexus, navel, and root chakras. Then, hold your hands over the knees on the front and the back (palms facing each other) and hold for a few minutes. Turn the palms up and slowly lift the energy up to the crown chakra. Sweep down the aura, smoothing the energy, moving down to the knees. Snap your fingers to end the energetic connection.

EXERCISE: Seventh Level Technique

There is an important energy gateway at the base of the skull, sometimes referred to as the "zeal point chakra" or the "mouth of god." This technique activates and sends energy via this gateway. Hold one hand at the base of the skull and the other at the crown of the head, holding for five minutes. Keep one hand at the base of the skull and move the other to the third eye, holding for five minutes. Finish with one hand on the crown and one on the third eye, again holding for five minutes.

EXERCISE: Six-Point Energy Meditation for Energy Awareness

This technique is designed to harmonize the flow of energy through the body. Center yourself with three even breaths, then bring your awareness to your crown chakra, noticing any energetic sensations. Repeat this process at your third eye, then your throat chakra, heart chakra, solar plexus, and finally the chakras on the palms of your hands.

Crystal Healing Techniques

The following techniques combine the power of crystals with reiki healing.

EXERCISE: Cleansing and Charging Crystals

Before using crystals, it's helpful to cleanse them, removing any unwanted energy they may have collected over time. I like to do this when I first acquire a crystal, and then I periodically clean them, especially before and after using them for healing and other purposes. There are a number of ways to cleanse your crystals, from submerging them in a bowl of salt or spring water (not all crystals can withstand the same treatments, so make sure to do a little research to see if it's safe to get your crystals wet), passing them through sage or other sacred smoke, placing them in the sun (again, make sure the type of crystal you're using won't be damaged by this), putting them in a bowl of uncooked rice, or burying them in the earth. Dispose of the water, salt, or rice after using, as it contains the energies cleansed from the crystal.

You can use reiki to cleanse your crystal by simply holding the crystal in both hands and setting the intention that reiki is cleansing all harmful and unwanted energies from the stone. Let reiki flow, filling the entire crystal with pure energy. The process of filling the crystal with reiki energy is also considered a form of charging, and you can fine-tune this process, if you like, by adding another layer of intention. For example, while filling the crystal with reiki, you can hold the intention that this crystal will channel reiki as needed by whoever is using it. You can charge the crystal with other intentions, too, perhaps for specific occasions, such as programming a stone to help you find calm in stressful situations. Periodically cleanse your crystals and recharge as needed.

EXERCISE: Crystal Chakra Healing

There are numerous ways to incorporate crystals into a chakra-healing session, but one simple way is to place an appropriate stone on each of the chakras before giving a reiki treatment. Alternatively, you can administer reiki, and after treating a particular chakra, place a stone there to continue and enhance the treatment before moving on to the next chakra. Use your intuition to determine which stone is needed where, or experiment with some of these crystal-chakra pairings. (Note that some of these suggestions differ from the crystal-chakra pairings listed in chapter 3, to give you additional options for your explorations.)

> **Root Chakra:** Garnet, hematite, ruby, red jasper, red calcite
>
> **Navel Chakra:** Carnelian, orange calcite, sunstone, amber
>
> **Solar Plexus Chakra:** Citrine, topaz, yellow tiger's eye, pyrite
>
> **Heart Chakra:** Green calcite, emerald, rose quartz, green kyanite
>
> **Throat Chakra:** Celestite, lapis, blue lace agate, sodalite
>
> **Third Eye Chakra:** Amethyst, sugilite, purple fluorite, lepidolite
>
> **Crown Chakra:** Clear quartz, Herkimer diamond, selenite, moonstone

EXERCISE: Crystal Grid

Grids are a popular way of using crystals, and there are numerous grid patterns that you can use. A simple yet effective grid utilizes five crystals, ideally with a pointed end, or termination. Mentally trace out a five-pointed star, and place a crystal at each of the star's points with the crystal's terminated end pointing inward. In the center, you can place a photograph of the recipient or something that you wish to charge, such as a piece of jewelry or a deck of tarot cards. Connect to the flow of reiki in whatever way feels best. You might bring your hands into gasshô, centering and calming yourself, then raise your arms to the sky, arms shoulder width apart, palms facing, and open to receive the flow of reiki, down your arms, into your crown, and through your entire body.

Activating the Grid

This is typically done by tracing the geometric shape of the grid, and methods vary. I like to trace in threes, so using the above five-pointed star as an example, I would trace out the pattern of the star, starting at the top point (use your intuition—other starting points are equally valid), tracing to the bottom right, top left, top right, bottom left, and ending back at the beginning. This would constitute one pass, and I would repeat this for a total of three passes. If you're using a circular grid, you might pass around the circle three times, then trace from each of the crystals toward the center, like the spokes of a wheel. Again, use your intuition to find the activation pattern that feels right for you. Imagine the center of the grid filling with reiki, which is then transmitted to the recipient or absorbed into the object being charged. The grid will deactivate once the person or object has received the proper amount of reiki. You can continue sending healing on consecutive days by reactivating the grid each day. You can also experiment with drawing the symbols of your choice over the grid or create a grid in the shape of a symbol.

EXERCISE: Crystal Jewelry

I love charging crystal jewelry with reiki; it's such a great way to carry a little reminder of my True Self with me throughout the day. Use whatever technique you prefer to connect to the flow of reiki (see an example method in the Crystal Grid Exercise), and hold the jewelry in both hands, envisioning the piece filling completely with reiki. Set the intention that the jewelry will emanate reiki as needed. If you have a specific intention, you can focus on that now to charge the jewelry. Examples of intentions include "I am in the right place, at the right time, doing the right thing" and "I am connected to Higher Guidance." Jewelry provides a wonderful touchstone, allowing you to tap into the healing power of both reiki and crystals during your daily activities.

Distance Healing Techniques

These techniques are suitable for administering reiki to a person who is not physically present or to a time in the past or future.

EXERCISE: Standard Distance Treatment

Get situated in a comfy place where you won't be disturbed during the treatment. You can use a photograph of the recipient, or write their full name, age, and location on a piece of paper. If you don't know all these details, simply visualizing the recipient works just as well in my experience. Some practitioners visualize the recipient in tiny form in the palm of their hand, so they can give reiki to all parts of the recipient's body simultaneously. You can also use what's called a

· · · · · · · ·

"correspondence." A teddy bear is a common correspondence, but you can use a pillow or your thigh, too. The idea with the correspondence is to visualize this as a stand-in for the recipient; you can move your hands over the teddy bear, pillow, or your thigh, representing different areas of the recipient's body. One note: take care with the correspondence during the treatment; don't toss the teddy bear aside, for example, to grab a drink of water, as energetically sensitive people can perceive this movement and may find it jarring or otherwise unpleasant.

Take a few minutes to center yourself and connect to reiki. Draw Symbol Three over the photograph, paper, or correspondence, if using, saying the mantra three times. I like to state the person's name in the following format: "Reiki is now connecting me to [name]," repeated three times. Draw Symbol One over the correspondence, saying the mantra three times and the recipient's name three times. You can imagine Symbol One entering the person's aura or surrounding them. Set the intention that this person will receive whatever they most need right now, in accordance with the highest good. You can then carry out the treatment, either by holding the photo or paper in your hands, or moving through the standard hand positions (see chapter 11) on the correspondence. If you feel guided to do so, you can also move through the hand positions in the air above the photo or paper. When the treatment is complete, smooth over the person's aura (over the photo, paper, or correspondence, or in your mind's eye), and draw Symbol One over the recipient, saying the mantra three times with the intention of leaving the person balanced on all levels and ending the treatment. You can use a variety of methods to end the connection. This is one of my favorites: snap your fingers or clap your hands three times, bring your hands into gasshô, and give thanks, stating, "This session is now done." Finish with kenyoku hô if you like.

EXERCISE: Mental-Emotional Distance Treatment

This technique is a great way to shift habitual thoughts, behavioral patterns, and other energetic ruts. Prepare for the session as outlined above for the Standard Distance Treatment by readying a photo or other correspondence and connecting using Symbol Three, its mantra, and the recipient's name. Draw Symbol Two, visualizing it going into the recipient's crown chakra while you chant the mantra three times. Draw Symbol One, again imagining it entering the crown chakra while you chant the mantra three times. Place the photo or paper between your palms, or place your hands on the forehead and back of the head if using a teddy bear or other correspondence. Allow reiki to flow, and if you are working on a particular mental-emotional issue, you can use an affirmation at this stage. The affirmation should be worded in the first person and in the present tense, for example, "I am in the process of positive change," or "I am open to love and support." Focus on this affirmation for three breath cycles (or longer, if you feel guided). An alternate method is to focus on the five precepts. When the process feels complete, end the session by drawing Symbol One into the recipient's crown chakra, saying the mantra three times, and intending that the session has ended. Use whatever techniques work best to end the session for yourself (e.g., gasshô or kenyoku hô).

EXERCISE: Healing the Past or Future

This versatile technique can be adapted to a variety of situations, but the basic process is choosing an event to focus on, connecting using the symbols and intention, and sending reiki. For the past, you may already have a specific event in mind, or you can choose an issue in your present life and meditate with reiki, perhaps using a technique like hatsurei hô, asking to be shown the past event or events that are influencing this current-day issue. Once you've chosen a past event, connect with reiki in whatever way works best (again, hatsurei hô is one option here), and bring the event to mind, filling in as many details as needed to help you feel connected. Draw Symbol Three onto the scene, chanting its mantra three times, and see the energy of the symbol infusing the entire scene. Draw Symbol One and chant its mantra three times, again seeing the energy completely filling the scene. Give reiki for as long as the energy continues to flow.

This step is optional, but I find it to be quite useful: Throughout the treatment, observe the scene and notice if and how it changes. You might see events unfolding in an alternate way or receive insights that you can apply to your present-day life. Feel free to ask any questions about the event, such as "What effect has this event had on my romantic relationships?" or "Is this event impacting my current physical health in any way?"

When the process feels complete, draw Symbol One over the situation with the intent that this session is now ended. Bring yourself back to the here and now, and use any techniques that feel right to finish, such as gasshô or kenyoku hô.

EXERCISE: Distance Treatments for Multiple Recipients

You can use a photo of each person or a piece of paper, one per person, with their name, age, and location. You can also pair these tools with a correspondence, such as a teddy bear or pillow. To begin, connect with reiki in whatever way feels best to you. Working with one photo or paper at a time, draw Symbol Three over the paper and say the mantra three times, the name of the person three times, and their location once. Then, draw Symbol One over the paper and say the mantra three times. Repeat this for each person. If using a correspondence to represent the recipients, at this point you would draw Symbol Three over it, saying the mantra three times, followed by, "This [teddy bear, pillow, etc.] represents [say each person's name three times and their location once] for this session only." For example, "This pillow represents Tina Martin, Tina Martin, Tina Martin in Chicago and Lee Henley, Lee Henley, Lee Henley in San Diego, for this session only." Then, draw Symbol One over the correspondence, chanting its mantra three times. Allow reiki to flow, either hovering your hands over the stack of photos or papers or the correspondence. You can also simulate moving through the standard hand positions over the papers or correspondence. When the treatment is complete, draw Symbol One over the correspondence and/or stack of photos, chanting its mantra three times while intending that the session has now ended. Finish with any techniques that feel best, such as gasshô and kenyoku hô.

In the next chapter, we'll look at different ways to incorporate reiki into your daily routines, because you will reap the most benefits of this powerful healing system through regular use.

CHAPTER 16

Reiki as Daily Self-Practice

This book is filled with techniques and principles that you can use to transform your life, but finding a way to incorporate them into your daily activities can be challenging. This chapter will help you do just that with programs focused on different goals, starting with morning and bedtime reiki routines and programs to improve physical health, build a regular meditation practice, and boost your divination skills. You'll also find programs for bringing more prosperity into your life, harmonizing relationships, enhancing focus and concentration, cultivating self-love, and working with spirit guides. By using these programs you forge healthy habits rooted in a regular reiki practice.

I see reiki as a way of remembering the True Self. Each and every time we interact with reiki, we encounter who we really are, beneath the layers of persona and other egoistic obstructions. When we embody our True Self—and this might happen for just a few minutes a day at first—we make different choices, choices that are aligned with our highest good. The more often we remember the True Self, the more often we make these aligned choices, and the effects begin to snowball. Step by step, choice by choice, we can change the trajectory of our life by interacting with reiki—by remembering our True Self—as often as possible. Note that these programs can be adapted however you like, perhaps by substituting different techniques from this chapter and chapter 17 or using alternate symbols. At the end of the chapter, I also provide guidelines for crafting a program of your own.

Rise and Shine Morning Routine

Before getting out of bed, start with a short and sweet round of tanden chiryô hô: Place one hand on your forehead, the other on your tanden (just below the navel). Stay here for three breath cycles, then bring both hands over your tanden, resting here for nine breath cycles. Get out of bed, and get your energy moving with some light movement for your physical and energy bodies. Start with shoulder circles: shrug your shoulders close to your ears, and circle them back and down, repeating a few times before reversing direction and circling your shoulders forward and down. Bring your arms into play by making arm circles on the sides of your body, as small or as large as you like. Do a few rounds in both directions, forward and back, imagining that your energy field is getting cleared out with each arm sweep. Now, letting your arms hang by your sides, start to rotate your upper body side to side, letting your arms swing. When your torso moves to the left, your right arm will swing in front of your body, perhaps tapping your left hip, while the left arm swings behind you, perhaps meeting your right hip. Again, feel your energy receiving a clean sweep with the movements.

Raise your arms overhead, shoulder width apart, palms facing each other. Open to a shower of reiki, coming down your arms, into your crown, filling your entire body and aura with an invigorating white light. If you have an intention for your day, repeat it now three times. Remember to phrase your intentions in positive language (e.g., "My relationships are healthy and harmonious" instead of "I am not fighting with my partner today"). Finish with your hands in gasshô. Draw a large Symbol One in front of you, and step through the symbol to start your day.

Commit to doing this practice every morning for seven days, and notice how you feel by starting your day intentionally, with reiki.

Peaceful Bedtime Routine

Before getting into bed, bring your hands into gasshô and take a few rounds of breath, gradually lengthening the inhales and exhales. Perform kenyoku hô (page 229) with the intention to release anything from your day that no longer serves. Prop yourself up in bed so you can sit comfortably with an upright spine. Bring your arms overhead, shoulder width apart, palms facing each other, and feel reiki flowing down your arms, entering your crown chakra. Intend that reiki will flow down your spine, cleansing this channel of any unwanted energy, flowing out through your tailbone and into the earth, where it is neutralized and energetically composted. Allow this flow to continue for as long as feels necessary (you can relax your hands on your lap at any point).

Bring your hands to crown level, palms facing toward you with middle fingertips touching, and slowly sweep them down the front of your body and over your lap, finishing by planting your palms flat on the bed. As you perform this sweep, intend that your energy is perfectly balanced on all levels. Bring your hands into gasshô and give thanks before lying down for bed. Commit to this practice for a full seven nights, and notice how your quality of sleep changes and how that affects your waking hours. I like to establish this routine at home, and then when I'm on the road I can tap into the energetic habit that I've built to help me sleep, even in unfamiliar surroundings.

· · · · · · · ·

Bedtime Box Ritual

Choose a special box to use, as simple or elaborate as you like. I bought an inexpensive wooden box from the craft store and decorated it with paints and glitter. You can also paint or draw reiki symbols inside the box if you like. Have slips of paper (colored paper can be fun) and a special pen ready for this bedtime routine. Each night, take a few moments to calm and center yourself, hands in gasshô, eyes closed, focusing on your breath for a few cycles. Bring to mind something from your day that you feel grateful for, big or small. Allow the feeling of gratitude to grow in your heart space, and write down the focus of your gratitude on a slip of paper. Draw Symbol One over the paper and place it in the box while chanting the mantra three times, intending that reiki will expand this feeling of gratitude in your life.

Climb into bed and perform a few rounds of breathing with reiki. Place one hand over your heart, the other just below the belly button on your hara. Allow reiki to flow, and tune in to the sensation of your hara hand gently rising and falling with the breath. Then, tune in to the heart hand and the rhythm of your heartbeat. Feel as the breath and the heartbeat begin to harmonize, and continue to give yourself reiki. When the process feels complete, allow yourself to drift off, feeling gratitude for your day, knowing that this feeling is expanding with the support of reiki.

Continue this practice for a full week (or as long as you like), and whenever you're feeling out of sorts, open your gratitude box and pull out a slip of paper at random. Soak in the grateful sentiment, and allow it to trigger this feeling of gratitude in the present moment. You can "activate" this feeling more powerfully by tracing Symbol One over the paper, chanting the mantra three times, and intending that reiki will connect you with the feeling of gratitude. Breathe for a few rounds, allowing this feeling to blossom and expand within you. Replace the paper in the box, close it, and once more draw Symbol One, chanting the mantra three times.

Physical Healing

You can use this process for general healing or to focus on a specific issue. To receive the most benefit, as with the other programs in this chapter, commit to the practice for a full seven days (although you can do it longer, too, if you feel guided to do so). You'll need a notebook, and if you already journal, you can record your insights there—no need to get a separate one for this program. Write out a health affirmation, which will serve as a focal point throughout the next seven days. Remember to phrase your affirmation in the present tense and positive language: for example, "I am enjoying healthy digestion" or "I love my strong, healthy bones." For general healing, try "I am physically healthy in every way" or "I make healthy choices every day."

Choose a specific time of day, and ideally, the same location, to do these exercises. For me, doing them in the morning, immediately after brushing my teeth is best. If I wait too long, I'm liable to get distracted by other things. Start by connecting to reiki: bring your hands into gasshô and open your crown chakra to the flow of reiki. With each inhale, bring reiki down into your hara (lower belly), and with each exhale, reiki travels into your hands and radiates from your palms. Do this for nine breath cycles.

Release your hands, and bring your affirmation to mind; you will use this statement as you go through a tapping sequence. Draw Symbol One on the palm of each hand, chanting the mantra three times per hand. To tap, bring the fingers of one hand together, like you're forming a bird's beak, or bring the index and middle fingers of each hand together if that's more comfortable. Use your "beak" or fingers to tap firmly on each point, like you're thumping a watermelon to see how ripe it is. Don't use enough pressure to hurt or bruise yourself. Tap each of the following points, while stating your affirmation at each point.

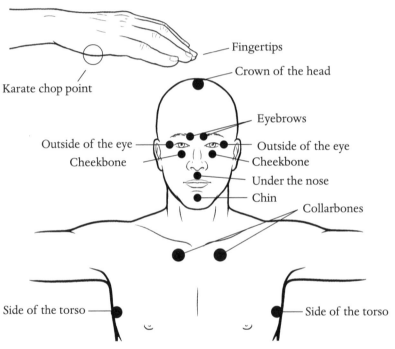

Figure 124: Tapping points

- Crown of the head
- Eyebrows
- Outside of the eyes, on the temples
- Cheekbones, in line with the pupils
- Under the nose (use one hand here)
- Chin (use one hand here)
- Just below the inner edge of both collarbones (you'll feel a little divot here)

• • • • • • • •

- Sides of the torso, level with nipples
- Karate chop point (tap the pinky edges of your hands together)

Finally, sit with an upright spine, eyes closed, hands resting on the knees, palms facing up in a receptive gesture. Allow reiki to flow down through your crown, filling your entire body, and ask, "What next step can I take to improve my health?" (You can be more specific here, too, substituting "digestive health" or "bone health," depending on your affirmation.) Stay in meditation, opening up to higher guidance. When an insight arises, bring your hands into gasshô, give thanks, and write this action step in your journal. Decide how you will take this action step today (or tomorrow, if you are doing the practice before bed). For example, if the action step is "walk 30 minutes," decide when you will do this—say, on your lunch break or after work. If you need to, you can break it up, taking a fifteen-minute walk during lunch and another walk after work. Trust that you would not be given this step if it weren't possible for you to carry it out, so gently yet firmly move through any resistance the ego churns out. Continue this practice for a full seven days, taking action steps each day in service of your health. Once you've finished the program, unless you are receiving guidance to the contrary, stick with the health-boosting practices that you wrote in your journal. Notice how you feel when you use these practices versus when you don't.

Other options: Feel free to combine this process with a standard reiki treatment on days when you have more time, moving through the hand positions for self-healing (chapter 11). My recommendation is to do the self-treatment before you start the tapping sequence, as a way to enhance the effects of the tapping. You can also adapt this process for mental-emotional healing by choosing an applicable affirmation, then drawing Symbol Two on your palms and chanting the mantra three times, followed by drawing Symbol One and chanting its mantra three times prior to beginning the tapping sequence.

Build a Meditation Practice

Take some time to connect with your reason for building a meditation practice. Do you want to enjoy more mental clarity or calm, heighten your intuition, or connect with spirit guides? While you may have multiple reasons that can change over time, choose one to focus on for this twenty-one-day practice, modeled after Usui's twenty-one-day experience on Kurama-yama. Ideally, pick a time at which you'll meditate every day, but if on some days that time simply isn't an option, fit your meditation into the day whenever you can over skipping the practice. If you like, burn incense while you meditate, using the same scent each time to support habit formation. Choose any incense you like. Some of my favorites are sandalwood, frankincense, and dragon's blood. Another option is to use a timer. When I first started meditating, knowing that the timer would go off in ten minutes helped me let go of the thoughts: "Am I done yet? Am I done yet? How about now?" There are also smart phone apps with meditation timers.

Once you're settled into a comfortable spot where you won't be disturbed, begin with hands in gasshô, eyes closed, breathing here for a few rounds until you feel calmer and more centered. Draw Symbol Two on your palms and chant the mantra three times. Draw Symbol One on your palms and chant the mantra three times. Place one hand on your forehead, one hand on the back of your head, and state an affirmation that reflects your reason for meditating, three times. For example, try "My meditation practice brings me peace and clarity of mind."

Reach your arms up to the sky, shoulder width apart, palms facing, and feel a flow of reiki washing down your arms and into your body. Bring your hands in front of your heart, palms facing down, elbows out to the side, fingertips touching. Breathe in deeply, then exhale out through the mouth, making a "haaa" sound, like you're trying to fog up a mirror, as you push the hands down to your lap. Breathe in as you move the hands, still in the same position, up to the third eye, and exhale with a "haaa" sound again as you push the hands down to your lap. Bring the hands back to the forehead and repeat the exhale and push-down four more times.[137] Let the hands rest on the knees, palms facing down, and stay here in meditation until the timer goes off. Bring your hands in gasshô and restate your affirmation three times.

Supercharge Your Divination Skills

Take a few moments to calm and center yourself in a place where you won't be disturbed. Draw Symbol Two on your palms, chanting the mantra three times. Follow with Symbol One, chanting its mantra three times. Place one hand over your forehead and third eye and the other hand over your divination tools (tarot cards, runes, scrying mirror, etc.). Feel the flow of reiki mediating a clear connection between you and your tools, and hold the intention that your divination skills be activated in accordance with the highest good (you can substitute a more specific phrase here, like "tarot skills" or "scrying skills"). Remain here for at least nine breath cycles or until the energy flow tapers off, then do a brief reading for yourself, asking any specific questions you have or simply asking, "What do I most need to know right now?" to nurture your connection with your tools. End with hands in gasshô, giving thanks, and repeat this process every day for seven days.

Another option: For seven days, start the practice with one hand on your tools and one hand on an individual chakra, starting with the crown chakra and working your way to the root chakra, one chakra per day. While we tend to associate the third eye with divination work, in truth, all the chakras play a role, and you can round out your perception by connecting through each of the chakras in turn.

---

137. This technique is from Gendai Reiki and is called *hadô meisô hô*.

• • • • • • • •

Magickal Money Jar

This is a reiki twist on a magickal practice I learned from Christopher Penczak.[138] Get a large jar and draw Symbol One on a piece of green paper. You can use a special pen or your favorite writing tool (a gold paint pen would be a nice money correspondence boost!), but any implement will do. Place this on the bottom of the jar, and add any or all of the following:

Herbs for Prosperity: Alfalfa, cedar, cumin, lavender, and moneywort (choose one herb or a combination, depending on what's available to you, and add one or two pinches of each, dried; they can be bundled into a sachet)

Crystals for Prosperity: Pyrite, green aventurine, citrine, and jade

During the waxing moon phase (from new moon to full moon), charge the jar. Draw Symbol One on both palms, chanting the mantra three times, and hold the jar in both hands. Allow reiki to flow, filling the jar, and hold the intention that for every bit of currency that is placed in the jar, your wealth will increase a hundredfold. Each time you add spare change to the jar, draw Symbol One into the jar and chant the mantra three times. End with hands in gasshô, giving thanks. When the jar is full, roll the change and, if desired, restart the process with a new batch of dried herbs, cleansed crystals (see page 238 for crystal cleansing tips), and a fresh piece of green paper with Symbol One drawn on it.

Harmonize Relationships

This program is best used either on one relationship or on one common aspect of multiple relationships. You can always repeat the process to address more than one relationship or multiple aspects, but there's benefit to narrowing your focus each time you do it. On a piece of paper, write down "my relationship with [name]" or briefly describe an aspect of your relationships that you wish to address, such as "my ability to actively listen" or "my fear of abandonment."

Take a few moments to calm and center yourself with hands in gasshô. Draw Symbol Two on your palms and chant the mantra three times, then draw Symbol One and chant its mantra three times. Hold the paper in both hands, and begin a variation on jôshin kokyû hô. Inhale through your nose and envision drawing reiki into your body through the nose. You might feel reiki entering as tingling, heat, vibration, or waves, or you can visualize it as white light. Envision pulling the breath and the reiki down to your hara (area slightly below the navel) with this inhale. On the exhale, visualize the reiki streaming out through your hands, into the paper with the intention that it is healing the issue. With each successive inhale, focus your awareness on

---

138. Christopher Penczak, *The Outer Temple of Witchcraft: Circles, Spells, and Rituals* (Woodbury, MN: Llewellyn Publications, 2008), 339.

• • • • • • • •

reiki flowing down into your hara, followed by reiki expanding and healing the issue on the exhale. Repeat this process for up to five minutes, stopping at any point if you feel light-headed.

Set the paper down, and end with hands in gasshô, giving thanks. Repeat this process for seven days, and during this time, pay attention to any insights that arise, suggesting changes you can implement to positively affect your relationship. The guidance might reflect necessary shifts in your behavior toward the other person and/or it might be related to self-care practices, which will support you in bringing your best self to the relationship. Know that reiki and your higher self are partnering throughout this process to help you see and heal relationship patterns that no longer serve your growth and well-being, and you will be invited to live out this guidance through your choices and actions.

Improve Focus and Concentration

The traditional technique of jôshin kokyû hô is designed to focus the mind through the breath, and this seven-day program harnesses this focused energy by pairing it with a mudra (hand gesture). First, experiment with the following three mudras, all of which can aid in focus and concentration, to see which one feels best. This is the mudra you will be using for the seven-day practice.

Gyan Mudra: Index fingertip touches thumb tip while the rest of the fingers are held together and straight.

Figure 125: Gyan mudra

Dhyana Mudra: Rest your right hand on top of your left hand, both palms facing up. Touch your thumb tips together.

Figure 126: Dhyana mudra

Rudra Mudra: Connect the tips of your thumb, index, and ring fingers while keeping the other two fingers as straight as you can.

Figure 127: Rudra mudra

Once you have chosen your mudra, begin jôshin kokyû hô: Inhale through your nose and envision drawing reiki into your body through the nose. You might feel reiki entering as tingling, heat, vibration, or waves, or you can visualize it as white light. Envision pulling the breath and the reiki down to your hara (area slightly below the navel) with this inhale. On the exhale, visualize the reiki streaming out through your hands, which are in your chosen mudra. With each successive inhale, focus your awareness on reiki drawing down into your hara, followed by reiki expanding and radiating outward through your hands on the exhale.

During this process, set the intention that this mudra will instantly improve your focus and concentration anytime you use it. Continue jôshin kokyû hô for anywhere from five minutes to half an hour, focusing on the mudra and its ability to hone your concentration. Repeat this process for seven days, and then use this mudra throughout your daily activities whenever you find your attention wandering. I like to periodically "refresh" the mudra by going through this seven-day practice again, but know that every time you use this mudra for focus and concentration, you are also adding to its energetic power, creating a positive snowball effect.

Bathe in Self-Love

This practice is a beautiful way to regularly commit to self-care, and I recommend doing it every month on the full moon, as often as you possibly can. Draw up a warm bath, adding a sachet of herbs (e.g., rose petals, hibiscus, jasmine) if you like. On a pink candle, carve Symbol Two on one side and Symbol One on the other with a pin, nail, or other suitable tool, chanting each mantra three times as you carve. Hold the candle in both hands and allow reiki to flow, filling the candle while you focus on the energy of self-love. If it's difficult for you to connect with this energy, focus on an affirmation, such as "I love myself in every way" or "My ability to love myself expands every day."

Light the candle and get into the bath. Draw Symbol Two and Symbol One on your palms, chanting the mantras three times each. You can also draw the symbols into the bathwater. Take this time to give yourself a reiki treatment while you enjoy this nice, relaxing soak, using the standard hand positions or any positions that intuitively feel best, all the while focusing on love. You might thank each area of your body as you give it reiki, ending with thanking your mind and your spirit. When you're done, trace a large Symbol One over your body, sealing in the energy of self-love as you chant the mantra three times. When you drain the tub, set the intention that any obstacles to self-love are draining away into the earth, where they are neutralized and composted. End with hands in gasshô, giving thanks.

Working with Spirit Guides

Start by choosing one of the following contact methods: automatic writing, a pendulum, or meditation. If using automatic writing, have a stack of paper and a writing implement, and number each page in case they get shuffled around in the process. If using a pendulum, you can buy a ready-made one or make your own from a cord or chain and something that has a bit of heft to it. I use a stone that I found on a hike that has a natural hole in it, but you can use a jewelry charm or even a metal washer from the hardware store. Cleanse your pendulum by holding it between your palms and filling it with reiki. Set the intention that this pendulum will only communicate with the entities who are aligned with your highest good.

• • • • • • • •

Prepare yourself and the space: Perform kenyoku hô. Draw Symbol One on your dominant hand palm, chanting the mantra three times, and use this hand to trace out an energetic circle of protection around yourself, moving clockwise around the space three times. Envision this circle expanding above and below, creating a protective sphere. When done, stand in the center of the circle and draw a large Symbol One in front of you, chanting the mantra three times as you envision the symbol expanding to fill the entire sphere with the energy of protection. Stand in the center and say, "The circle allows only entities who enter in perfect love and perfect trust, and blocks out all other entities. And so it is."

Get settled in the circle, and draw Symbol Four in the air in front of you. Bring your arms above your head, shoulder width apart, palms facing, and connect to the flow of reiki. Feel it cascading down your arms, through your crown, filling your entire body and energy field. Bring your hands into gasshô, and ask to connect with the entity that is correct and good for you right now, in accordance with the highest good, harming none. Spend a few rounds here, breathing and waiting to feel a sense of connection. If you are using the medium of meditation, you will stay here for the duration of the session, asking any questions once you have made contact and getting to know this entity.

If using automatic writing, place the pen to paper, ready to write. You can experiment with either looking at the page, perhaps with a soft focus, or closing your eyes. Ask a question and allow your hand to move. Toss pages aside as you write and move on to the next to stay in the flow. (This is why it's helpful to number the pages first!)

If using a pendulum, the process is similar. Hold the pendulum in one hand (I favor my dominant hand, but the opposite is true for some practitioners). I like to loop the chain or cord over my hand once so the chain is secure without my having to grasp it. Let your muscles relax, ask to be shown what a "yes" response looks like, and wait for the pendulum to move, indicating the pattern corresponding to an affirmative answer. Do the same for a "no" response. Then, ask any questions you have. When you're done, thank the spirit for meeting with you and, if you feel called to do so, ask if it would be willing to work with you again. End with hands in gasshô, giving thanks. Draw Symbol Four once more, chanting the mantra three times while intending that your spirit contact session has ended. Perform kenyoku hô, then use the opposite hand used to cast the circle, and move once around the circle in a counterclockwise fashion, envisioning the circle opening, perhaps like energetic drapery.

When working with a new spirit contact, I like to work within the safety of a circle, as directed above, and once you have developed a relationship in which you feel comfort and trust, you can begin to work outside the formality of a circle, always trusting your intuition and ending a session if you become uncomfortable. Working with spirit guides is much like human relationships: they benefit from mutual respect, give and take, and a regular commitment of some kind,

· · · · · · · ·

which can vary depending on the relationship. I work with some of my guides every single day, whereas other guides appear only under certain circumstances.

Building Your Own Reiki Program

1. Decide on a focus for your program. This might be a specific goal, such as finishing a work project or engaging a healthy movement practice for a designated time period.

2. Look through the reiki techniques and choose one or two that intuitively feel like a good fit for your program focus. This is also a great way to learn new reiki techniques, so don't be afraid to experiment with ones you haven't used before.

3. Clarify your intention so that you can focus on this during your practice time. You might choose to turn your intention into an affirmation.

4. Decide on the number of days or frequency of your program. For example, you might do the practice every day for a week or a month, or you could commit to doing it every full moon, the first day of each month, or another interval that feels meaningful to you.

5. Write down a simple sequence outlining what you will be doing each time you practice. As a general guideline, connect with reiki, focus on your intention while you do a reiki technique, and end the practice in a meaningful way.

6. You might choose to journal your experience so you can get a feel for what works well for you personally, fine-tuning as you go.

A program could be as simple as choosing a reiki technique and using it every day for a set length of time. You could do the same with the symbols, choosing one symbol to use or meditate on every day. Ditto with the five precepts. Here are additional focus ideas to get you started:

- Increasing self-awareness
- Boosting memory
- Developing energy sensing abilities
- Enhancing dream recall or interpretation
- Starting a healthy habit
- Releasing an unhealthy habit
- Increasing your confidence, perhaps leading up to a presentation
- Supporting you in learning a new skill
- Boosting creativity
- Opening yourself up to healthy new friendships or romantic relationships

• • • • • • • •

• Creating healthy relationship boundaries

• Enhancing manifestation

Now that you've learned numerous ways to incorporate reiki into your daily routine, choose one method that resonates with you right now and dive in! Remember, you'll reap the most benefit from your reiki practice if you use it regularly, and the programs in this chapter give you plenty of material to get you started.

• • • • • • •

PART III
Professional Reiki Practice

In part 3, we look at reiki in a professional light, covering the specifics of creating your own healing practice, from finding and setting up your treatment space to developing effective healing plans with your clients. We also cover special uses for reiki, everything from medical to magickal applications, including, in chapter 19, reiki healing for pets and using reiki with and for children. Finally, we'll discuss the practice of teaching reiki with a look at curriculum suggestions for all three levels of traditional instruction and ways to make the information engaging and useful for your students.

CHAPTER 17

✺

Your Healing Practice

Becoming a reiki practitioner, whether as your full-time job or a part-time pursuit or hobby, can be an incredibly rewarding experience. You have the opportunity to help others remember their True Self and facilitate body-mind-soul healing, while also deepening your personal practice with reiki. Opening a healing practice also comes with its fair share of challenges, and in the next few chapters we'll cover everything from client communication and ethics to space and legal requirements to help you put your best foot forward.

Getting Started

First things first, if you want to set up shop as a reiki practitioner, a basic level of knowledge is required. Most people attend a course, perhaps following the traditional three-level structure described in chapter 9. We might categorize the areas of required knowledge in the following way:

1. The system of reiki (what is reiki, historical overview of reiki, five precepts, hand positions, symbols and mantras, reiki techniques, etc.)

2. Conducting a healing session (client communication, intake and documentation, performing the treatment, aftercare, etc.)

3. Running a business (setting up the space, legal requirements, record keeping, accounting, marketing, etc.)

A well-taught course will cover the first point thoroughly, and you will typically be taught the basics of conducting a healing session as well. How much individual teachers discuss the business aspect varies. In earlier chapters, we covered the first category at length. In this and the

• • • • • • • • •

following chapter, we'll explore points two and three, starting with choosing the right space for your practice.

Choosing a Space

The first consideration is whether to operate out of your home or a separate business location. While each situation is unique, here are some points to help you make an informed decision.

Safety

Do you want clients knowing where you live? If you work only via word of mouth and clients must be referred or vetted by someone you know, this might not be an issue, but if you promote your services via a website or other publicly available medium, this is definitely something to think about.

Personal versus Professional Space

Will clients have to walk through personal areas of your home to reach the treatment room? Those areas would need to be kept clean and free from tripping hazards and other liabilities. Also, consider any decor or other items that may present an image counter to the tone you wish to set for your business.

Client-Household Interactions

Will other household members be present? The treatment room needs to provide privacy and some measure of separation from distracting sounds. Clients might not want to have to interact with other household members before or after their session.

Facilities and Access

Is there a clean restroom available? Is there a safe place for your clients to park? Will clients' vehicles pose an issue with your neighbors? Is the entrance to your home clean and free of hazards?

Environment

Do you have pets? Some clients are allergic to or uncomfortable around animals, and some pets make noise that can be distracting during a treatment. Do you smoke? Again, some clients are allergic or simply dislike the smell of smoke.

There is also the challenge of maintaining professional boundaries when working out of your home. Some practitioners have a separate entrance to their treatment space or a detached building on their property, both of which create an added layer of separation between work and home, but if that setup isn't available, you will need to be particularly attentive to boundaries. If you offer clients a cup of tea in your kitchen afterward, they might come to expect an extra twenty to thirty minutes of your time after every session, and this also blurs the separation between your office space and your personal living areas. Do clients have to walk through your

· · · · · · ·

bedroom to access the bathroom? To me, this invites a layer of intimacy that is inappropriate in client relationships.

If you opt for a separate business location, here are some points to consider:

• Rent (Does this include utilities? Internet access?)

• Location (Is it safe? Convenient for you and your clients?)

• Is there parking?

• Is this a private or shared space? If shared, who are your officemates?

• What's the noise level like?

• Is there a restroom?

• Is the space accessible (elevator, ramp, etc.)?

• Do you have to commit to a lease? If so, for how long?

• Who takes care of repairs?

• Is there sufficient room for your treatment table and any other supplies that you use?

Setting Up Your Space

Once you've secured a location for your practice, it's time to get the room set up for business! Here are tips for making the space as comfortable and inviting as possible.

Treatment Table

Look for a massage table or reiki table, which can be found online, at some massage/salon supply retailers, or, if you're lucky, on Craigslist or yard sales. A reiki table differs from a massage table in that it's missing the lower cross beam or panel at the head, making it easier for you to sit at the client's head without bumping your knees into the table. I have a massage table, since I also offer bodywork, and, quite honestly, the panel has never been an issue, but ideally, test out a table before you buy to see if it's a good match for your body. Tables are adjustable in height, so be sure to experiment to find a setting that works best for you. A general rule of thumb is to stand next to the table and let your arm hang freely. In this position, set the table at the height where your knuckles are brushing the tabletop. Many tables include a face cradle or headrest, which is used when the client is prone (face down), and some companies offer packages that include a stool and various bolsters.

Stool

You'll need something to sit on for part (or all) of the treatment, and I like to use a stool with wheels so I can maneuver without taking my hands off the client to drag a chair around. I only use a stool when working at the head and sometimes at the feet, preferring to stand for the rest of the session, but do whatever feels best for your body.

· · · · · · · ·

Linens

Some practitioners use a bare table, wiping it down with a cleaner between clients (make sure to check which cleaners are suitable for your table so you don't damage the upholstery). Personally, I don't like the feel of the bare table when I'm receiving a reiki treatment, so I prefer to use linens. You can buy linens especially for massage tables, although most twin sheet sets will also fit. With sheet sets, you would need to buy face cradle covers separately. Use clean linens for each client. Another nice option is to buy a table warmer, which is a heating pad sized to the table and designed to be used under the fitted sheet. Do not use a regular electric blanket, as many of them come with instructions to not place the blanket under the body and to only use it as a covering.

Bolster

While there are many options available, the only bolster I use for the majority of my sessions is a round bolster designed to fit under the knees when the client is supine (face up) or under the ankles in the prone position (face down). You can buy fabric bolster covers, or you can slide the bolster underneath the bottom sheet so it's not touching your client's skin or clothing directly. You might also have a pillow handy for clients who wish to have something under their head when they're supine. Be sure to have extra pillowcases and change them between clients.

Temperature

In my office, I have a fan and a space heater so I can adjust the temperature of my room independent of my officemates, and I can also alter the temperature throughout the session to suit the client. Some people tend to run hot or cold, and it's nice to be able to adjust as needed. Comfy blankets are also good to have on hand.

Lighting

I like to find a happy medium between bright enough to safely see and muted enough to create a relaxing atmosphere. I have a few tabletop lamps situated around the room, as well as a string of white lights around the ceiling. Fluorescent lighting is, in my opinion, a major bummer, from the glaring light to the distracting hum, so I avoid using it in my treatment spaces.

Music

I love creating playlists, and I use a subscription service that allows me to play an unlimited number of songs for a flat, low monthly fee. Regardless of what you use, choose music that is soothing, unobtrusive, and instrumental, as most lyrics can be distracting. Remember, too, that you will be listening to this music, sometimes all day, which is why I like to regularly create fresh playlists!

Storage

Clients often like a place to sit while they're taking off their shoes, as well as a spot to store their belongings during the session. I like to have a couple of wall hooks for coats and purses, as well as a little table with a tray for jewelry, watches, and so on. Having a special area for these items reduces the chance of them getting lost or forgotten when the client leaves.

Mirror

This is optional, but many clients like to give themselves a once over when they get off the table, smoothing down their hair, and so on.

Toiletries

In the session space there should be tissues and a trash can. Make sure there is an accessible restroom that is clean and well-stocked.

Safety

Go over the room and make sure there aren't any hazards, such as cords or rugs that someone might trip on. Is your office equipped with working smoke detectors? Make sure you regularly refresh the batteries. This responsibility might fall on the building manager or owner, but is the entrance clear and free of hazards, such as ice and snow? Is the parking area safe and well lit?

Fun Details

What sort of decor will you include in your space? Plants and crystals are a natural choice for healing rooms, but get creative! Some practitioners like to have a picture of Mikao Usui in their office or a copy of the five precepts.

The Energetic Space

In addition to the physical space, your healing practice consists of the energetic space you create. The physical details influence the energy, of course, which is why it's so valuable to attend to those details with care and intention. In Jikiden Reiki (see appendix A), the placement of the scroll containing the five precepts and the head of the treatment table are taken into consideration by orienting them in the area with the highest energy, known as the *kamiza*. I like to move through the space and intuitively get a sense of the energy flow in the room. For example, is there a path that you tend to travel whenever you enter the room? If so, try to avoid blocking that path with furniture or clutter. What is the first area that draws your attention when you open the door? That might be a wonderful spot to place the precepts, pleasing artwork, plants, or eye-catching crystals. Is there a spot that feels a little blah or easily overlooked? Spend some extra time there when cleansing the space (instructions follow).

I like to do more involved energetic cleansings at regular intervals, along with smaller cleansings on a daily basis. I time my major cleansings with the sabbats or seasonal holidays, but you can choose any dates that feel significant or that will be easy for you to remember, such as four times a year at the start of a new season or every new moon.

Energetic Deep Clean

Draw Symbol One on both palms, chanting the mantra three times, and then start by physically cleaning the space, wiping down all surfaces with a natural cleanser, sweeping or vacuuming the floor, and taking out the trash. Get into all the nooks and crannies, vacuuming under any rugs, opening drawers and wiping them down, and so forth. As you clean, intend that you are removing any unwanted or harmful energies. Once that's complete, draw a large Symbol One in the center of the room, and see it expanding to fill the entire space as you chant the mantra three times, intending that reiki is purifying the space on all levels. I like to pair this with smudging using sage smoke, but that's entirely optional. If you do use smoke, make sure you don't set off any smoke alarms. You could also use sage or Florida water spray instead.

Once the space has been energetically cleared, I like to fill the space with reiki, and I do this by drawing Symbol One on all the walls, the floor and the ceiling, and in the corners. I then stand in gasshô, eyes closed, and envision a beautiful web-like matrix of reiki filling the entire space. You might also charge some crystals (see chapter 15) and place them around the room. I like to take crystals like black tourmaline, smoky quartz, or hematite and charge them with the intention of absorbing and neutralizing any harmful energies, and I situate them about the room, including underneath the treatment table. Be sure to cleanse any crystals on a regular basis (see chapter 15).

Energetic Touch-Ups

Each day when I arrive at my office, I take some time in my treatment space, hands in gasshô, eyes closed, practicing jôshin kokyû hô (page 230), intending that reiki is purifying me and the space. I call upon my spirit guides to be present, I give thanks for my work, and I set my intention to be of divine service through my every thought, word, and deed. The entire process need take no longer than five to ten minutes. You might use this time to recite the precepts or any other practices that feel meaningful for you, intending that these practices are cleansing and raising the vibration of you and your healing space. In between clients, I like to use kenyoku hô (page 229) to make a clean break and transition. If the energy in the room starts to feel off and you don't have time to do a more thorough cleansing, draw Symbol One, and see it expanding to fill the room with the intention that all harmful energies are neutralized and reiki is permeating the space.

· · · · · · ·

Legal Requirements

In addition to setting up the space, you also need to ensure that you're complying with local and state regulations, and these can be divided into general business requirements and reiki-specific requirements. Very few areas currently have legal guidelines specific to reiki practice, but be sure to check your local governing bodies to make sure. A good place to start is the local massage therapy board, if this exists. They should be able to point you toward any legislation relevant to reiki practitioners. In particular, find out if you are permitted to place your hands directly on the client or if you need a license to touch in order to do so. Many states allow physical contact without a license (excepting privacy areas, of course), provided you are not manipulating the tissue in any way, which would be classified as massage.

Insurance

It's a very good idea to obtain insurance for your practice, and there are many affordable options available. Do an online search for "reiki practitioner insurance" to see what's available in your area. A suitable plan will include both professional liability (protects against malpractice, meaning errors or negligence on your part) and general liability (protects against accidents, injury, or damage that occurs while the client is at your place of business), and some plans also include product liability, which covers your treatment table and other equipment. Be sure to check the specifics of the coverage limits. Some companies offer what's called a "shared limit," meaning that the money available is shared by everyone insured by this company, while others set an individual limit.

Business License

In terms of business requirements, even if you are operating out of your home you may need to secure a business license. As a massage therapist, I need to have a business license from the state massage board and a separate business license issued by the city. If I were only practicing reiki, I would need to have the city business license, even if my practice was in my home. If you sell products, you will also need a sales tax license, sometimes called a reseller's license. In most cases, licenses can be easily obtained, often online, so don't let these requirements scare you. I was able to take care of the majority of these things in an afternoon.

Taxes

And on the topic of taxes, make sure you are tracking your income so you can remit the appropriate tax. If you're new to business ownership, it's a good idea to meet with a qualified accountant or get a good book on basic business finances (look for books tailored to the sole proprietor, which is what you are considered if you're running a practice on your own), so you know the basics of how much money to set aside for taxes and how often you need to remit them. Depending on where you live, reiki may or may not be considered a taxable service. In many areas, physical products are taxable, so if you sell products, you'll need a method for separating any sales tax collected from your business funds so you can remit it at the proper time.

Charging for Your Services

To determine a price for your services, start by doing a little research into what other practitioners in your area are offering. If you can't find reiki locally, you can compare to massage prices. In many areas, reiki treatment prices are a bit less than massage, perhaps 10 to 20 percent less. Once you get a general sense of the going rate, now it's time to decide what length of session you would like to offer, with standard treatments often falling in the thirty-minute to ninety-minute range. The length depends on a variety of factors, such as these:

- Your physical and energetic stamina
- What you intend to offer in each session and allowing yourself enough time to do so
- Adequate time to discuss the client's intake form, questions, and concerns

Also, consider what length of time would be worth commuting to your office for, if applicable, before offering very short treatment times. If it takes you forty-five minutes to get to your office, and you're at a stage of your business where you only see one client a day, you might not want to offer thirty-minute sessions.

Once you decide on the session lengths you will be offering, it's time to set your prices. Here's one process for calculating smart prices:

1. Decide on your desired annual income from your practice. How much do you want to make in a year? This number should be achievable and sustainable, meaning you can live off of this amount without running yourself into the ground with overtime.

2. Decide on how many weeks per year you would like to be able to take off for vacation. This is important! Your self-care practice is vital to the success of your practice, so don't skip this step. Subtract the number of vacation weeks from fifty-two to determine the number of weeks you'll be working each year.

3. Divide your desired annual income by the number of working weeks. This is how much you would need to make each week.

4. Determine what feels like a good number of sessions to perform each day. I limit myself to four sessions, which can range from an hour to two hours each, with a total daily limit of eight hours. Once you have your daily number, multiply that by the number of days you'll be working in a week.

5. Take the number from step 3 (your weekly desired income) and divide it by the number from step 4 (hours worked per week). The result is the hourly rate you would need to charge to reach your desired annual income.

This process gives you a good starting point, and it can provide a helpful reality check, too. If your desired annual income is $100,000, you may find this isn't reasonable for your first year in practice after you run these numbers, and this allows you to make some adjustments to your business plan. How does this number compare to the rates of other local practitioners? While there are many ways to differentiate your services and thereby justify higher rates, if your prices are *significantly* higher than the average, you will need to effectively communicate the added value that your services offer—and deliver on those claims!

On the topic of charging, you'll need to decide which forms of payment you accept. While credit cards do come with a transaction fee, I find that the convenience they offer your clients far outweighs the fees. The vast majority of my clients prefer to pay with a card, and as someone who rarely carries cash myself, I appreciate not having to run to an ATM prior to visiting other practitioners. Some clients will pay cash, though, so be sure to have some smaller bills handy in case you need to make change. If you're accepting cards, there are many convenient card processing options available now, and an internet search will help you decide which one has the features you need. If you decide to offer an online appointment booking option, many of those systems come with a built-in payment option that will allow the client to prepay online, or, depending on the system, in person as well, generally via a smartphone app with a card reader.

Now that you know the ins and outs of setting up shop, in the next chapter we'll explore the basics of conducting a reiki healing session.

CHAPTER 18

Conducting Healing Sessions

In this chapter, we'll look at best practices for preparing for and conducting reiki sessions with clients, because once you have your physical and energetic space established, it's time to flesh out the details of a healing session, which starts before your client even walks through the door. Make sure you arrive early enough that you have time to prepare the room (for example, turning on space heaters or putting fresh linens on the table) and yourself. I don't like feeling rushed before sessions, so I always aim to give myself a full twenty minutes before my clients arrive to ground and center, use the restroom, and practice any energy techniques that will leave me feeling present and energized.

When your client arrives and you've made your introductions, help them orient to the space, offering them the restroom and showing them where to put their things. I highly recommend keeping records for all your clients, and I have an intake form that I require people to fill out online beforehand or at the start of their first session. Make sure you store these records in a secure place, either in a locked cabinet or encrypted, digital format. The online booking program I use also includes secure storage of client records. At a minimum, the intake form should have sections for the following:

- Contact info, including emergency contacts
- Health history
- Current issues or complaints (including medications and supplements being used)
- Allergies or sensitivities (including scents or touch)
- Informed consent agreement (see next page)
- Client's signature and date

Following is a sample informed consent agreement, and you can ask your client to initial each statement and sign at the bottom of the form. This example may not cover circumstances specific to your practice or local requirements, so be sure to adapt as needed, consulting a professional legal advisor if necessary.

Informed Consent Agreement

____ *I understand that the reiki treatment given to me by [your name] is for the purpose of stress reduction and relaxation.*

____ *I understand that the reiki practitioner does not diagnose illness or disease and does not prescribe medical treatment or pharmaceuticals.*

____ *I understand that reiki treatment is not a substitute for medical care and that it is recommended that I work with my primary caregiver for any condition I may have.*

____ *I have stated all my known physical conditions and medications, and I will keep the reiki practitioner updated on any changes.*

____ *I understand that reiki treatment is therapeutic and completely non-sexual in nature.*

Be sure to go over the form with your client, asking any necessary clarifying questions about their health history and current health concerns. Discuss what they hope to achieve by working with you, and clarify the scope of your practice and discuss reasonable expectations when needed, for example, if your client is expecting to be cured of a terminal illness after one session. This is not to say miraculous healing cannot happen, but we should not make claims that we can cure or fix our clients.

It is also illegal to diagnose any physical or mental health conditions, unless you possess the required licensure in a relevant field. If you suspect a health condition, recommend your client see their physician or other healthcare professional. One more legal note: in some states, you may be considered a "mandatory reporter," which legally obligates you to report suspected child abuse or neglect to an appropriate agency (or elder abuse or neglect depending on the jurisdiction). Additionally, some states require reporting if a client expresses an intent to self-harm or harm others.

Developing a Holistic Healing Plan

While not required, it can be beneficial to develop a treatment plan with your client, giving you both a means of tracking change over time. Some clients prefer to come in sporadically, as

· · · · · · · ·

needed, and don't want the added involvement of a longer-term plan, but it's nice to offer this to interested clients. I would highly recommend keeping your own notes, though, even for clients who don't want to create a healing plan. These notes help you provide continuity in your sessions by, for example, following up on issues addressed in previous treatments to see if and how things have changed or recognizing when certain techniques are more or less effective with certain clients so you can adjust accordingly.

To develop a healing plan, draw up a standard document that you will use with every client to streamline the process. These are some helpful fields to include:

- Reason for this session: stress reduction/relaxation and/or a specific complaint?
- Changes since last session
- What do you observe/energetically sense and what is your client experiencing *before* the treatment?
- What do you observe/energetically sense and what is your client experiencing *after* the treatment?

If you wish to get more specific with client treatment goals, these additional fields are useful:

- What is your goal for our work together? If there are multiple goals, focus on no more than three, and complete the following questions for each goal individually.
- Do you have a desired time frame for reaching this goal? If the time frame is more than two to three months, I recommend breaking the goal into smaller milestones to maintain momentum and a sense of accomplishment.
- How will you know when this goal has been met? If the goal is too vague, this question will require that you get more specific. For example, instead of "I want to feel better," work with something more focused, like, "I want to improve my digestion." In this example, possible answers to the question "How will you know when this goal has been met?" include "I no longer have constipation" or "I don't feel bloated and gassy after meals."
- What is your in-session plan—i.e., which reiki techniques (or other methods) will best support this goal?
- What is the client's take-home plan—i.e., how will they support the work in between sessions? It's nice to give your client either a copy of the full plan or a written reminder of their take-home actions. Remember that these recommendations must fall within your scope of practice (e.g., you cannot send your client home with a meal plan unless you have the relevant training and licensure).
- At subsequent sessions, you'll indicate how the client did with their take-home actions and make any necessary adjustments for future assignments.

• • • • • • • •

This brings up the topic of recommended number of sessions. Many practitioners advise scheduling three sessions in close succession (i.e., one week to no more than one month apart) when the client first begins treatment. If this is an option, time- and budget-wise for your client, this is a great rule of thumb, as it allows you to maintain momentum with the changes underway while supporting your client through this initial stage.

Reiki can sometimes heighten issues on a physical, mental, or spiritual level for a period of time after the first treatment. Some practitioners see this as a form of detoxification whereby reiki, in the process of healing, temporarily stirs up energetic "ick" before it is cleared out. Discuss this possibility with your client so they aren't alarmed if this occurs, and if they do experience these effects, know that they are typically reduced with subsequent treatments. Depending on what your client is experiencing, it may be advisable for them to utilize additional forms of support, such as a physician or mental health professional.

Ultimately, the number of treatments depends on each client's unique situation. If you are using a treatment plan, as outlined earlier in this chapter, you can base the number of treatments on the rate of progress toward a client's goals. If you aren't using a treatment plan and the client doesn't have any specific concerns they wish to address, once or twice a month is a great frequency for "maintenance" and general stress reduction, and this can be increased during times of higher stress or when dealing with specific health concerns to once or twice per week.

Ethics and Client Communication

We've briefly touched on ethics in this chapter, but here, let's look more closely at how to clarify your ethics and implement them in your practice. Ethics are the principles that govern how you behave and how you conduct your work, and they help to ensure that you do not knowingly inflict harm on others or yourself. The following are what I consider to be core ethics for healing professionals.

Maintaining Clear Boundaries

Physical Boundaries: Touch and physical space. For example, not touching clients without their consent, and then, only within the bounds of the treatment. Give the client privacy before and after the session so they can get on and off the treatment table.

Emotional Boundaries: How much information is shared about feelings and personal information. As a general rule, I minimize the amount of time I spend talking about myself unless it is directly relevant to the treatment, and I do not use sessions to discuss my personal problems, gossip, and so on. By the same token, if you are uncomfortable about information the client is sharing with you, you have the right to ask them to stop. Emotional boundaries also touch on something called "transference," in which a client redirects feelings for someone else, such as a parent or spouse, onto the practitioner, and countertransference is the reverse:

· · · · · · · ·

when a practitioner redirects these feelings onto a client. Unless you are a licensed mental health professional, it isn't appropriate to process transferred feelings with your client, but you can set kind-yet-firm boundaries if you see this occurring, either from your client's end or your own. In extreme cases, it may be necessary to refer the client to another practitioner.

Intellectual Boundaries: Having respect for one another's thoughts and ideas, as well as having a sense of what is and isn't appropriate to talk about in different circumstances, politics and religion being two examples that commonly fall on the list of topics best avoided in many situations!

Sexual Boundaries: Not only physical touch but also sexual comments, such as jokes or descriptions of sexual acts. I make it very clear that sessions are strictly non-sexual, and I reserve the right to terminate a session or refuse service if a client is behaving in a manner that makes me uncomfortable.

Material and Time Boundaries: Physical possessions, money, and time. Setting clear prices is one form of material boundary, and starting and ending sessions on time is a form of a time boundary. It's useful to determine your policy for late or no-show clients before this occurs and clearly state this on your website, intake form, or both.

Offer Referrals

Know your scope of practice and refer to other qualified professionals when needed. For example, if a client becomes aware of past abuse during a reiki session, unless you are a mental health professional, it is outside your scope of practice to help your client process this experience. Refer them to a qualified therapist. It can take time to build a network of practitioners for referrals, and if you don't know any therapists, an internet search is a good place to start. Don't hesitate to introduce yourself to other healthcare practitioners and ask if you can refer clients to them when needed. It's helpful to ask what type of clients they work with and any areas they specialize in so you can tailor your referrals to different client needs. If a client has a serious physical condition that they are not seeking medical treatment for, I like to make it clear that reiki is meant to be a complement to, not a substitute for, professional medical treatment. It's smart to have a list of practitioners in various fields to whom you can refer clients when needed.

Honor Confidentiality

Honor and protect your client's confidentiality. Store all health records securely, and never share your client's personal information or the details of your sessions together with anyone without the client's written consent (for example, a client might give written consent for you to share treatment information with their doctor).

Follow Credentials and Permissions

Do not use modalities or techniques without proper training and practice. Do not administer treatment of any kind without the client's informed consent.

Effective client communication is supported by maintaining clear boundaries, which requires us to, one, know what our boundaries are, and two, develop the skills to communicate and, when needed, reinforce those boundaries. As this is something that is not frequently taught in mainstream education, it can be worthwhile to seek out supplementary training. See the recommended resources for suggestions.

In the next chapter, we look at using reiki with specific populations, such as children and animals, and in different contexts, such as for environmental healing, political harmony, and other applications.

Chapter 19

Special Uses for Reiki

There are many contexts in which reiki is used, and in this chapter we'll take a look at some of the unique settings in which reiki is practiced. Reiki does not require a specific belief system in order to be effective (beyond a willingness to receive the energy); thus, people from all walks of life seek out and benefit from reiki treatment. In my own practice, I see clients who have wide-ranging spiritual beliefs, such as devout Christians, practicing witches, and atheists. People come for many different reasons, too. Some seek guidance on an important decision, need physical healing, desire improved focus and concentration prior to an important event, or feel energetically "off" and want to hit the reset button. Others simply wish to relax and let go of stress.

Medical Reiki

One prominent organization for medical reiki is Raven Keyes Medical Reiki International. Reiki master Raven Keyes developed a set of protocols, which she calls the "Gold Standards and Best Practices," for practitioners working in medical settings, and she pairs members of her organization with surgeons and healthcare facilities that wish to use reiki during medical procedures. Reiki master Pamela Miles also has extensive experience working in medical settings, has participated in clinical research on the healing effects of reiki, and teaches a course for those who wish to take their reiki practice into the world of conventional healthcare. More hospitals are offering reiki to their patients, citing benefits like stress reduction, pain relief, improved quality of sleep, decreased muscle tension, and accelerated wound healing. A 2017 article in *The Cut* states that "about 60 U.S. hospitals offer reiki sessions, including New York-Presbyterian, Memorial Sloan Kettering, and UCLA Medical Center; as of 2014, over 800 hospitals offer reiki training."[139]

If you are interested in pursuing reiki training for medical applications, look for a course that will help you hone your ability to present the benefits of reiki to medical professionals and collaborate with healthcare providers to best serve the needs of the patient. Courses will often cover scientific research, allowing you to present well-rounded information about reiki treatment without making claims regarding specific outcomes. Typically, you will learn how to work safely in a medical environment, including adhering to Standard Precautions, which are designed to minimize the transmission of infectious conditions, and administering reiki effectively without obstructing any medical interventions.

One very exciting aspect of bringing reiki into medical facilities is the blending of spiritual and scientific perspectives. Some practitioners feel this compromises or dilutes the practice of reiki, but in my view, reiki is more than robust enough to handle enquiry from many different angles, including a scientific one. It's likely that we will never definitively answer all our questions about how reiki effects healing, but the process of asking these questions and bringing practitioners from many different disciplines together to explore them, I feel, honors the holistic, collaborative energy of reiki.

Reiki for Children

Most of the techniques already presented in this book can be used with children, using your discretion and based on the child's comfort level. With reiki treatments, it's often a good idea to start with shorter sessions, from 5 to 30 minutes, adjusting as needed if the child wants to stop. As with adults and animals, always ask permission before giving reiki. Take some time to explain why you'd like to administer reiki and what the child might expect, such as sensing warmth in your hands or tingling in their body. I also like to show kids how to give themselves reiki. While some feel that the child must be attuned in order to do so, in my experience we are all natural conduits of reiki, and this seems particularly true for children, who typically have less of the energetic filters and blockages that many of us develop throughout life. Whether or not you agree, showing a child how to soothe themselves by placing their hands on their body in a therapeutic manner is a beautiful practice.

Space Cleansing
Turn physical cleaning into an energetic cleanse by charging cleansing implements (dust pans, brooms, spray bottles of natural cleaners, etc.) with reiki: Simply place your hands over the tool

---

139. Arianna Rebolini, "What the Heck Happened to My Body During Reiki?" The Cut, September 25, 2017, https://www.thecut.com/2017/09/what-the-heck-happened-to-my-body-during-reiki.html.

and allow reiki to flow. It can be fun (and effective) to chant a mantra together while you do this (see page 152), supercharging the flow of reiki. Then, use your magickal cleaning tools to physically and energetically cleanse the child's room and play spaces.

Morning and Bedtime Routines

Explore fun and easy-to-implement ways to incorporate reiki into your child's morning and evening routines, such as beginning the day with a little mantra chanting to wake the mind and balance the energy field. Show children how to draw a reiki symbol over their breakfast (Symbol One is a good choice due to its simple design; see page 153), that day's outfit, homework, or athletic equipment. Before bed, a short reiki treatment is a great way to let go of the day and transition into a peaceful night's sleep.

Reiki Boost

To create a healing touchpoint that can be used throughout the day, charge a piece of jewelry, a favorite writing pen or pencil, or other object that your child has ready access to. You can set an intention for the item together, such as "I feel calm and know that I can ask for help anytime" or "I love myself no matter what happens." With this intention in mind, hold your hands over the object (you can do this with your child), and allow reiki to flow. Whenever the child needs a little reiki boost, simply holding the item will initiate a healing flow of energy.

Working with the Precepts

The reiki precepts (see chapter 13) are a wonderful tool for spiritual growth for kids and adults alike. You might recite them together, perhaps each morning, or use them as a focus for discussion. For example, at the end of the day, you might have a family check-in and reflect on any challenging situations that triggered anger or worry and how you handled it, listing what you're grateful for and why, and so on. Kids can also use a precept as a journal or art prompt, helping them go deeper with the concept in a more self-directed manner.

Reiki for Animals

There are numerous practitioners bringing reiki to the animal world, such as the Animal Reiki Alliance, founded by Kathleen Lester, which offers in-person and distance reiki treatments for animals and their caregivers. Lester also provides reiki services through the Loving Pet Care Hospital in Baltimore, MD, as standalone sessions or as a pre-, intra-, and post-operative treatment.

Kathleen Prasad is the founder of Animal Reiki Source and developer of the Let Animals Lead method, which encourages a meditative approach of collaborating with the animal over doing reiki "to" them. On her website, she outlines seven guiding principles for working more

. . . .

effectively with animals, starting with intent.[140] Prasad advocates always asking the animal for permission before administering reiki. Allow the animal to initiate touch, and let the animal guide you in where it wants to be touched, if at all. Allow the animal to move freely during the treatment, and relax your focus rather than trying to "beam" or "send" energy to the animal or its specific health issues. Be mindful of your body language, adopting a non-threatening, open attitude without prolonged eye contact or other domineering cues. Release expectations of how the treatment should unfold, including duration and desired behavior, and end with gratitude to the animal for participating in the treatment.

Prasad, with Elizabeth Fulton, is the author of *Animal Reiki: Using Energy to Heal the Animals in Your Life*, which outlines how to adapt your reiki practice for animal clients. They advise setting aside an hour for each treatment, but stay flexible: some animals may require a longer treatment, while others may only be able to tolerate short sessions. Get comfortable so you can relax and stay focused on the treatment. Ideally, work in a quiet area that is familiar to the animal and where it is able to move freely. Not all animals wish to receive hands-on treatment (and this will not be practical in all cases, either, such as with fish), and the session will be most effective if you allow the animal to dictate the level of contact.

Reiki can be given sitting near the animal, and you needn't hold your palms out, either, which can feel threatening to some animals and will likely lead to muscle fatigue on your part. Simply rest your hands in your lap, palms facing up, and allow reiki to flow. Further, Prasad and Fulton advise that you always respect the animal's boundaries, introducing yourself from five to ten feet away, keeping your hands down by your sides, palms forward, allowing the animal to approach you. If the animal is uncomfortable around people, they advocate keeping a safe distance over attempting physical contact.[141] Sometimes during a treatment, a formerly skittish or standoffish animal will initiate contact, but it is recommended that you release expectations of how the session will unfold and focus on being a conduit for reiki, delivered in whatever manner is most appropriate for your animal friend.

As with reiki for humans, treatments are meant to be a complement to, not a substitute for, medical care. Coordinate your treatment with veterinary care, and do not advise clients to stop any conventional treatments without the recommendation of their veterinarian.

Food and Water

Draw the reiki symbol of your choice (see chapter 12) with your finger over an animal's food and water bowls, then hover your hands over the bowl and allow reiki to flow. You can pair this

---

140. "The *Let Animals Lead* Approach with Reiki," Animal Reiki Source, accessed June 2, 2019, https://www.animalreikisource.com/animal-reiki-information/the-approach/.

141. Elizabeth Fulton and Kathleen Prasad, *Animal Reiki: Using Energy to Heal the Animals in Your Life* (Berkeley, CA: Ulysses Press, 2006), 84.

• • • • • • • •

with specific healing intents if you like: for example, "strong and healthy bones" or "calm during travel."

Housing and Habitat

Cleanse the animal's space with reiki: Draw Symbol One (page 153) or any symbols of your choosing in all four corners or cardinal directions of the animal's space. See the symbols creating a grid of energy that permeates the entire area, cleansing and harmonizing the energy.

Toys and Accessories

Energetically cleanse and charge pet leashes, toys, and other accessories by holding the object in your non-dominant hand and place your dominant hand about four inches above the object. Focus on your hara (lower abdomen) and make three horizontal chopping motions over the object with your hand, stopping abruptly after the third chop. Give the object reiki for a few minutes.

Reiki for the Environment

In chapter 15, we covered methods for giving reiki to plants and seeds, and you can expand this work to entire areas and ecosystems, or the earth as a whole. I believe in cultivating a harmonious relationship with the land I'm living on, so I advocate starting in your own backyard. Don't have a yard? Not a problem. Cultivating a relationship with the land on which your home sits, no matter how urbanized, is just as powerful. In fact, I have found that these urban spaces are often more in need of healing yet are often overlooked, so your efforts here are likely to be quite beneficial.

There is no one right way to give reiki to the land, but I like to start by asking permission. If this is part of your spiritual practice, you can commune with the land spirits, perhaps using the technique on page 255, Working with Spirit Guides, and specifying that you wish to connect with the spirits of the land. Ask these land spirits to share their story—in what ways do they need healing? How can you aid in this process? You might be guided to take additional steps beyond giving reiki treatments. Once you have permission, you can use a technique like jôshin kokyû hô (page 230), intending that, on each exhale, reiki beam outward, into the land, sky, and everything contained within. I like to envision this energy soaking into the ground, the plants and stones, permeating the air, and so on. You can pair this technique with symbols, too, perhaps drawing Symbol One in the four directions, above and below, chanting its mantra as you intend reiki to heal the land.

This process can be adapted to distant locales by using Symbol Three. Connect to reiki in whatever way works best, perhaps using hatsurei hô or simply hands in gasshô, opening to the flow of reiki. Draw Symbol Three, chanting its mantra three times, as you intend to connect

• • • • • • •

with the location in need of healing. Visualize Symbol Three forming a bridge from here to there, then draw Symbol One, chanting its mantra three times, seeing the energy move across this bridge, bringing with it the powerful flow of reiki. Continue to give reiki until the process feels complete, then redraw Symbol One with the intention that the bridge dissolves, ending the connection and bringing the session to a close. You can finish with kenyoku hô and hands in gasshô, giving thanks.

Local and Global Events

Reiki can be sent to situations in need of healing, such as political conflict or disaster areas. Set the intention that the healing unfold for the highest good, harming none, then use the same method as outlined above for distant environmental healing. For human affairs, I like to use Symbol Two and its mantra for added mental-emotional healing, and this can be done by drawing the symbol and chanting the mantra three times after you use Symbol Three. Follow with Symbol One and proceed with the rest of the instructions.

Reiki helps us remember our True Self. The more ways we have of consciously interacting with this powerful energy, the more we remember who we really are, and the more we live from this expansive, enlightened place. Find ways to work with reiki that feel meaningful for you, and don't be afraid to make it fun! Sometimes reiki practice is approached with so much reverence, which is beautiful and well-deserved but can sometimes cause us to feel separate from this energy that exists within each and every one of us. Find ways to bring reiki into the very stuff of your life. Yes, respect it, honor it—but *live* it. Don't keep it up on a shelf, only to be taken down for special occasions. Or, more accurately, reveal every moment to be the special occasion that it truly is by weaving reiki into all that you do.

If teaching reiki is something you feel called to do, in the next chapter we look at the content typically covered in the various levels of instructions, along with practical tips for leading engaging courses for your reiki students.

CHAPTER 20

❧

Teaching Reiki

In most systems, teaching reiki is a responsibility reserved for those who have completed all levels of training and have been practicing for some time. In this chapter, we'll look at basic requirements for standard reiki instruction, which you can adapt as needed to suit your own teaching style and the needs of your students.

Due to the many variations of reiki systems that exist today, requirements for and methods of teaching are equally varied, but there are basic considerations that need to be addressed:

- Will the instruction be divided into different levels, and if so, how many?
- Which topics will be taught in each level?
- How long will each course be?
- Is there a minimum amount of time required before students can progress to the next level?
- Are there certain proficiencies students must demonstrate before they are permitted to progress to the next level?
- What is the cost of each course?
- Where will the course be taught?
- What materials and supplies are needed (e.g., treatment table[s] for practice sessions, manuals, etc.)?
- What is the class size limit?
- Will support be provided to students after the course, and if so, via what means (email, private Facebook group, in-person community meetings, etc.)?

Once you've nailed down the basics, it's time to flesh out the course material—what will you be teaching, exactly? You might work from an existing text, or you can create your own course manual, which you might offer in combination with one of the texts in the recommended resources section to add your own thoughts about reiki, student exercises, and space for in-class note taking.

Here's an overview of material typically covered in each level according to the standard three-level system, but know that a *great* deal of variation exists, depending on the teacher.

Level One

Students receive their first attunement at this level (some teachers give as many as four level-one attunements) and learn the basics of working with energy, both for self-healing and working with family and friends. A brief history of reiki is given, and time is spent discussing how reiki is used. In Gendai Reiki, the system created by Hiroshi Doi, the following topics are covered:

- Summary of reiki, including its history and philosophy (e.g., the Five Precepts)
- Hands-on healing basics (e.g., hand positions, aura cleansing)
- Administering self-healing and healing for others
- Basics of a reiki session
- Plant and animal applications
- Purifying spaces and objects with reiki
- Basic healing techniques (e.g., reiki mawashi)
- Self-growth and purification techniques (e.g., kenyoku hô, gasshô breathing)
- How to practice reiki after finishing the level one course

Level Two

Some teachers (myself included) require students to spend at least a month giving reiki to themselves and, optionally, family and friends before progressing to level two, but there are many courses available now that combine levels one and two into a single day or weekend seminar. In level two, students receive another attunement (or multiple attunements) and learn how to work with the symbols and mantras. Many teachers cover only the first three traditional symbols, leaving Symbol Four for level three. In addition, more time is spent learning how to administer reiki treatments for others, in contrast to level one, which usually has more of a focus on self-healing. This is also the level during which distance healing is typically taught, in conjunction with studying Symbol Three. In Gendai Reiki, the following topics are covered:

- Healing with the first three symbols and kotodama (mantras)
- Healing distantly, healing the past and future
- Additional reiki techniques (e.g., grounding yourself, charging objects)

• • • • • • • •

- Traditional Japanese techniques for self-growth and purification (giho)
- How to practice reiki after finishing the level two course

Level Three

Students typically receive one attunement at this level, and some courses teach Symbol Four and its mantra, along with methods for performing attunements on others. Some teachers will provide instruction on how to teach reiki and business considerations for opening a reiki practice. Still others divide this level into two parts: the first for those interested in practicing reiki at the master level, and the second for those who also wish to teach. In Gendai Reiki, this level is divided into two levels, and the topics covered in each are as follows:

Level Three

- Usage of Symbol Four and its mantra
- Connecting to higher dimensions, including one's higher self
- Deepening your meditation and self-growth practices
- Furthering your understanding of Usui's philosophy
- Using reiki in daily life
- Additional techniques for self-growth and purification

Level Four

- Theory and practice of performing attunements for each level
- Living as a reiki master
- Deeper understanding of all four symbols and mantras
- What to teach in each level

When I'm teaching, I like to mix hands-on practice with lecture, both to keep things interesting and because reiki is *meant* to be experienced; it's not solely an intellectual exercise. Using the guidelines above or books listed in the recommended resources, map out the topics and skills you wish to cover in each level, then brainstorm ways to convey this information in a manner that will keep the energy in the room up and engagement high, while providing multiple avenues for students to grasp the content. For example, when teaching core topics that students need to remember, you might present it multiple ways: visually, including giving students text or diagrams that they can refer back to later, and asking them to draw or write the information in their own notes; aurally, through spoken lecture and through having students repeat information back to you or to each other, perhaps in breakout groups where they practice teaching each other the content; and kinesthetically, through hands-on practice sessions. If attention starts to

· · · · · · · ·

wane, take breaks and get people up and moving, perhaps using this time to practice techniques like kenyoku hô or reiki undô. Be sure to leave plenty of time for questions and discussion. It's also great to offer a means (anonymous, if possible) for students to provide feedback on the course, helping you continually improve your teaching methods.

If you feel called to teach, it can be a very gratifying way to help others on the path of healing and self-discovery. Remember, you don't have to (nor can you) know everything about reiki before you start teaching, so while it is advisable to give yourself plenty of time to practice and study before embarking on the teaching path, don't hold yourself back by waiting until you feel like you've mastered everything. There's always something more to learn, and by adopting a beginner's mind, even while teaching, you open the dialogue to learn from and with your students.

PART IV
Reiki Complements

There is truly no limit to the ways in which you can incorporate reiki with other healing tools and techniques, and in part 4, we explore a variety of options to get you started, such as aromatherapy, crystals, bodywork, magickal practices, and sound therapy, to name just a few. No doubt this section will spark fun ideas of your own that will enable you to personalize your reiki practice to your specific needs and healing aims, while keeping your practice fresh and engaging.

· · · · · · · ·

CHAPTER 21

❧

Enhancing Your Reiki Practice

Over the years, reiki has been integrated with numerous healing practices, and in this chapter, we'll take a look at a handful of modalities that are easy to explore with little to no prior experience. On a basic level, I see reiki blending with other techniques in two ways: One, using reiki beforehand is a way to prime your energy system to receive the full benefit of other treatments; and two, reiki serves as an energetic mediator of sorts, guiding other techniques toward the highest good. Of course, we still need to use common sense to avoid harm, but on an energetic level, reiki brings everything we do into greater alignment with the True Self. It also enhances our intuition, so if we're paying attention to our inner voice as we engage in various healing practices, we'll get a sense, based on what we're drawn to, of which methods are most needed on our healing journey. Another reason for integrating reiki with other techniques is that it's fun! Reiki transforms our life the more we use it, so finding different ways to incorporate reiki into your day gives you more opportunities to work with this powerful energy.

Essential Oils and Aromatherapy

Aromatherapy is the practice of using essential oils, which are volatile, plant-derived aromatic oils, for healing, and it is thought that basic methods for distilling essentials oils were practiced in ancient Persia, Egypt, and India thousands of years ago.[142] These oils are extracted from plant materials in a variety of ways, distillation being the most common, and the method of preparation will change the therapeutic efficacy of the finished oil. Most aromatherapy practitioners advise using oils that have not been adulterated (for example, not combined with alcohol or

---

142. Shirley Price, *The Aromatherapy Workbook: Understanding Essential Oils from Plant to User* (London: Thorsons, 2000), 8.

· · · · · · · ·

other cheaper oils) and are natural, not synthetically produced. To extend the life of your essential oils, store them in tightly closed, dark-colored glass bottles, out of the light, in a cool, dry area.

Various chemical compounds are present in essential oils, such as terpenes, phenols, and aldehydes, each of which have different healing effects. For example, aldehydes are known to counteract inflammation and infection, reduce fever, calm the nervous system, and act as a tonic (tones and restores, improves overall well-being) and hypotensive (lowers blood pressure).[143] In addition to the direct effects of the chemical compounds, the smell of the oil also plays a role in healing, triggering a release of neurochemicals that can relax or stimulate the nervous system, depending on the aroma, which, in turn, can affect other body systems. Inhaling oils can also affect the mucous membrane of the nose and lungs, potentially providing relief from bronchitis, asthma, and so on.[144]

The amount of essential oil to be used varies based on the application, and many oils need to be diluted in a neutral carrier oil, such as almond or jojoba oil, or some other medium to prevent adverse reactions, such as skin irritation. It varies by recipe, but one common dilution is three to five drops of essential oil per teaspoon of carrier oil. If you're new to aromatherapy, it's a good idea to stick with recipes created by trained aromatherapists before getting experimental, and patch test with a small amount of the product before slathering it all over your body! Some oils, such as those in the citrus family, are considered phototoxic, meaning that they can make the skin more sensitive to sunlight, so they are not good candidates for, say, homemade sunscreens or use before heading to the beach. *With proper use and dosage,* many oils are safe to use during pregnancy, but it is advisable to work with a trained aromatherapist during pregnancy and breast-feeding if you are new to oils. (See recommended resources for additional recommendations.)

Choosing essential oils to work with is both an art and a science. There are many reference books listing essential oils and their healing applications that can help you find the right oils for what ails you (see recommended resources). You can also tap into your intuition, boosted with the power of reiki, to help you choose.

EXERCISE: Choosing Oils with Reiki

Start by taking a few deep, cleansing breaths to calm and center yourself. Close your eyes and bring your hands into gasshô. Visualize Symbol Two in front of you, and see it entering your third eye as you chant the mantra three times, with the intention of activating your intuition in accordance with the highest good. Visualize Symbol One in front of you, and see it entering and filling your aura as you chant the mantra three times, with the intention that reiki will con-

---

143. Price, *The Aromatherapy Workbook*, 64.
144. Price, *The Aromatherapy Workbook*, 201.

• • • • • • • •

nect you with the essential oils that are correct and good for you at this time. If you have a specific health condition you wish to address, you can add that to your intention. Bring your arms above your head, shoulder width apart, palms facing, and allow a flow of reiki to cascade down through your arms, into your crown, filling your entire body and energy field. Bring your hands back into gasshô, and stay here as long as you like. You might receive intuitive guidance in this space, or you can continue the process in any of the following ways:

- Look through a book of essential oils until your intuition calls out, directing you to one or more particular oils. You can also draw Symbol One over the book, chanting its mantra three times while focusing on your intention to find the correct essential oils.

- If you have a collection of essential oils, interact with them in this space, perhaps moving one hand over the bottles until you feel intuitively drawn to one, or opening the bottles and seeing how the aromas affect you.

- You can also do this exercise before heading to the store, and use the same process as above, moving your hands over the bottles (this can be done discreetly, if needed, to look like you're simply browsing the selection) or smelling tester oils to see which ones speak to you.

When you've found the essential oils that you'll be working with, here are practices for enhancing their effects with reiki. These are by no means the only way to incorporate reiki into your aromatherapy time, so use your imagination to come up with additional techniques that work well for you.

- Trace Symbol One over the bottle while chanting the mantra three times and holding the intention that this essential oil will interact with you in accordance with the highest good. If you have a specific health concern, you can add that to your healing intention. If you are addressing a health issue with a mental-emotional component, you can use Symbol Two before using Symbol One.

- I like to connect with the spirit of any plants I am working with, and reiki can facilitate this connection. You can use the Working with Spirit Guides technique on page 255, or simply place your hands in gasshô, allow reiki to flow through you, and then ask to be connected to the spirit of the specific plant in accordance with the highest good. In this place, you can ask the plant for any healing guidance, and be sure to thank it for working with you. At the end of any session in which you've connected to a plant spirit, finish with hands in gasshô, intending that the session has ended, and give thanks.

- Draw symbols over aromatherapy diffusers before using, setting any healing intention you like, such as purifying self and space or filling the room with unconditional love, healing, and so on.

· · · · · · · ·

- Prepare batches of body lotions, oils, scrubs, or other products containing essential oils, and before gifting them to friends and family (or using them yourself), charge them with reiki by drawing Symbol One over the container, chanting the mantra three times, and then holding it in your hands, allowing reiki to flow until you can sense that it has completely filled the substance with healing energy.

- Use diluted oils during a reiki self-treatment, perhaps choosing one for each chakra and rubbing them onto the body before placing your hands on the area for self-treatment. You can also add a few drops of diluted oil to your palms before giving a treatment.

Here are some simple recipes to get you started. Use any of the above methods for adding reiki.

Gel Face Mask

2 ounces aloe vera gel

1 tablespoon jojoba oil

2 drops essential oil

Stir the aloe vera gel and jojoba oil together in a small bowl, then add the essential oil of your choice and stir to incorporate. Apply to clean skin, leaving on for no more than ten minutes, then wash with warm water. Finish with the facial oil or lotion of your choice.

Facial Steam

4 cups water

Heat-safe bowl

2–3 drops essential oil(s) or 2 tablespoons fresh or dried herbs

Towel

At-home facial steams are very easy to do: Simply boil water, pour into the bowl, add any oils or other ingredients, such as fresh or dried herbs, and drape the towel over your head, tenting the bowl with the towel so the steam is trapped inside. Use common sense and let the water cool down a bit if it feels too hot or increase the amount of space between the water and your skin. You can use any essential oil you like, perhaps selecting one using reiki, as outlined earlier, but here are some options to get you started:

Normal Skin: Lavender, rosemary, geranium, jasmine

Dry Skin: Sandalwood, neroli, clary sage, chamomile (German or Roman)

Oily Skin: Ylang-ylang, bergamot, frankincense, lemongrass

Acne: Thyme (linanool), lavender, chamomile (German or Roman), juniper berry

• • • • • • • •

Money Freshener

Apply eight drops (a number said to increase wealth) of essential oil (single plant or a combination of different oils) on a small piece of paper. Draw Symbol One, chanting the mantra three times, with the intention of attracting wealth in a manner that is correct and good for you, harming none. Fold it up and tuck it into your wallet with paper bills. Some good essential oils for money magick are frankincense, myrrh, spikenard, patchouli, clove, sweet orange, and pennyroyal. You can combine this with the technique outlined on page 291 to connect with the plant spirit, asking for guidance in your relationship to money or with a specific financial issue.

Bodywork

Reiki is a wonderful complement to bodywork, and as a massage therapist, I offer sessions that combine reiki treatment with relaxation massage. You don't have to go to a professional massage therapist, though, to benefit from reiki and bodywork. There are numerous methods that you can perform on yourself, and here, we'll look at techniques from different bodywork modalities, such as Thai massage and reflexology, that are easily done at home.

Thai Massage

Thai massage, sometimes known as Thai yoga massage or Thai yoga therapy, is traditionally called *nuat phaen boran* ("traditional style massage") or *nuat thai* ("Thai massage"). It combines influences from Thailand, India, and China, and it utilizes acupressure techniques along energy lines (*sen*) and at specific energy points, along with various passive stretches to clear and harmonize the flow of energy.[145]

The navel is an important energy point in many traditions, which makes sense, given that it was the conduit for our original source of nourishment via the umbilical cord. The following technique from Thai massage involves gentle massage and pressing of the abdomen.

EXERCISE: Energetic Abdominal Clearing

Find a comfortable place to lie down where you won't be disturbed. Do a round or two of jôshin kokyû hô (page 230) to bring yourself into a deeper state of relaxation and to connect with reiki. Begin by using one palm to gently circle around the navel clockwise (i.e., from center, circle over to and down the left side, then travel up and around the right side). You can start with smaller circles closer to your navel and gradually move outward. When this feels complete, use the heel of your hand to gently yet firmly press the following points.

---

145. C. Pierce Salguero and David Roylance, *Encyclopedia of Thai Massage: A Complete Guide to Traditional Thai Massage Therapy and Acupressure* (Forres, Scotland: Findhorn, 2011), 23.

• • • • • • • •

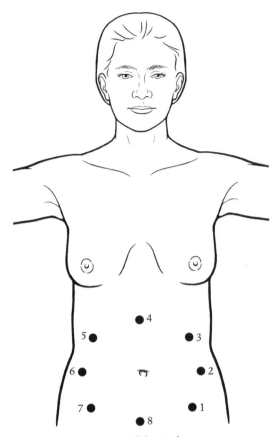

Figure 128: Abdominal points

While some points might be a little tender, don't use enough pressure to cause pain. The points are arranged as if on a clockface:

- Point one, a couple of inches above your left hip point.
- Point two is horizontally in line with your navel, a couple of inches to the right of point one.
- Point three is roughly in line with point one, a few inches higher than the navel.
- Point four is above the navel, just below the sternum. (Note: At the bottom of the sternum is a small bony projection called the xiphoid process. Use gentle touch here as it is possible to break this bone with excessively heavy pressure.)
- Points five, six, and seven are right-side mirror images of the three left-side points.
- End at point eight, below the navel, just above the pubic triangle. End with heso chiryô hô, the navel healing technique (page 230).

Herbal Steam Compress

Thai medicine uses hot herbal compresses for a variety of conditions, ranging from sore muscles and arthritis to digestive disorders and skin issues. While the process is a bit involved, if you're feeling motivated, these compresses are a wonderful way to combine herbs, bodywork, and reiki. You will need a means of steaming the bundles, such as an electric rice or vegetable steamer or a lidded pot with a metal colander set inside, and you will need fresh or dried herbs to fill the compress. Many recipes exist, but below are two to experiment with. You can also use herbs that might be more readily available in your area, such as plantain, chamomile, lavender, sage, calendula, or peppermint, to name just a few.

To integrate reiki into the process, you can use the compresses after giving yourself a reiki treatment (this feels really lovely!), or you can connect with the plant spirits using the method outlined in the aromatherapy section earlier. You could also draw Symbol One on the compress, chanting the mantra three times, with the intention of fully activating the healing powers of the herbs in accordance with the highest good.

Shivagakomarpaj Blend[146]

Handful of dried cassumunar ginger (common ginger may be substituted)
Handful of dried kaffir lime (leaves and rind)
Handful of eucalyptus leaves
Handful of cinnamon leaves
Sprinkling of natural camphor crystals (do not use synthetic substitutes)

Fresh Warming Compress[147]

2 parts galangal
1 part lemongrass
1 part mint
1 part shallots
1 part ginger (fresh root, not powdered)
1 part turmeric (fresh root, not powdered)
1 teaspoon camphor
1 teaspoon salt
½ part kaffir lime leaves or peel

---

146. Salguero and Roylance, *Encyclopedia of Thai Massage*, 545.
147. Nephyr Jacobsen, C. Pierce Salguero, and Tracy Wells, *Thai Herbal Medicine: Traditional Recipes for Health & Harmony* (Forres, Scotland: Findhorn Press, 2014), 132.

• • • • • • • •

Lay the herbs out on a piece of cotton muslin, one square foot in size, place the herbs in the center, wrap, and secure with cotton twine. You can also recycle clean, old sheets for these compresses. If you want to get fancy, there are YouTube videos outlining how to wrap and tie these bundles in the traditional manner. If you used dried herbs, briefly dip the bundle in water to wet it before placing it in the steamer. For fresh herbs, steam for five minutes; steam for twenty minutes if using dried herbs.

Before using, test to make sure the compress isn't hot enough to burn your skin. You can dip it lightly in sesame or coconut oil before applying to the skin, or use as is. Press the ball against your skin using pressure that feels firm enough to be therapeutic without causing discomfort. As a general rule, for a more stimulating experience, work from the extremities toward the core of the body using a faster rhythm. For a more relaxing experience, work from the core outward with a slow and steady pace. I like to do this in the bathroom, as it's easiest to perform while undressed in an area that won't be damaged if any herbal liquid or oil gets on the floor. The compresses can be returned to the steamer and reused throughout the session, but if you're using them on someone else, always use fresh compresses for each person, and clean the steamer thoroughly between sessions.

Reflexology

This modality uses the thumb or fingers to apply pressure and/or massage certain points on the hands and feet, which are said to correspond with different areas of and systems in the body. By stimulating these points, it is believed that energy blockages can be cleared in the corresponding body areas. There are numerous books available, with detailed maps of the hands and feet, showing which points are connected to which organs and other bodily structures (see recommended resources). Here, we'll look at some basic sequences to enhance your well-being. To integrate reiki into the practice, you can give yourself a treatment first, followed by reflexology, or you can start with jôshin kokyû hô (page 230), seeing reiki streaming from your fingertips, before beginning the reflexology.

The following headache sequence is from *The Touch Remedy* by Michelle Kluck-Ebbin.[148]

148. Michelle Kluck-Ebbin, *The Touch Remedy: Hands-On Solutions to De-Stress Your Life* (New York: Harper Elixir, 2016), 69.

Headache Remedy

Brain Reflex Point: Pinch the end of both big toes between your index fingers and thumbs, holding for ten seconds. It's optional to make small circles with the thumb in the fleshy pad of the big toe.

Eye Reflex Point: Locate the area at the base of the second and third toes on both feet. Pinch this spot between thumb and index fingers, holding for ten seconds. Then, finish with a round of circular motions made with the thumb.

Neck Reflex Point: Apply pressure to the base of the big toe on both feet, holding for ten seconds, then do a round of small circles with the thumb.

Union Valley Point: Grasp the webbing at the base of the thumb and index finger with the thumb and index finger of the opposite hand. Pinch here for ten seconds, then make circular motions with the thumb, moving first in one direction and then the opposite. Repeat on the other hand.

Drilling Bamboo Point: Find the indentations where the bridge of the nose and the eyebrows meet, and use your index fingers to apply pressure for ten seconds. Release and repeat.

Gates of Consciousness Point: Bring your index and middle finger of each hand together, then press them into the hollows on either side of your neck at the base of the skull. Use an upward pressure for ten seconds, release, and repeat.

Digestive Boost

Start on the right hand, and locate the knobby bone at the inside base of your palm (see figure 129). Go just above this and apply pressure to the ileocecal valve / appendix point for ten seconds (point 1). Caterpillar crawl with your thumb an inch upward from this point (ascending colon), along the outer edge of the palm, then make a 90-degree turn, crossing your palm to the opposite side (transverse colon) (arrows 2 and 3). Do the same on the left hand. (Note: the one-inch path above the ileocecal point represents the descending colon on the left hand.) Return to the right hand, and apply pressure on the meaty pad at the base of the thumb (point 4). Hold for ten seconds and repeat on the opposite hand. Finally, press and hold the gallbladder point on your right hand by tracing down from the base of the pinky, halfway down the palm (point 5).

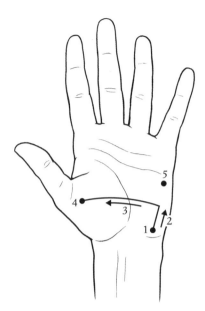

Figure 129: Digestive reflexology

Scalp Massage

You don't need to follow any particular method for this, doing whatever feels good to you, but I've also provided a sequence if you need some ideas. Start by drawing Symbol One on both palms, chanting the mantra three times while intending to receive whatever it is you most need right now. Place one palm over your forehead, the other over the back of the head and hold until the flow of reiki feels complete. Rub your temples with the pads of your fingers, using slow, circular movements. Move above your ears, again using slow, circular movements. Travel behind the ears along the base of the skull, stopping to massage each area as you do so. From the base of the skull, move upward, over the back of the skull, massaging all the way to the crown of the head. Use your finger pads to move the scalp and scalp fascia on the crown in a circular motion, perhaps working on one side at a time if that feels best. Continue working forward to your hairline, then lightly smooth your fingers over your head and down the back of your neck, repeating three times. Close your eyes and make a few sweeps over your forehead, starting at the midline and moving out to your ears. Repeat on the cheeks, then smooth from the jawline down the front of the neck.

Color Therapy

Color has been used throughout history to communicate, to create beauty, to honor the living and the dead, to attract a mate, and so much more. The effect of color on human psychology has been studied by many, such as Dr. Max Lüscher, who developed the Lüscher Color Test, matching colors with different personality traits, and Hermann Rorschach of Rorschach Ink-

• • • • • • • •

blot Test fame.[149] In ancient Greece, Hippocrates created a diagnostic system based on the four humors—black bile, yellow bile, phlegm, and blood—each associated with a different color, and the patient's condition was assessed, in part, by examining the color of their hair, skin, and eyes.[150] Many traditions associate the elements with different colors, such as Traditional Chinese Medicine, which associates wood with green, fire with red, earth with yellow, metal with white, and water with blue/black.

In energy work, different colors have been assigned to the chakras and layers of the aura, and types of energy are sometimes perceived in color. For example, heavy or slow-moving energy might appear darker or more opaque than other energies. Color can also be used to initiate healing in a variety of ways, such as working with colored crystals or visualizing colored light in meditation. Below, I list common associations for each color, but keep in mind that there is often a good deal of variation in how individuals respond to color, based on culture, personal experiences and preference, so trust your intuition.

Red: Stimulating, energizing, passionate, outgoing; sex, anger, strength, action, drama, revenge; increases temperature, boosts circulation

Orange: Joy, enthusiasm, wisdom, courage; adventurous, assertive, having a sense of humor, sociable, uplifting; stimulates appetite

Yellow: Intellectual, open minded, attentive to details, enthusiastic, cheerful, confident, nervous; excess mental activity; heals digestion and depression

Green: Calming, soothing, grounding; harmony, balance, equilibrium, wealth, abundance, hope, faith; reduces inflammation, relaxes the mind

Blue: Spirituality, intuition, communication, tranquility; cooling, relaxing; soothes inflammation, relieves insomnia, lowers temperature

Violet: Dignity, royalty, wealth, healing, creativity; self-worth, self-respect, dignity; balances the nervous system, works on the unconscious self, reduces irritability

There are endless ways to incorporate color into your healing routines. Here are some suggestions to get you started:

• Perform a variation on chakra kassei kokyû hô: Raise your arms to the sky, hands shoulder width apart, palms facing each other, and connect to reiki. Feel the flow of energy down through your arms and into your head. Place your hands, palms facing up, on your knees. With each inhale, visualize the color associated with each chakra as you bring energy and

---

149. Howard Sun and Dorothy Sun, *Colour Your Life: How to Use the Right Colours to Achieve Balance, Health and Happiness* (London: Piatkus, 2014), 10.

150. Sun and Sun, *Colour Your Life*, 101.

· · · · · · · ·

breath to that area. You can also start by setting the intention to see the health of each chakra, noting the color and vibrancy first, then sending extra healing energy to any chakras that seem dull, dim, or otherwise lackluster. The traditional color associations for this exercise are as follows:

Root: Red
Navel: Orange
Solar Plexus: Yellow
Heart: Green and/or pink
Throat: Sky blue
Third Eye: Indigo
Crown: Violet and/or white

• When drawing the symbols, either in your mind or on paper, incorporate color. For example, if you were performing the Money Freshener technique on page 293, you could draw Symbol One in purple or green to enhance the effects. Use colored symbols on chakras or any area of the body to add the healing power of color. You can also send healing color using various distance techniques presented throughout the book to a person, plant (green and yellow are especially nice for plants), animal, or place.

• Charge a colored candle with reiki by holding it between your hands and allowing reiki to fill the candle from top to bottom, and light it to experience the healing effects of reiki and color. Pair this technique with a specific intention, if desired, such as soothing anxiety (try blue, green, or pink), deepening meditation (try purple, white, or indigo), or connecting with spirit guides (white) by focusing on the intention while charging the candle. You can also draw any of the symbols into the wax using a warm pin or nail.

• Consciously choose your outfits, accessories, or makeup based on the qualities you wish to enhance that day. You can use symbols on any of these items, too, paired with an optional intention, such as confidence building before presentations, harmony and clear communication before a meeting, energy boosting before going to the gym, and so on. A great resource to help you tap into the healing and magickal potential of fashion is Tess Whitehurst's *Magickal Fashionista*.

Crystals

In addition to the techniques starting on page 238, here are fun and effective ways to use crystals in your reiki practice.

Making a Crystal Essence

Sometimes referred to as a crystal elixir, this method allows you to transfer the healing energies of crystals to water, which can then be rubbed on an area of the body in need of healing, sprayed in a space for cleansing and healing, added to a bath, or incorporated into personal care products, such as face masks and lotions (for lotions made with oil, not water, you can infuse your oil with crystal energy instead).

First, make sure that your crystals are safe to use in water and do not contain any toxic chemicals. You can research your crystals online or reference a crystal book (see recommended resources) for potential safety concerns. If your crystals do contain potentially hazardous chemicals, you can still prepare an essence using the indirect method.

For either method, start by washing the crystal with dish soap and water (unless it's of a type that will be damaged by water), then cleanse and charge your crystals with reiki using the instructions on page 238. Proceed with the direct method (for non-toxic crystals) or the indirect method (for toxic crystals).

Direct Method: Place your crystals in a bowl, ideally glass, and add enough spring water to cover the crystals. Place the bowl in sunlight or moonlight for a few hours. You can draw any symbols you choose over the bowl, sending any intention that feels appropriate into the essence. If you don't plan to use the essence within a few days, mix one part essence with two parts brandy, vodka, or apple cider vinegar, which acts as a preservative.

Indirect Method: Place the crystal in a small bowl, then place this inside a larger bowl. Fill the larger bowl with spring water, and place in sunlight or moonlight for a few hours. (Note: some crystals will fade in sunlight.) You can draw any symbols you choose over the bowl, sending any intention that feels appropriate into the essence. Preserve as outlined above if you don't plan to use the essence within a few days.

I like to store my essences in a colored-glass dropper bottle labeled with the type of crystal and the date it was bottled.

Crystal Healing Circle

You can create a circle of crystals, similar to a crystal grid (page 239), in which to perform a self-healing or treatment for others. You can also meditate in the circle, perform divinatory readings, connect with spirit guides (page 255), or use it for magickal purposes (page 317). For overnight healing, create a crystal circle around your bed (you can also create a grid underneath your bed if you're worried about people stepping on or tripping over the circle). Or place four crystals in each direction, perhaps on windowsills or bookshelves to keep them out of the way, connecting them into a circle using the activation method outlined below.

Choose the appropriate crystals using your intuition or by researching crystal properties. You could also adapt the process on page 290, outlining how to choose essential oils with the guidance of reiki, for your crystal search. Cleanse and charge the crystals using a specific intention if desired (page 238), and place them on the floor in a circle. To activate your circle, draw

Symbol One on the palm of your dominant hand, chanting the mantra three times, and move your hand clockwise around the circle, palm facing the crystals, intending that each crystal is activated and connected to its neighbors with reiki. I like to move around the circle three times.

When done, stand in the center and perform jôshin kokyû hô, filling the space with reiki. Use this circle as desired, and if you need to leave the circle at any point, imagine pulling open a set of curtains, stepping through, and closing the curtains behind you. Do the same when you reenter the circle. To release the circle, draw Symbol One on your dominant palm, and move in a counterclockwise direction, sweeping your hand around the circle, envisioning it opening and sending healing energy out into the cosmos. Stand once more with hands in gasshô, setting the intention that your session is now over. Cleanse your crystals before using for other purposes.

Crystal Reminders

Like using sticky notes on the bathroom mirror, crystal reminders help you maintain focus over time on a desired intention. First, choose your crystal, perhaps using reiki to guide you. Cleanse and charge the crystal with your desired intention (page 238). This can be a short-and-sweet word or phrase—self-love, confidence, healing, releasing fears—or a fully fleshed-out affirmation, such as "I enjoy eating in a way that deeply nourishes my body" or "I am communicating my needs kindly and effectively." I like to finish by drawing Symbol One over the crystal, chanting the mantra three times with the intention that it will emanate reiki to support my intention. You can also use Symbol Two for mental-emotional support (or use any the non-traditional symbols that connect with your intention). Place the crystal somewhere conspicuous, like your work desk or on the bathroom sink. Know that every time you see the crystal, you are supported in living out your intention in accordance with the highest good.

I generally work with one crystal at a time in this manner, to maintain more singular focus when establishing new habits, but it's also possible to use multiple crystal reminders for well-established intentions that you've been working with for a while. For example, if you're already in the habit of eating healthy, you can place crystal reminders in the cupboards to support staying on track. Or if you've been working with the intention of body self-love for a while, you might place a reminder crystal among your morning personal care products to keep you aligned with that energy. Use your intuition to determine when a crystal is no longer needed or when it needs to be refreshed. For the former, simply cleanse the crystal so it's ready to use for other purposes; for the latter, draw Symbol One over the crystal (and any other symbols used for the original charging), chanting the mantra three times while focusing on your intention.

Flower Remedies

Perhaps the most well-known line of flower essences is that of Dr. Edward Bach (pronounced BATCH), an English surgeon and pathologist who experimented with thousands of plants before creating his system of thirty-eight flower remedies. This was not the first use of flower essences, however. Paracelsus, a Swiss physician living in the sixteenth century, prescribed the dew of specific flowers for different illnesses, and earlier still, Hildegard of Bingen, a twelfth-century abbess and polymath, recorded the energetic healing capabilities of flowers.[151]

A flower essence is made by letting fresh flowers steep in spring water, using the light of the sun or the moon to transfer the plant's life force into the water. Katie Hess, flower alchemist and founder of LOTUSWEI, a floral apothecary, explains that essences are made according to lunar cycles, with flowers collected on the full or new moon, when more of the plant's life force is concentrated in the blossoms.[152]

Choosing a Plant

Whether you're seeking a plant from which to make an essence or you're wondering which essence is best for you to use right now, it's helpful to partner with the energy or spirit of the plants to aid in this process. To choose from already-made elixirs, you can use the technique outlined on page 290 for choosing essential oils. I often make my flower essences while out on hikes. I take a few mason jars of spring water and scissors with me, and I connect with reiki before heading out on my walk, asking to be led to the plants that are correct and good for me. You could follow the same process before walking in your garden.

Once I've found a plant, I sit nearby and ask to connect with its spirit. Use your intuition, or follow this simple process. Bring hands into gasshô and introduce yourself to the plant, stating your desire to partner with it to create a flower essence. Ask permission. You may hear an affirmative response or simply get a sense that it's okay to proceed. In cases where I am not granted permission, I often feel a block or "emptiness," like there's nobody on the other end of a metaphorical phone line. In these instances, thank the plant, and if you feel called, try working with it again on another occasion.

If you do have permission, you can take this time to ask the plant for messages: Does it have a preference for how many flowers you collect or any other particulars for preparing the essence? What is its medicine—in other words, what issues can its essence be used for? You can also meditate with the plant after making the essence to get further clarity on the latter question if you're not able to spend a lot of time with the plant now. Always remember to thank the plant spirit for working with you, and be sure to positively identify any wild plants to ensure they're not toxic. Some practitioners make essences from toxic plants, reasoning that there is so little of the physical compounds present in the final essence that it will do no harm, but in these instances,

---

151. Katie Hess, *Flowerevolution: Blooming into Your Full Potential with the Magic of Flowers* (Carlsbad, CA: Hay House, 2016), 37.

152. Hess, *Flowerevolution*, 38.

· · · · · · · ·

I prefer using the indirect method as outlined under Making a Crystal Essence (page 300). Also, make sure the flowers you're collecting aren't endangered or considered species of concern, and never take all the flowers in a given area.

Make Your Own Flower Essence

Once you've decided on a plant to work with, you'll need:

Glass bowl (some practitioners set one aside to use solely for essences)

Scissors

Spring water

Mesh strainer (tea strainers work well)

Funnel

Jar and bottles

Brandy, vodka, or distilled white vinegar

I like to give myself a reiki treatment before making flower essences, but if you don't have time, start with kenyoku hô (page 229), then use any technique that allows you to connect with reiki, such as seishin toitsu (page 230). Pour spring water into the bowl and draw Symbol One over the water, chanting the mantra three times with the intention that this process is unfolding according to the highest good. Ask permission of the plant, then use scissors to snip three flowers into the bowl of water. Many practitioners recommend that you not allow any of your energy to "contaminate" the essence by touching the flowers or the water. I have found that partnering both with the plant (see below) and reiki results in powerful essences, without my needing to obsess over contamination, but I do avoid touching the water as much as possible. Place the bowl in sunlight, avoiding any areas of shadow or cloudy skies, for three hours. For night-blooming plants, carry out this process in moonlight (you can let it steep overnight, but take the bowl inside before the sun rises).

Strain out the flower matter, and, ideally, return it to the plant. If this is not possible, I like to set the flowers in my garden instead of throwing them in the trash. In a jar, combine the strained essence with an equal amount of preservative (brandy, vodka, or vinegar), and label with the plant name, date collected, and "mother essence." From this mother essence, you can now make a stock bottle; I like to use a fifty-milliliter bottle for my stocks. Fill the stock bottle with a fifty-fifty mix of spring water and preservative, then add ten drops of the mother essence. Finally, to make a dosage bottle (this is what you'll actually use when taking your flower essence), take a fifteen milliliter glass dropper bottle filled with fifty-fifty spring water and preservative, and add one drop from your stock bottle. Make sure you label all of your bottles.

. . . .

Note: While it's best to stick with the fifty-fifty ratio of water to preservative, there is flexibility in the number of drops used to make the stock and dosage bottles. Use your intuition, following the guideline of using less drops in the dosage bottle than you do for the stock bottle. Why less? I was taught that with higher dilutions, there is less of the physical constituents of the plant present and therefore more of the spiritual essence.

Using Flower Essences

Essences can be taken in a variety of ways, such as adding them to a beverage, bathwater, or beauty products. To take directly, place three to five drops under or on the tongue. Katie Hess of LOTUSWEI recommends five drops, five times per day. Ultimately, use your intuition. Unless guided otherwise, I tend to use flower essences for a minimum of one week, as I find I get more benefit by allowing the energy to build and increase in my system over time. You can also combine multiple essences, and if there's a combination that works particularly well for you, consider creating a dosage bottle of this mixture. Flower essences are also safe to use with children, pets, and plants.

Bedtime Practice

You can incorporate essences into your bedtime routine by placing three drops on the tongue before performing any nighttime rituals (see page 246 for ideas), or simply before going to bed. Use your intuition to choose the right essence for you, or experiment with red or white chestnut, vervain, aspen, or Bach Flower Remedies Rescue Sleep.

Movement Practices

Reiki helps remove obstructions and return our energy to a state of harmonious flow, which makes it an ideal complement to movement practices, which are, in and of themselves, very beneficial for improving energy flow. You can integrate reiki into any movement practice of your choice in any number of ways. Here are some ideas to get you started:

- Perform a mini self-treatment following the cool-down phase of your workout, allowing your hands to be drawn to any areas most in need of reiki.
- Use symbols on movement equipment and in the space, setting any specific intentions that are relevant to your practice. A good general intention would be, "I am honoring my body, mind, and soul through this _____ (yoga, walking, soccer, etc.) practice."
- Take a few moments with eyes closed, hands in gasshô, and connect with the flow of reiki. Draw a large Symbol One in front of you, chanting the mantra three times, then walk

through it with the intention that you will be guided by reiki throughout your movement practice.

Yoga

Here are some of my favorite ways to integrate reiki with yoga practice:

- Start by chanting one or more of the mantras continuously for five minutes. I find this to be a wonderful way of breaking loose "sticky" energy that will then be released through my physical practice, and it also clears my mind and prepares me to be fully present in my body. You might experiment with different mantras to see how they affect you.
- If you normally do *pranayama* (breath work) as part of your practice, experiment with some of the reiki breathing techniques, such as jôshin kokyû hô (page 230) or Breath of the Fire Dragon (page 235).
- Physical yoga practice consists of asanas, or postures, and after this more regimented style of movement, it's wonderful to let your body move in an uncontrolled fashion by practicing reiki undô (page 233).

The following is a variation on the yoga sequence known as Sun Salutation A, or *Surya Namaskar* A. You can pair it with an intention of your choice, in essence dedicating your practice to the intention by focusing on it throughout the movements. Draw a large Symbol One over your mat, chanting the mantra three times while focusing on the intention of your choice or the intention, "I am connecting deeply with reiki through my movements." Another option: create a Crystal Reminder (page 302), and place this a few feet from the top of your mat to serve as a focal point for your *drishti* (gaze), throughout the practice.

Stand at the top of your mat, feet hips width apart, feeling all four corners of the feet grounded into the mat. If your knees are locked, move your shins forward ever so slightly to bring softness to the knee. Close your eyes, bringing your hands into gasshô. Feel reiki entering your crown, moving down your spine, through the legs, and out through the feet. Feel how this increases your sense of connection to both earth and sky.

Figure 130: Mountain pose with prayer hands

· · · · · · · ·

Sweep your hands over your head with upward-facing palms, looking skyward without straining the neck until your palms join at the top. Feel reiki coursing down the arms and into the back, and allow your shoulders to relax down for one breath.

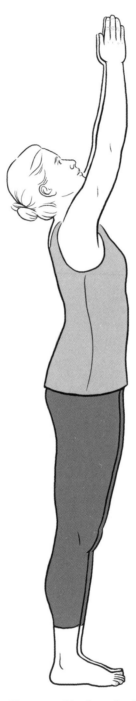

Figure 131: Hands overhead

Glide your gasshô hands in front of your face through heart center, then start to bend your knees slightly (or a lot, if needed) and hinge at the hips. Move your butt back in space and gently engage your abdominal muscles to provide support as you fold over. Bend your knees as much as you need to and plant your palms on the earth, head hanging heavy, and feel reiki washing down your back like water. Feel the energy traveling down your arms and into the earth, releasing anything that no longer serves you. Notice if there's any tension in your neck, and see if you can breathe into it, softening and releasing.

Figure 132: Forward fold

Lightly engage your abdominals again and bring your palms to your shins or a yoga block as you look at the floor a few feet ahead of you. Don't worry about having perfectly straight legs; focus on lengthening from your tailbone to the crown of your head, feeling the energy running along the spine. Notice if you're holding any tension in your throat; breathe and soften into it.

Figure 133: Halfway lift

Return to a forward fold, head hanging heavy, then plant your palms on the mat and step back into a pushup position. Engage your trunk, tapping into the powerful energy of your hara to keep from sagging in the low back. Engage your upper arms to stabilize the shoulder joint. This often involves a slight external rotation at the shoulder, which will point the inner crease of your elbow more toward the top of your mat. Energetically lift up through the armpits so you're not sagging into the shoulder joints.

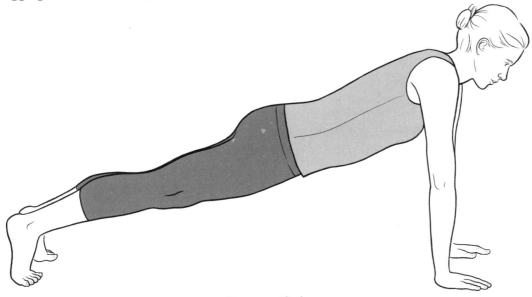

Figure 134: Plank pose

Maintaining engagement of the trunk, lower your knees to the floor while keeping the integrity of the shoulders established above. Shift forward slightly and start to bend your elbows, keeping them tucked into the sides of your ribs.

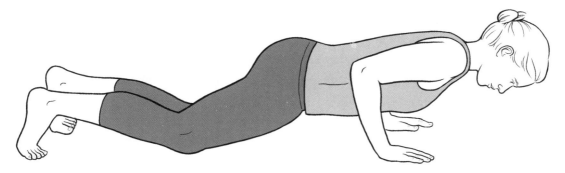

Figure 135: Modified Chaturanga

If your shoulders creep toward the ears, gently move them back. Lower all the way down to the ground and place your forehead on the mat. Take a few breaths here, really enjoying your contact with the earth and feeling appreciation for its constant presence and support. Feel the energy swirling at your hara, and on each breath, expand it to fill your entire body.

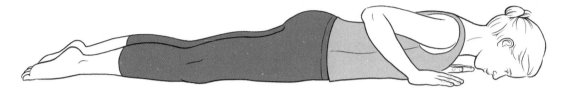

Figure 136: Face down

When you feel ready, plant your palms on the side of your body, level with the nipples, and feel engagement beginning at the pubic bone, extending up the torso to the sternum, lifting you into a Low Cobra Pose, keeping the tops of your feet firmly pressed into the ground.

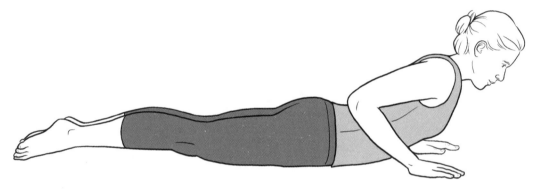

Figure 137: Low Cobra

You don't need to go very high to experience the benefits; focus more on lengthening through the front of the body without crunching in the low back. You can energetically pull back through anchored palms to assist in this lengthening. Look to a point on the floor a few feet in front of you, as opposed to looking skyward, to facilitate length and ease in the back of the neck, and breathe through your heart space. Release and return to forehead on the floor, once more appreciating its solidity and calming effect.

Plant your palms by your sides once more, and engage your trunk to lift into a push-up position on bent knees. Start to move your hips back, as if you're going to sit on your heels, then press firmly into your palms, lifting the hips into downward-facing dog pose, keeping your heels lifted and/or bending the knees slightly if you need to.

- - - - - - - -

Figure 138: Down Dog

Stabilize the shoulders as before with a slight external rotation, bring the elbow pits more toward the front of the mat, armpits lifting. Take three breaths here, and visualize Symbol One. I like to picture the symbol under my body, buoying me up, and I inhale its energy through the nose with each breath.

Step forward to the top of your mat, feet hips width apart, and plant your palms on your shins, lengthening through the entire spine, noticing if the energy flow feels different now. Release into a forward fold, bending your knees as much as you need to, then move your butt back, really pressing into your feet, and use this grounding force to move into standing, rising through the strength of your feet and thighs over relying primarily on your back muscles. Lift the arms overhead once more, palms touching, then bring them into gasshô at heart center. Draw Symbol One in your mouth with the tongue, then let it go with a long, open-mouthed exhale, filling your aura with the energy of the symbol and the focused power you created through your mindful movement.

Sacred Dance

As with yoga, there are endless ways to incorporate reiki into a sacred dance practice. The key is to allow your body to move naturally rather than forcing it to follow a prescribed sequence. As Leslie Zehr writes in *The Alchemy of Dance*, "Sacred Dance is dancing for expression rather than performance."[153] I like to create a sacred space for dancing using the method for purifying space on page 214, the circle-casting steps in Working with Spirit Guides on page 255, or the Crystal Healing Circle on page 301. You might choose a theme or intention you'd like to explore through your dance, spending some time journaling any insights that arise when you're done moving. Select music that feels appropriate. Generally, I like to use instrumental music for sacred dance, but you might find that carefully chosen vocal composition works for you as well.

Perform kenyoku hô (page 229), then use any practice that allows you to connect with reiki, really feeling the energy moving throughout your entire body. Options include (but are certainly not limited to) the Seventh Level Technique (page 238), Reiki Boost (page 238), or tanden chiryô hô (page 232). Standing with feet slightly wider than hips width apart, start to sway gently back and forth, perhaps with eyes closed. Gradually allow your arms and head to join in the movement. Begin to move more organically, letting the rhythm of the music take you into whatever expression feels good. Notice how the energy is moving through your body. Are there any areas that feel harder to reach with your awareness? If so, gently introduce movement to those areas, allowing this to initiate a clearing influx of energy.

Continue dancing for as long as you like, perhaps varying the tempo to include faster, more staccato movements interspersed by slower, more fluid expression. When done, take some time in *Shavasana*: lie on your back, legs straight, feet naturally falling out to the sides, arms by your sides, shoulders soft and relaxed. Close your eyes and stay here for at least a few minutes. Then, place one hand on your hara, the other on your forehead, allowing reiki to flow as long as needed. Sit up, bring your hands into gasshô, and give thanks.

Dance is also wonderful when experienced with others, and the ecstatic dance movement is a great way to find communal dance spaces that don't require going to a bar. While I love dancing at nightclubs and bars, too, it's nice to have the option to dance in a space where no talking or photos are permitted and participants are committed to creating a safe space for all bodies. For example, to honor personal space, the ecstatic dance guidelines remind participants "that we all have different levels of comfort when it comes to being approached and touched. Please be mindful and make sure the way you approach other dancers is resonant with them. If somebody offers you a shared dance and you are not interested, simply give them a bow with hands at your heart to say, 'no thank you.'"[154]

Feldenkrais

The Feldenkrais Method was developed by Dr. Moshé Feldenkrais (1904–1984) through his personal journey of healing from physical injuries, combined with his knowledge of physics,

153. Leslie Zehr, *The Alchemy of Dance: Sacred Dance as a Path to the Universal Dancer* (New York: iUniverse, 2008), 6.
154. "About," Ecstatic Dance, accessed June 2, 2019, https://www.ecstaticdance.com/about.

biomechanics, neurology, and psychology. It utilizes gentle, often slow, movements performed with focused attention to improve coordination, range of motion, movement efficiency, and self-awareness. He saw natural movement being restricted in numerous ways by social conditioning, whittling down an individual's possible avenues of expression until they fit the mold dictated by society. By rediscovering natural movements, one can change their self-image and realize their full potential, all of which is a wonderful complement to reiki's ability to align us with the True Self.

The following exercise is a sample of the method, focusing on an exploration of eye movement.[155] To integrate reiki, begin with hands in gasshô and perform jôshin kokyû hô. Spend a few breath cycles, feet hips width apart, swaying from side to side and front to back, maintaining awareness on your hara, noticing what you feel at this center of gravity as you move. Then, proceed with the exercise.

Stand with feet roughly hip width apart and begin to rotate your upper body from left to right, allowing your arms to hang without effort. As you move, the arms will naturally follow, the right swinging behind you, perhaps even touching your left glute or hip, while the left arm swings freely over to the right. Continue moving back and forth, and close your eyes. Allow the head to move naturally and with ease. Fine-tune your awareness to focus on the transition from one direction to the other. Which part of you begins this transition: the hips, the head, the eyes? This can be trickier to discern than you might think. If you're like me, it will be necessary to practice this movement many times before you can tell which part of you is initiating the switch from left to right. Finally, open your eyes and continue the movement. For many people, this leads to less fluidity, if only slightly, than moving with the eyes closed. Practice until you experience the same level of smoothness with the eyes open as you do with the eyes closed (or vice versa if the opposite is true for you). As an experiment, try this exercise once as described, then perform tanden chiryô hô (page 232) and try it again. Did this alter your movement in any way?

Meditation, Visualization, and Thought Practices

Many of the traditional and non-traditional techniques presented in earlier chapters incorporate meditation and visualization, so here, we'll look at additional ways to introduce reiki into what we might call "mentally based practices."

Symbol Meditation

This is a practice introduced in my first book, *Living Reiki*, and it's one I like to use from time to time to deepen my relationship with the symbols. You will likely find that your experiences

---

155. Moshé Feldenkrais, *Awareness through Movement: Health Exercises for Personal Growth* (New York: Harper-Collins, 1990), 145.

change over time, yielding different layers of understanding. Start with hands in gasshô, and perform jôshin kokyû hô (page 230) or hatsurei hô (page 229), coming into a calm, centered state. Draw the symbol you wish to work with, chanting its mantra three times while holding the intention to connect with the energy and teachings of the symbol. On the screen of your mind, call up the symbol, and enter meditation using one of the following techniques (or whichever method comes to you intuitively):

- See the symbol carved or painted on a doorway, chant the mantra three times to open the door, and step through into your meditation. Be sure to exit through the same door to end the meditation.

- See the symbol in the form of a hedge maze from an aerial viewpoint, then start at the entrance of the maze and move toward the center. Notice any details as you travel through the maze, including animal, plant, or other spirit guides who might appear. Is it night or day? A particular season? Is one of your senses more acute than the others? Do you notice a predominance of any one color? If a detail catches your eye, ask reiki or any guides you meet for messages. What do you find at the center of the maze? Allow the experience to unfold naturally, and when you're done, see yourself standing at the entrance to the maze once more before returning to a normal state of consciousness.

- See the symbol in front of you, like a gateway of light, and step through it, entering your meditation. Exit through the same symbol to end the meditation.

Seeing Blind Spots

We all have gaps in our awareness, which can act as potholes, causing us to trip, often over the same things, again and again. The following meditation will help you partner with reiki to find and heal these blind spots. Keep in mind that you won't be seeing *all* your blind spots in a single session, rather reiki will lead you to the areas that are most in need of attention right now. Begin with hands in gasshô, taking a few breaths to calm and center yourself, then begin the Seventh Level Technique (page 238). In your mind's eye, see a path taking shape. It might be a dirt trail, gravel, asphalt, and so on. Make note of any details that seem important as you step onto the path. Draw Symbol One in front of you, stepping through with the intention of being guided to your blind spots that are most in need of healing right now. Begin to walk on the path. Stop when you reach a pothole, mirage, obstruction, or other area that you intuitively recognize as a blind spot.

Conjure up the image of a lantern, flashlight, candle, or magnifying glass, intending that this instrument be made of reiki, and use it to explore the blind spot. What do you see? What do you feel? Do any memories or thoughts arise? Ask any questions you might have. When you feel ready, dissolve the instrument you created, reabsorbing the energy, and place your hands over the blind spot, allowing reiki to flow. You can also stand in or near the spot, allowing reiki to radiate out of your entire body, filling the area with its light. Continue until the spot feels healed, and return the way that you came, bringing yourself back to a normal state of consciousness. Bring hands into gasshô and give thanks. Take some time to journal about the experience. What do you know about yourself that you didn't before? Find ways to integrate this new awareness into your daily life. Is there an action you can take, a habit that wants to be shifted, a conversation that needs to take place? Embody this forgotten part of you in whatever ways feel best.

Seiheki Chiryô (Habit-Healing Technique)

Choose an affirmation to work with. It should be worded in the first person and in the present tense. For example, "I am in the process of positive change," or "I am healing on all levels." Then, place your non-dominant hand on your forehead and the other hand on the back of your head. Focus intently on your affirmation while allowing reiki to flow for a few minutes, then release concentration on the affirmation and continue giving reiki until the process feels complete.

Deprogramming Technique

This is an alternate version of seiheki chiryô using the traditional symbols. Choose an affirmation, then draw Symbol Four, Symbol Three, and Symbol Two on the head. I find this difficult to do on myself, so two options that work just as well in my experience are, one, draw the symbols on your non-dominant palm before placing it on your forehead, or two, look at yourself in a mirror and draw the symbols on your head in the reflection. Place the non-dominant palm on your forehead and the other hand on the back of the head, seeing reiki fill your entire being, especially the head. State the affirmation three times, and repeat this exercise for six consecutive days.

Magickal Practices

Entire books could be written on the topic of integrating reiki into a magickal practice, and indeed, they already have. One great reference is Christopher Penczak's *Magick of Reiki*. Here, I present a handful of ways to get started, but let the creative energy flow and use your intuition to weave reiki into your magick however you like. I incorporate reiki into virtually all aspects of my spiritual practice, and it can be incorporated into a wide variety of magickal pursuits, such as:

- Cleansing self and space before casting a circle for ritual
- Cleansing your altar and magickal tools
- Enhancing meditation and out-of-body experiences
- Protection when exploring new techniques or new spiritual realms
- Boosting energy flow, such as during ritual or spellcasting

• • • • • • • •

- Connecting with spirit guides
- Enhancing the efficacy of potions, herbal sachets, magickal inks, incense, and so on.
- Charging crystals, talismans, and amulets
- Activating psychic abilities: for example, before using divination tools

Spellwork

One of the components of successful spellcasting is raising energy to fuel your spell, and reiki is a wonderful way of doing so. There are many ways to perform spells, but here we'll look at the basic steps in casting a petition spell with reiki.

1. Write down the desired outcome. This should be specific, so rather than casting a spell for "abundance" or "health," use language that clearly states your desire: "I have a new car that is perfect for me in every way" or "My [body part or system] is perfectly healthy." Another way to develop your wording is to ask yourself, "How will I know when my spell has been fulfilled?" Describe whatever conditions will indicate the spell was a success and craft that into a concise statement.

2. Insert your statement into a petition. Here's the format that I learned from my teacher, Christopher Penczak, with some minor changes, but you can adapt as needed, substituting any higher powers that you work with, such as reiki, the universe, and so on: *I, [state your name], ask in the name of the Goddess, God, and the Great Spirit of Reiki to be granted [state your desired outcome]. I thank the Goddess, God, and Reiki, and I ask that this be correct and for the highest good, harming none. And so it is.*

3. Take a piece of paper and charge it with reiki by holding it in both hands, allowing reiki to flow. Write your spell on the paper, then draw Symbol One over the paper with your finger, chanting the mantra three times with the intention that your spell unfolds in the highest way possible.

4. You can prepare a sacred space using the method for purifying space on page 214, the circle-casting steps in Working with Spirit Guides on page 255, or the Crystal Healing Circle on page 301. I find this enhances my ability to build and temporarily contain energy prior to releasing during spell casting. Cleanse yourself using kenyoku hô (page 229).

5. Perform jôshin kokyû hô (page 230), and concentrate on creating a cone or ball of energy, which expands in strength and power with each exhale.

6. Continue until it feels like the energy is ready to "pop," then loudly, confidently read your petition spell three times. Immediately release the energy with a forceful exhale, perhaps tossing your arms up into the air and turning your face up to the sky, seeing and feeling the energy traveling out into the cosmos, carrying out your spell. Bring your hands into gasshô,

• • • • • • • •

signaling that you are letting go of attachment to the energy, allowing the spell to unfold in the best way possible.

7. In the days to come, resist obsessing over your spell, which can serve to call the energy back to you. Use techniques like tanden chiryô hô (page 232) to calm and center yourself whenever you're tempted to worry about the outcome.

Protection Magick

In my experience, the best form of protection magick is regular self-care and healthy boundaries, but sometimes it's useful to boost our natural protection, and the following is an easy yet powerful way of doing so.

Start by performing kenyoku hô (page 229), intending that you are releasing all things that no longer serve your highest good. Visualize a rain of reiki falling gently over you, permeating your entire body and energy field with light. Starting in front of your body, use both index fingers to trace the Angel Wings symbol (page 176). Begin with each finger at the end of the spirals, tracing the path around until both fingers meet at the top of the symbol. Turn to your right and repeat. Make two more turns to draw the symbol on all four sides, returning to face the front once more. You can also draw the symbol above and below, if you like. Close your eyes, hands in gasshô, and set the intention that reiki protects you from harm on all levels. Give thanks.

Using a Pendulum

I love using a pendulum to connect with my higher self and spirit guides, and I have a necklace that doubles as a pendulum, allowing me to use it on the go. You can buy pendulums at metaphysical stores or make your own. You'll need a chain or cord—mine is about two feet long, which works really well for me. Play around with different lengths, but I've noticed that too-short chains or cords can restrict movement in a way I don't like. Choose an object to string on the cord. It should have a little bit of weight to it (i.e., not a feather) so it's easier to sense when and how it's moving. Cleanse the pendulum using jakikiri jôka hô (page 232), and as you give reiki, set the intention that the pendulum will connect you with your higher self and higher guides.

The first time you use it (or anytime you're working with new guides), establish what "yes" and "no" answers look like. Hold the pendulum in one hand (I favor my dominant hand, but the opposite is true for some practitioners), and loop the chain or cord over your hand once so the chain is secure without needing to grasp it. Let your muscles relax, and ask to be shown what a "yes" response looks like. Wait for the pendulum to move, indicating the pattern corresponding to an affirmative answer. Do the same for a "no" response.

You can use your pendulum in any number of ways, starting, of course, by asking any yes-or-no questions you have. Rather than letting the pendulum dictate your choices, see this as a

· · · · · · · ·

way of cutting through the clutter and getting clear on what your higher self thinks in order to support informed decision-making. I've used my pendulum to check in with my body, to see if a particular food or supplement would be good for me, to choose tarot cards, essential oils, crystals, and so forth. You can also go on a "spiritual hike" with your pendulum when you want to deepen the connection to your intuition. Whenever you come to a crossroads in the trail, use the pendulum to choose a direction, perhaps combining this with the sensory explorations on pages 64–66. This is a great way to practice honoring your intuition in a low-stakes manner, making it easier to do so with more important decisions.

Sound Therapy

Humans have been using sound to heal and connect with one another throughout history, beginning with claps and percussive body movements; humming, chanting, singing, and speaking; and the drumming and songs of shamans. Sound is a vibration that travels through the air or another medium, like water, in the form of a wave, and we perceive these waves as sounds via the ear, but they can often be felt by other parts of the body as well. Sound is measured in terms of cycles per second, known as *hertz*. Like any other wave, a sound wave consists of crests and troughs, and you can think of a hertz as "the number of waves that reach your ear in one second."[156]

Resonance is an important principle in sound healing, and it can occur in different ways: On a basic level, the vibrations of one body can travel to another body and set off matching vibrations. This is known as *free resonance*. When a body sends out vibrations, they can trigger vibrations in another body that aren't an exact match, but instead are in harmony with the original vibration. This is known as *sympathetic resonance*. And finally, certain bodies (the human body being one example) are able to resonate at a variety of frequencies, and this is known as *forced resonance*. The word *entrainment* is often used in conjunction with resonance, and this occurs when one object's powerful vibrations changes the vibration of another object, causing it to vibrate in sync with the first. "Our internal biological rhythms are also subject to entrainment. Our heart rate, breathing rate, and brain wave activity all entrain with each other in a powerful feedback loop."[157]

One possible mechanism for sound's healing effects is described by Bruce Lipton in *The Biology of Belief*. He writes that various receptor antennae existing on the outer membrane of cells are able to "read vibrational energy fields such as light, sound, and radio frequencies. The antennas on these energy receptors vibrate like tuning forks. If an energy vibration in the environ-

156. Joshua Goldman and Alec W. Sims, *Sound Healing for Beginners: Using Vibration to Harmonize Your Health and Wellness* (Woodbury, MN: Llewellyn, 2016), 35.
157. Goldman and Sims, *Sound Healing for Beginners*, 42.

ment resonates with a receptor's antenna, it will alter the protein's charge, causing the receptor to change shape.… Biological behavior can be controlled by invisible forces as well as it can be controlled by physical molecules."[158]

Healing through Humming

Humming is perhaps one of the easiest ways to explore sound healing, and studies have shown it to be effective in lowering blood pressure and heart rate; increasing lymphatic circulation; boosting melatonin levels, which can help to relieve insomnia, improve immune function, and decrease inflammation; and generating natural endorphins, neurotransmitters that block pain and contribute to feelings of happiness.[159] To experiment with humming, try using the sounds associated with the seven chakras in the Hindu system. Below, I've listed both the *seed sound* (single-word mantras said to activate energy) and the vowel sound for each chakra. Begin by bringing your hands into gasshô and taking some deep, calming breaths. You might also open your connection to your chakras with a technique like chakra kassei kokyû hô (page 236).

Root Chakra: LAM (pronounced *lum*, rhymes with *drum*) or O (as in hope)

Navel Chakra: VUM (pronounced *vum*, rhymes with *drum*) or OO (as in due)

Solar Plexus Chakra: RAM (pronounced *rum*) or A (as in father)

Heart Chakra: YAM (pronounced *yum* as in yummy) or AY (as in day)

Throat Chakra: HAM (pronounced *hum* as in humming) or EE (as in free)

Third Eye Chakra: OM (pronounced *aum*) or U (as in glue)

Crown Chakra: Silence (some traditions associate this chakra with OM)

Tuning Forks

Another tool for working with healing sound is a tuning fork. These can be found at metaphysical stores and online, and they're available singly or in sets. Sound healer Eileen Day McKusick, author of *Tuning the Human Biofield*, recommends aluminum, not steel, and machined, not molded, forks for the best sound quality and healing effects.[160] One way to use tuning forks in your reiki practice is in conjunction with byôsen reikan hô (page 67). After scanning the body with your hands, looking for energetic imbalances, use a tuning fork on any areas you find by striking the fork and holding it over the area. For areas that seem especially stuck, give hands-on

158. Bruce H. Lipton, *The Biology of Belief: Unleashing the Power of Consciousness, Matter & Miracles* (Carlsbad, CA: Hay House, 2016), 82.

159. Jonathan Goldman and Andi Goldman, *The Humming Effect: Sound Healing for Health and Happiness* (Rochester, VT: Healing Arts, 2017), 26–35.

160. Eileen Day McKusick, *Tuning the Human Biofield: Healing with Vibrational Sound Therapy* (Rochester, VT: Healing Arts Press, 2014), 259.

· · · · · · · ·

reiki first and then use the fork. You can also purchase sets of forks tuned to the frequency of individual chakras, which would be wonderful to use with a technique like chakra kassei kokyû hô (page 236).

Singing Bowls

The most common form of singing bowl is a Tibetan singing bowl made from metal, although crystal singing bowls are also quite lovely to work with. Sound is created either by striking the bowl to create a single sound or by running the striker or mallet around the rim of the bowl, creating continuous sound via friction. Bowls come in a range of sizes (available singly or in sets), each creating a different sound, and they may be unadorned or decorated with sacred symbols, patterns, and other imagery. Unless you need a bowl that creates a specific note, use your intuition to choose the best bowl for you. Before using a bowl for the first time, I like to cleanse it using jakikiri jôka hô (page 232), and I also do this periodically, just as I do with crystals. To heal with bowls, you can simply play the bowl and allow the sound to wash through your body, perhaps bringing you into a meditative state where further healing can transpire. This is really wonderful at the start of a reiki treatment. You can also tone a bowl and place it directly on the body for a "sonic massage." I like to use bowls to start and end meditations or reiki practices, such as in conjunction with hatsurei hô (page 229).

Reiki Mantras

Traditional reiki practice offers us a powerful method for healing with sound: mantras. Chanting the mantras, either in repetitions of three or continuously for a period of time, is a great way of clearing your energy and going deeper with the teachings. I find the latter to be especially true when chanting continuously. After a number of repetitions, my awareness shifts and it's as if I can hear between or beyond the sound. I encourage you to experiment with chanting the mantras (I like to focus on one at a time) to see how they affect you. You can also work with the five precepts (page 217) and waka (page 222), reciting them at the start of healings, attunements, or meditation sessions to clear and focus the mind.

This chapter is merely a taste of the myriad ways of integrating reiki into other healing practices, and I have found that the more I work with reiki, the more the energy itself leads me intuitively to new applications. I have a reiki journal where I record what works (and for what circumstances) and what flops so I can refine my practice over time. Reiki is meant to be lived, and we can enrich our practice by weaving this powerful energy into everything we do, working with mindfulness and curiosity. Have fun, and don't be afraid to experiment!

CHAPTER 22

⁂

Other Healing Modalities

There are many different systems of vibrational medicine, and you might choose to comple-ment your reiki practice with study in another branch of energy healing. This section will give you an overview of the more well-known systems.

Barbara Brennan School of Healing

Brennan, whose work was discussed in the chapters on auras and chakras, created an energy healing school for the study of human energy fields and systems and hands-on techniques for healing and personal transformation. Brennan, a former NASA physicist, spent decades research-ing and working with the human energy field, developing a system for perceiving energy, diag-nosing imbalances, and facilitating healing through hands-on techniques. The school offers a Bachelor of Science degree in Brennan Healing Science and a diploma in the Brennan Healing Science Professional Studies, with instruction covering a variety of topics, such as anatomy and physiology of the human energy field, healing with color and sound, ethics and professional boundaries, and self-care for healers.

Craniosacral Therapy

Cranial osteopathy was developed by William Garner Sutherland, DO, who, in studying the cranium, posited that the bones were not ossified and rigidly held in place, as was the con-sensus view of the time, but rather were designed for respiratory motion, which he called the "Primary Respiratory Mechanism."[161] Through light touch, a practitioner can sense the move-ments of contraction and expansion, influenced by the fluctuating flow of cerebrospinal fluid

---

161. Michael J. Shea, *Biodynamic Craniosacral Therapy*, vol. 1 (Berkeley, CA: North Atlantic Books, 2007), 3.

(the "cranial wave"), and reintroduce functional movement as needed to return the system to balance. Sutherland's methods were further developed by Dr. John Upledger, founder of the Upledger Institute International and creator of CranioSacral Therapy. The method has been adapted in various ways by other practitioners, such as Hugh Milne, creator of Visionary Craniosacral Work, and Franklyn Sills, founder of Biodynamic Craniosacral Therapy. Craniosacral therapy works to bring the entire human system into balance, mirroring our discussion of the holographic perspective of healing in chapter 4. Hugh Milne writes, "Craniosacral work is based on the understanding that any one bone is a hologram of the … mind-body-spirit unity. When it is balanced, it exerts a profound balancing effect on the whole."[162]

Eden Energy Medicine

Created by healer and clairvoyant Donna Eden, Eden Energy Medicine blends techniques from yoga, acupuncture, qigong, and other modalities to return the human energy system to a state of balance and health. According to Eden Energy Medicine, there are nine major systems composing the human energetic anatomy, many of which have been covered elsewhere in this text. The meridians are responsible for moving energy throughout the entire system as needed, including bringing in nourishment and removing waste. The chakras are energetic hubs, each of which resonates with a different frequency of energy, therefore influencing different areas of life experience, such as relationships, sexuality, communication, and psychic development. The aura is the multilayered container of the human energy system, each layer corresponding to different functions; the Celtic weave patterns and brings together your different energy systems, creating harmonious communication and dynamic equilibrium when it is functioning properly; and the electrics "emerge from the electrical dimension" of the body's various energy systems, and they "serve as a bridge that connects all the energy systems."[163] The Basic Grid is what Eden describes as "the foundation of your energy centers," and she perceives it as a graph of intersecting lines.[164] Unlike the chakras, which interface with energies in the surrounding environment, the Basic Grid is entirely contained within the body, and issues at this level can severely compromise the other energy systems. The Five Rhythms aren't a distinct energetic system but, as the name suggests, a rhythm that runs throughout the body's energies, and they are synonymous with the five phases or five seasons of Traditional Chinese Medicine. Eden describes them as leaving a "vibratory imprint on your physical attributes, health patterns, and personality traits."[165] The

162. Hugh Milne, *The Heart of Listening: A Visionary Approach to Craniosacral Work*, vol. 1 (Berkeley, CA: North Atlantic Books, 1998), 6.
163. Eden and Feinstein, *Energy Medicine*, 196 and 198.
164. Eden and Feinstein, *Energy Medicine*, 204.
165. Eden and Feinstein, *Energy Medicine*, 213.

Triple Warmer is found in Traditional Chinese Medicine, and it is considered to be both a meridian and a radiant circuit, which is more diffuse than a meridian and connects various energetic pathways and centers together. Eden also sees Triple Warmer as intimately connected with the immune system, helping the body ward off invaders while ensuring this response doesn't go into hyperdrive, resulting in allergies or autoimmune disorders. And finally, the radiant circuits are tasked with harmonizing all the organs and energy systems, redistributing energy where it is most needed and coordinating the various functions within a living system. Eden Energy Medicine works to bring balance to these nine systems through various hands-on techniques and simple movement exercises.

Emotional Freedom Technique (EFT)

EFT combines principles from Traditional Chinese Medicine and acupressure with affirmations, and it was pioneered by psychologist Roger Callahan, who paired different ailments with specific tapping sequences based on the Chinese system of meridians. The tapping was performed in conjunction with different statements or thoughts, and he called the system Thought Field Therapy. One of his students, Gary Craig, went on to simplify the tapping sequence and affirmations, making it more accessible for laypeople and creating the Emotional Freedom Technique (EFT). It is said to support health by maintaining or reintroducing a healthy flow of energy through the meridian system, and practitioners recommend tapping daily to reap the most benefit.[166] See page 247 for a tapping exercise.

Traditional tapping is usually paired with an affirmation using the following phrasing: "Even though [state issue], I deeply and completely love and accept myself." For example, "Even though I feel fearful about my doctor's appointment, I deeply and completely love and accept myself," or "Even though I have a strong desire to overeat, I deeply and completely love and accept myself." Ideally, the affirmations are stated aloud as you move through the tapping sequence, but you can also say the affirmations silently if you don't have privacy. EFT is currently being used for a variety of applications, such as pain management, weight loss, and treatment of depression, anxiety, and PTSD.

Energy Medicine Yoga

Created by Lauren Walker, a student of Donna Eden and yoga teacher Rod Stryker, Energy Medicine Yoga combines Eden's energy healing techniques with mat-based yoga sequences. In addition to traditional yoga poses, or asanas, EM Yoga incorporates tapping, holding, stretching,

---

166. *EFT and Tapping for Beginners: The Essential EFT Manual to Start Relieving Stress, Losing Weight, and Healing* (Berkeley, CA: Rockridge Press, 2013), 11.

· · · · · · · ·

and massaging of acupressure points to facilitate a clear flow of energy.[167] Walker offers EM Yoga teacher trainings and is the author of *Energy Medicine Yoga* and *The Energy Medicine Yoga Prescription*.

5Rhythms

Developed by Gabrielle Roth, 5Rhythms is a movement practice centered on the embodiment of the following rhythms: flowing, staccato, chaos, lyrical, and stillness. Flowing is associated with flexibility, surrender, fluidity, and connection to one's inner truth. Staccato is all about boundaries and strength, connection to the world through the heart, and the inner warrior standing up for one's values. Chaos is associated with release, letting go, and breaking free of limitations and illusions to make deeper contact with one's authentic nature. Lyrical is the emergence from chaos, where one has broken free of destructive patterns and is aligned with the fundamental pulse of existence. Stillness merges the experience of duality—receptive and active, stillness and motion—distilling one's life experiences into a higher wisdom.[168] Classes are available through the Moving Center, founded by Roth in 1977, and at locations worldwide.

Healing Touch

Created in the 1980s by nurse Janet Mentgen, Healing Touch utilizes intentional, heart-centered touch to bring harmony and balance to the human biofield. Similar to a reiki treatment, recipients often experience a sense of deep calm and relaxation. At times, symptoms may briefly intensify as healing is initiated and accelerated. Certification courses are available through the Healing Touch Program and cover a range of topics, such as energy anatomy, how to perform hands-on healing for self and others, meditation techniques, and performing Healing Touch case studies.

Polarity Therapy

This healing system was developed by Dr. Randolph Stone, a doctor of osteopathy, naturopathy, and chiropractic, who believed that life energy was composed of the elements of ether, air, fire, water, and earth. Each of these elements flows from opposing positive and negative poles aligned around a neutral center, and practitioners use bodywork and exercises to bring balance to an individual's life energy. Bodywork incorporates rocking, stretching, and acupressure techniques, while the exercises combine sound, breath, and self-massage. By balancing our personal

167. Lauren Walker, *Energy Medicine Yoga: Amplify the Healing Power of Your Yoga Practice* (Boulder, CO: Sounds True, 2014), 18.
168. Gabrielle Roth and John Loudon, *Maps to Ecstasy: Teachings of an Urban Shaman* (London: Thorsons, 1995), 54.

· · · · · · · ·

energy, we are able to respond to life experiences with greater equanimity, creativity, flexibility, and resilience.[169]

Pranic Healing

Founded by Choa Kok Sui, a Chinese-Filipino energy healer, Pranic Healing teaches a precise method, called scanning, for identifying energetic disturbances, which are classified as congestions, or energy blockages, and depletions, or energy deficiencies, and sweeping or energizing techniques are used to treat each condition, respectively. Specific healing sequences are employed to target the largest meridians, along which the major chakras lie, to produce the maximum benefit in less time.[170] Pranic Healing courses are available worldwide.

Pulsed Electromagnetic Field Therapy (PEMF)

In PEMF, a pulsing magnetic field with a precise intensity and frequency is applied to the body using different tools, from a pinpointed "pen" device to a full-body mat, and it is used to treat a variety of conditions and to maintain general health. On a cellular level, PEMF is said to improve the production of ATP (a molecule that provides energy for many of life's vital processes), increase oxygenation, enhance circulation and hydration, support detoxification, and improve nutrient absorption. PEMF has been extensively studied, and the FDA has approved various PEMF devices to fuse broken bones, accelerate wound healing, boost tissue growth, and treat depression, among other applications.[171]

Qigong and Tai Chi

Both qigong and tai chi are movement practices that work with chi or qi (energy), and they both incorporate breathing and meditation techniques. *Qigong* can be translated as "working with life energy," and it can be divided into two main categories: *dong gong*, which is more active, and *jing gong*, which is more passive. In the former, the body is visibly moving, while in jing gong, the body is still and qi is moved through precise breathwork, visualization, and mental focus. Qigong can be further categorized by application, such as medical qigong and martial qigong. One form is of particular interest due to its parallels with reiki practice: external qi healing, or *Wai Qi Zhi Liao*, which is the hands-on practice of transmitting qi for healing purposes.[172]

---

169. John Beaulieu, *Polarity Therapy Workbook*, 2nd ed. (Pennsauken, NJ: BookBaby, 2016), 14.

170. Stephen Co, Eric B. Robins, and John Merryman, *Your Hands Can Heal You: Pranic Healing Energy Remedies to Boost Vitality and Speed Recovery from Common Health Problems* (New York: Atria Paperback, 2002), 34.

171. Bryant A. Meyers, *PEMF—The Fifth Element of Health: Learn Why Pulsed Electromagnetic Field Therapy (PEMF) Supercharges Your Health Like Nothing Else!* (Bloomington, IN: Balboa Press, 2014), 12.

172. Kenneth S. Cohen, *The Way of Qigong* (New York: Random House International, 2000), 4–5.

* * * * * * *

Tai chi can be loosely translated as "The Grand Ultimate" or "The Superior Ultimate," and it is a form of martial arts that, like qigong, utilizes slow, flowing movements.[173] There are different styles of tai chi, named after their founders: Yang, Chen, Wu (or Hao), and Sun.[174] Precise movements are performed in set sequences, or forms, which are designed to cultivate and move chi throughout the body, removing energy blockages, and with practice, building power, coordination, and vitality.

Quantum-Touch

Created by Richard Gordon, this system utilizes life force energy to facilitate healing, and it is said to be useful in treating a myriad of conditions, such as scoliosis and other structural alignment issues, mental-emotional conditions, infections, cancer, and chronic pain. It is said to integrate well with other modalities, from reiki to chiropractic medicine, enhancing their effects, but it can also be used as a standalone treatment. Practitioners use breath and meditation techniques to raise the energetic vibration of their hands, which can then be used to elevate the client's frequency through the principles of resonance and entrainment.[175] Quantum-Touch teaches that we all have the ability to self-heal; hands-on healing for another is meant to facilitate and support this innate process. Thought is also an important component of the practice, as energy is seen to follow and patterns itself around our thoughts. By using intention and meditation techniques, thoughts can be a tool to elevate one's energy frequency, inducing healing.[176] Quantum-Touch training and a directory of certified practitioners can be found at www.quantumtouch.com.

Shamanic Techniques

Shaman is a Tungus word used by the Ural-Altaic tribal people of Siberia to describe someone who "enters a state of altered consciousness—at will—to contact and utilize an ordinarily hidden reality in order to aquire knowledge, power, and to help other persons."[177] The term is now widely used by practitioners of non-Siberian descent, although some anthropologists and modern practitioners have adopted the term "core shamanism" to differentiate the use of shamanic techniques, which are practiced by many cultures worldwide, from traditional Siberian shamanism.[178] These techniques involve the ability to enter what Michael Harner, anthropologist and founder of the Foundation for Shamanic Studies, refers to as a Shamanic State of Conscious-

173. Therese Iknoian and Manny Fuentes, *Tai Chi for Dummies* (New York: John Wiley & Sons, 2001), 14.
174. Iknoian and Fuentes, *Tai Chi for Dummies*, 48.
175. Richard Gordon, *Quantum-Touch: The Power to Heal* (Berkeley, CA: North Atlantic Books, 2006), 17.
176. Gordon, *Quantum-Touch*, 26.
177. Michael Harner, *The Way of the Shaman* (New York: HarperOne, 2011), 25.
178. Christopher Penczak, *The Temple of Shamanic Witchcraft: Shadows, Spirits, and the Healing Journey* (Woodbury, MN: Llewellyn Publications, 2010), 2.

ness (SSC). This mode of non-ordinary awareness allows the shaman to access hidden realms of reality that contain information and power, often sourced from animals, plants, and spirits, which can effect positive change, typically in the form of healing (physical, mental-emotional, and spiritual). Accessing the SSC is done through a variety of means, including meditation and breathwork, fasting, drumming and other sounds, ritual dance or other movements, and plant substances. See page 346 for a discussion of shamanic reiki.

ThetaHealing

Created by Vianna Stibal, ThetaHealing utilizes meditation techniques to enter a theta brain wave state, which is characterized by a frequency of around 6 to 7 hertz and a feeling of deep relaxation. In this state, one can release limiting beliefs and initiate healing on a physical, mental-emotional, and spiritual level. ThetaHealing also involves a process known as DNA activation, which is said to turn on dormant portions of genetic material, which leads to enhanced healing and intuition, accelerated detoxification, and the ability to access different planes of existence.[179] Stibal names seven planes, each of which has a distinct energetic vibration or frequency, from the first plane, which contains all the inorganic material on earth, to the seventh plane, the plane of the "Creator of All That Is" and the source of all energy. It is at the seventh plane that one can tap into immense source energy and transcend many of the limitations inherent in the lower planes.[180] The ThetaHealing organization offers classes for practitioners and a directory of certified ThetaHealers.

Touch for Health (TFH)

This modality is based on the work of chiropractor George Goodheart, who developed a system he dubbed applied kinesiology, which uses muscle testing as a way of diagnosing energy flow within the body. In massage school, an instructor demonstrated one way that she used muscle testing in her chiropractic work: She had the patient hold a bottle of supplements in one hand, close to their chest. Then, the patient extended their other arm in front of their body, and if the arm yielded easily when the doctor pressed down on it, the supplement in question was not recommended for this particular patient. If, however, the arm remained firm, the supplement was a good match. I might not have believed this had I not experienced it firsthand. While holding what turned out to be an ill-matched supplement for my body, when my instructor pressed down on my arm, in spite of my best efforts, it collapsed by my side like a wet noodle. When holding the

179. Vianna Stibal, *ThetaHealing: Introducing an Extraordinary Energy Healing Modality* (Carlsbad, CA: Hay House, 2012), 2.
180. Vianna Stibal, *Seven Planes of Existence: The Philosophy of the ThetaHealing Technique* (London: Hay House, 2016), 3.

appropriate supplement, however, my arm remained rigid and firm with little conscious effort on my part. Touch for Health uses the principles of applied kinesiology as further developed by Dr. John Thie (and later, his son Matthew Thie) to diagnose a wide range of imbalances. A sequence of muscles is tested, each corresponding to different Chinese meridians, and weakness in a particular muscle indicates an imbalance in the corresponding meridian. Balancing exercises, which include simple movements or holding of acupressure points, are used, after which the muscle is retested. Classes are available through the Touch for Health Kinesiology Association.

Reiki practice is meant to be lived, and sometimes this path will lead you to integrating reiki with other modalities, such as the ones covered in this chapter. Follow your intuition and give yourself permission to explore new ways of weaving reiki into diverse practices and healing traditions.

Conclusion

Reiki has the power to transform your life from the inside out, and the more you interact with this energy, the more profound and far-reaching the changes will be. My hope is that you will use the information in these pages to weave reiki into your daily life, from your morning commute to the moments before sleep. Reiki is a divinely intelligent energy flow that knows precisely what we need in each moment, and when we embody reiki, we tap into our own divine intelligence. This then guides us through the choices that are most in alignment with our highest good, leading to greater physical health, mental-emotional balance and resilience, and spiritual aliveness.

Know that reiki is always available to you—*healing is your birthright*. I wish you all the best on your journey!

APPENDIX A

Students of Hayashi and Takata

In our discussion of the history of reiki, we looked at three of the most important figures within the system of reiki: Mikao Usui, its founder, and Chûjirô Hayashi, one of Usui's students, who went on to teach Hawayo Takata, who was responsible for reiki's initial transmission to the West. In this section, we'll look at the different branches of reiki that have sprung directly from this original source, and in appendix B we'll look at further offshoots from these primary branches.

Chûjirô Hayashi, one of Usui's students, went on to teach, among many others, two women who are relevant to our discussion: Hawayo Takata and Chiyoko Yamaguchi. We'll look at Yamaguchi first, as Takata's "branch" leads to many sub-branches that we will discuss below.

The Yamaguchis: Jikiden Reiki

Chiyoko Yamaguchi took Reiki One and Two with Hayashi, and she and her son, Tadao Yamaguchi, went on to create what is now known as *Jikiden Reiki*, with Jikiden translated as "directly transmitted or passed down from one's teacher," in this case, Chûjirô Hayashi.[181] The Yamaguchis aim to replicate Hayashi's original teachings as closely as possible based on information from Chiyoko, as well as other family members who attended Hayashi's seminars. Tadao acknowledges that it is impossible to recreate the experience in full, but he strives to carry on the original teachings as best as possible.

Returning now to Hawayo Takata, the reiki tree branches into multiple offshoots, as many of Takata's master-level students went on to create their own system of reiki. To learn more about Takata, please refer back to chapter 7.

---

181. Yamaguchi, *Light on the Origins of Reiki*, 18.

• • • • • • • •

Phyllis Lei Furumoto: Usui Shiki Ryôhô

After Hawayo Takata's death, her granddaughter, Phyllis Lei Furumoto, hosted a gathering of Takata's master-teachers, and during this meeting, they compared class notes and decided to standardize the symbols. This group eventually became known as the Reiki Alliance, and Furumoto was given the title of Office of the Grandmaster (OGM), defined by the group as the "lineage bearer of the system of Reiki."[182] They called their system *Usui Shiki Ryôhô*, and there are four aspects to the practice: healing practice, personal development, spiritual discipline, and mystic order.[183] Healing practice centers around self-healing, augmented by giving treatments to friends and family and receiving treatments from others. Throughout this, the student undergoes personal development, perhaps by becoming more sensitive to the body's needs and making healthy changes, uncovering latent gifts, or finding meaningful work in alignment with the True Self. Spiritual discipline supports this change and growth, and students are asked to build and maintain a practice that deeply nourishes their whole being. And finally, the group defines a mystic order as a "group of people who share a common practice that brings them through experience to a reality beyond the realm of the five senses," and they see the touch aspect of reiki as a gateway to deeper union with the self and all beings.[184]

Beth Gray and John Harvey Gray

Beth and John lived in San Francisco and were students and practitioners of various metaphysical systems before studying reiki. Beth became a minister of the Universal Church of the Master, taking over a local chapter of the church as pastor in 1973. Initially, the services included a healing meditation, during which healers would demonstrate various techniques. John Harvey writes, "About one-third of the healers felt worse at the end of the healing meditation, while there seemed to be little improvement in the health of those who sat for healings."[185] It was during this time that the Grays first heard about Takata through a man named Wally Richardson, who was planning to host Takata in his home so she could teach reiki while visiting California. The Grays took the introductory level course with Takata and were attuned to reiki.

Shortly thereafter, they offered to host Takata's classes in their own home in Woodside, California, and during the next several years Takata would stay with them and teach, en route to visiting her daughter in Iowa. John became a master-teacher in 1976, and Beth's students claim that

---

182. Stiene and Stiene, *The Reiki Sourcebook*, 188.

183. "Four Aspects," Usui Shiki Ryoho, accessed June 2, 2019, https://www.usuishikiryohoreiki.com /usr-4%20aspects.htm.

184. "Four Aspects," Usui Shiki Ryoho, accessed June 2, 2019, https://www.usuishikiryohoreiki.com /usr-4%20aspects.htm.

185. "John Harvey Gray," The John Harvey Gray Center for Reiki Healing, accessed June 2, 2019, https:// learnreiki.org/reiki-master-teacher/john-harvey-gray.

· · · · · · ·

she received her master-teacher training at the same time; her official certificate is dated 1979. Beth taught Usui Shiki Ryôhô throughout the US and Australia and is said to have instructed over 20,000 level one and two students between 1973 and 1990.[186] John went on to create the John Harvey Gray Center for Reiki Healing, which teaches "the original Usui Reiki system, in its complete and authentic form and as further expanded by John Harvey Gray."[187]

Ethel Lombardi: MariEL

In 1983, Ethel Lombardi, one of Takata's master-teachers, diverged from the Reiki Alliance and created her own system of reiki: MariEL or Mari-EL, named after Mary in the Christian tradition. She taught only one teacher.[188] Information is difficult to track down, but various websites corroborate that the system was developed to balance patriarchal energies through the divine feminine. Healing focuses at the cellular level, as each cell is seen to hold memories, which, when negative, can block the flow of energy. Practitioner and client work together to release these memories and harmonize energy flow. Reiki master and scholar Robert Fueston writes that Lombardi was already a well-known healer in Chicago before studying with Takata.[189]

Barbara Weber Ray: The Radiance Technique

Weber was one of the few master-teachers who was not present at the initial meeting of what is now the Reiki Alliance. She claimed to be Takata's successor, which was disputed by the group, and went on to create the Radiance Technique, also referred to as Authentic Reiki and Real Reiki. In 1983, Weber published a book, *The Reiki Factor*, which triggered a resurgence of interest in reiki in Japan, thanks to the efforts of one of her students, journalist Mieko Mitsui (see chapter 7). In the first edition of the book, three levels of study are described, but this was later expanded to seven levels. Traditional and non-traditional symbols are taught.

Iris Ishikuro (with Arthur Robertson): Raku Kei Reiki

Also known as the Way of the Fire Dragon, *Raku Kei Reiki* was developed by one of Takata's original master-teachers and cousins, Iris Ishikuro, and one of Iris's students, Arthur Robertson (Robertson also studied with Virginia Samdahl, another of Takata's master-teachers). It is claimed that the system originated in Tibet, and there are four levels, with the first two combined into one course. *Raku* refers to the vertical flow of energy in the body, and *kei* is the horizontal

186. Stiene and Stiene, *The Reiki Sourcebook*, 190.
187. "John Harvey Gray," The John Harvey Gray Center for Reiki Healing, accessed June 2, 2019, https://learnreiki.org/reiki-master-teacher/john-harvey-gray.
188. Stiene and Stiene, *The Reiki Sourcebook*, 208.
189. Robert N. Fueston, *The History and System of Usui Shiki Reiki Ryoho,* vol. 1 of *Reiki: Transmissions of Light* (Twin Lakes, WI: Lotus Press, 2017), 166, Kobo.

flow. "Master Frequency plates" incorporating the *antahkarana* symbol are utilized to switch the polarity of the body, in addition to the use of other non-traditional methods, such as Breath of the Fire Dragon (page 235), chakra techniques, and the Johrei symbol ("white light symbol").[190]

Other Students of Takata

The rest of Takata's original twenty-two master-teachers went on to practice and/or teach in a variety of ways, but for some, very little information is known. Here is a bit about each of them:

- Before studying with Takata, Dr. George Araki founded the Institute of Holistic Health Studies in 1974, which is still in operation today at San Francisco State University. He is one of the founding members of the Reiki Alliance. Dr. Araki retired from the university in 1999 and passed away in 2006.

- Dorothy Baba was one of the master-teachers to attend the first meeting of the organization that was to become the Reiki Alliance. She was a social worker in Stockton, California, and passed away in 1985 after sustaining severe injuries in a car accident.[191]

- Ursula Baylow received her master attunement from Takata in either 1978 or 1979. Robert Fueston writes, "Takata secretly trained Ursula as a Master immediately after Ursula's Second Degree training in 1978," but she asked that Ursula not share this with anyone until, upon visiting with Ursula in 1979, Takata issued her master certificate, dated June 11, 1979. Baylow was the first reiki master in Canada; she also practiced reflexology.[192]

- Rick Bockner arranged a class of approximately fifty-four students in British Columbia to be taught by Takata in October of 1980, and a few days later, at Bethal Phaige's cabin, Bockner received his master attunement from Takata.[193] He is still active in the reiki community through his organization, Reiki Home.[194]

- Virginia Samdahl received her master attunement from Takata in 1976, prior to which she was a psychic healer in Chicago, Illinois. She introduced one of her students, Barbara Weber Ray, to Takata, and after Weber went on to form the American Reiki Alliance, Samdahl was initiated to the master level of Weber's system in 1981, before leaving the organization in 1983.[195]

---

190. Quest, *Reiki for Life*, 378.
191. Fueston, *The History and System of Usui Shiki Reiki Ryoho*, 175.
192. Fueston, *The History and System of Usui Shiki Reiki Ryoho*, 176.
193. Fueston, *The History and System of Usui Shiki Reiki Ryoho*, 183.
194. "Reiki Home: An Unfolding Journey," Reiki Home, accessed June 2, 2019, https://reikihome.org/.
195. Fueston, *The History and System of Usui Shiki Reiki Ryoho*, 151.

• • • • • • • •

- Patricia Bowling (Ewing) received her master attunement from Takata in 1980, and Fueston writes that she was also interested in meditation, channeling, soul retrieval, and other metaphysical modalities.[196]

- Barbara Brown received her master attunement from Takata in 1979 in British Columbia, Canada. She was one of the founding members of the Reiki Alliance, and she passed away in 2000.[197]

- Fran Brown received her master attunement from Takata in 1979 in Iowa, and she wrote the book *Living Reiki: Takata's Teachings*, published in 1992. She is the founder of the Reiki Center for Healing Arts. In 1999, she met with members of the Usui Reiki Ryôhô Gakkai in Japan, including Chiyoko Yamaguchi (see the earlier section on Jikiden Reiki), and she claims that, in comparing the teachings of the Gakkai with the material she learned from Takata, they found them to be similar: "Hayashi organized the hand placements taught by Usui so that it was easier to teach Reiki. Takata says that he never changed any of the teachings and asked her not to change them either, nor have I."[198] Brown passed away in 2009.

- Harry Masami Kuboi was attuned to the master level by Takata in 1977. A 2010 article by Susan Uyemura of the Japanese American Living Legacy describes Uyemura's interview with Kuboi at his home in Palolo Valley, Hawaii, during which they discussed Kuboi's psychic abilities, healing, and exorcisms. He published two books, *All of Reiki Book I* and *All of Reiki Book II*, along with an unpublished book called *Knowledge Beyond the Earthly Realm*, which expounds on his belief that 99 percent of human illness is caused by entities from other planets.[199] Kuboi passed away in 2013.

- Barbara Lincoln McCullough received her master attunement from Takata in 1977 in Iowa, and she taught a handful of students, including Helen Borth (1980), David G. Jarrell (1981), Judy Carol Stewart (1985), and Laryl Fett (1986).[200]

- Mary Alexandra McFadyen received her master attunement from Takata in 1980, and in 1990, she founded Reiki Outreach International, which describes its goal as "direct[ing] the healing energy of reiki in a specific healing transmission from thousands of practitioners every day toward famine, drought, flood, plagues, mass illness, wars, political turmoil, and

196. Fueston, *The History and System of Usui Shiki Reiki Ryoho*, 192.
197. Fueston, *The History and System of Usui Shiki Reiki Ryoho*, 183.
198. Fueston, *The History and System of Usui Shiki Reiki Ryoho*, 178.
199. Japanese American Living Legacy, "The Mystical World of Harry M. Kuboi: Reiki Master of Masters, Psychic and Professional Exorcist," news release, October 2010, http://www.jalivinglegacy.org/press/2010/12_Harry Kuboi.pdf.
200. Fueston, *The History and System of Usui Shiki Reiki Ryoho*, 174.

• • • • • • •

the suffering of all kind on the planet."[201] She was presumed dead in 2011, after a missing-person report was filed in Austin, Texas, where she lived.

• Paul David Mitchell received his master attunement from Takata in 1979 and was one of the founding members of the Reiki Alliance. In 1992, he became part of the Office of the Grand Master and was given the role of Head of the Discipline of Usui Shiki Ryôhô. Mitchell is the author of *The Usui System of Natural Healing*, sometimes referred to as the "blue book" of the Reiki Alliance, which includes content from Takata's diary. The version of the precepts given is slightly different from other sources: "Just for today do not worry. Just for today do not anger. Honor your parents, teachers, and elders. Earn your living honestly. Show gratitude to every living thing." Mitchell continues to travel and teach reiki around the world.

• Bethal Phaige ("Bethel" in some sources) was initiated to master level by Takata on 1979 (her certificate is dated 1980). She is the author of *Gestalt and the Wisdom of the Kahunas* (1983) and an unpublished work, *Journey into Consciousness*, in which she shared, "The lessons (in life that I needed to learn) may have been particularly painful because my initiations had been timed so closely together. I had left Hawaii that spring not knowing of Reiki. I return this winter as a Reiki Master, a very green one."[202]

• Shinobu Saito was attuned to the master level by Takata in 1980. Born in Japan, Saito survived the bombing of Hiroshima. She was a member of the Reiki Alliance and lived in Palo Alto, California.[203] Saito passed away in 2015.

• Wanja Twan, a founding member of the Reiki Alliance, received her master attunement from Takata in 1979 in British Columbia, with Bethal Phaige and Barbara Brown. Her daughter, Anneli Twan, compiled a series of interviews by a few of Takata's master-teachers, including Wanja Twan and Barbara Brown, entitled *Early Days of Reiki: Memories of Hawayo Takata*. Anneli was attuned to the master level by her mother in 1984 so she could assist in teaching courses.

• Takata's sister, Kay Yamashita, received her master attunement from Takata in 1975. According to Fueston, she may have been a member of the *Hayashi Reiki Kenkyû Kai* (research society) in Hawaii. John Harvey Gray was told by Takata that Yamashita was qualified to complete his master-level training, should anything happen to her.[204]

---

201. "Reiki Outreach International," The Reiki Association, accessed June 02, 2019, https://www.reiki association.net/reiki-outreach-international.php.

202. Stiene and Stiene, *The Reiki Sourcebook*, 365.

203. Fueston, *The History and System of Usui Shiki Reiki Ryoho*, 190.

204. Fueston, *The History and System of Usui Shiki Reiki Ryoho*, 163.

· · · · · · · ·

APPENDIX B

꧁

Other Branches of Reiki

In the previous section, we looked at students and branches of reiki with a direct connection to Chûjirô Hayashi and Hawayo Takata, and here, we'll explore the myriad reiki systems that have arisen from those initial offshoots. Keep in mind this isn't a 100 percent complete list of reiki systems, as there were some systems for which I could find nothing more than a name, and no doubt reiki branches exist without books, websites, or other publicly available sources of information.

Angelic RayKey: Sananda

This system is said to be the teachings of Archangel Michael as channeled by Sananda, and with the addition of the new material, she was guided to change the name to RayKey. There are three levels of study that incorporate a variety of non-traditional techniques, such as sealing the aura, healing with color, using intercessory prayer, and sending energy to individuals who have "crossed over."[205]

Ascension Reiki: Jayson Suttkus

There are ten levels of initiation in the Ascension Reiki system, which was developed by Jayson Suttkus, based on his work with the "Ascended Masters."[206] The different levels of initiation are said to attune various levels of the subtle anatomy as follows:

---

205. "Angelic RayKey—ARK," Of One Source, accessed June 2, 2019, https://ofonesource.com/school/class -list/reiki-and-angelic-raykey.

206. "Ascension Reiki," Ascension Reiki, accessed June 2, 2019, https://ascensionreiki.com/AscensionReiki -Introduction.html.

· · · · · · · ·

1. The Acting Body (conscious, unconscious, and physical body)

2. The Thinking Body (collective conscious, collective unconscious, seven auras, and five pranas)

3. The Feeling Body (universal conscious, universal unconscious, seven chakras along the spine, and five chakras on the front of the body)

4. The Karmic Body or Atmic Body (God conscious, God unconscious, eternal body, and the meridian system)

5. The Mind

6. The Soul

7. The Spirit

8. The Will

9. The Higher Self

10. The Sacred Heart

Celtic Reiki: Martyn Pentecost

This system originally used some of Usui's methods paired with "eighteen original essences," described as "the vibrations of trees," but over time the practice evolved until Pentecost reworked the teachings in 2009. On his website he writes, "Celtic Reiki Realm Mastery consists of different experiences and areas of knowledge, which combine into a powerful form of treatment style, method of spiritual growth, and personal-development system. These consist of: Essences, Techniques, Realms, Mystics, Lores, Orientations, and Calibrations." Training is divided into three programs: Foundation Mastery, Mystic Mastery, and Realm Mastery, with other courses offered on topics such as Celtic seership and karmic regression therapy.[207]

Gendai Reiki Hô: Hiroshi Doi

Hiroshi Doi was one of the first students of Mieko Mitsui, the journalist who has been credited with reimporting reiki to Japan in the 1980s. Mitsui was only permitted to attune students to levels one and two, so Doi began to search for teachers offering level three courses in Japan. He met Kimiko Koyama, the sixth president of the Usui Reiki Ryôhô Gakkai, and was permitted to join the Gakkai after being introduced by one of its members. He was taught and attuned by Koyama and was amazed at how different it was from the course he had taken with Mitsui. Interested in "whether Western reiki had improved or degenerated from Dento Reiki or had become a totally different practice," Doi also studied Neo Reiki in Osaka and attended many Western

---

207. "About," Celtic Reiki, accessed June 2, 2019, http://celtic-reiki.com/wp/index.php/about/.

reiki courses in Japan, including those taught by Frank Arjava Petter. [208] (*Dento Reiki* refers to the system practiced by the Usui Reiki Ryôhô Gakkai, as inherited from Mikao Usui.)

Doi eventually developed the system of Gendai Reiki Hô, which he defines as "a practical Reiki method for modern people." [209] The teachings are rooted in Usui's original methods and philosophy with Doi's additions. In a 2014 *Reiki News Magazine* article, Doi states that Western reiki tends to focus more on the healing aspects of reiki, and he feels that "the importance of spiritual advancement, which is the basic philosophy of Usui Reiki Ryôhô, was not exported to the West enough." [210] Thus, his system incorporates a number of practices for self-purification and spiritual growth. See chapter 20 for an overview of Gendai teachings specific to each level.

Golden Age Reiki: Maggie Larson

This system was channeled by Maggie Larson, also known as Shamara, and is said to be similar to the Tera Mai (included in this appendix) with additional symbols and a different type of elemental energy. [211]

Jinlap Maitri Reiki and Blue Star Reiki: Gary Jirauch

Training in both systems is available to already attuned reiki masters. *Jinlap Maitri Reiki* instruction is divided into five levels: Five Elements Practitioner, Medicine Buddha Practitioner, Medicine Buddha Master Practitioner, Jinlap Maitri Master Practitioner, and Jinlap Maitri Master Teacher. It is said to incorporate the use of sounds, colors, and elements to aid in healing, along with twenty-five symbols. [212] Blue Star Reiki is a variation of Blue Star Celestial Energy, which was said to have originated in ancient Egypt and channeled through a South African reiki master named John Williams. Jirauch added to the teachings and created Blue Star Reiki, which consists of two levels and fourteen symbols.

Johrei Reiki/Vajra Reiki

Johrei is a spiritual practice based on the teachings of Mokichi Okada, who founded the practice in 1935. Johrei is a means of focusing and channeling universal life energy. The Johrei Fellowship does not recognize Johrei Reiki as part of its teachings and has since trademarked the name, so Johrei Reiki is now known as *Vajra Reiki*. It is taught in three levels, and it is recommended

---

208. Doi, *A Modern Reiki Method for Healing*, 41.

209. Doi, *A Modern Reiki Method for Healing*, 6.

210. William Lee Rand, "Interview with Hiroshi Doi Sensei, Part One," *Reiki News Magazine*, spring 2014, 30, https://www.reiki.org/download/InterviewHiroshiDoiSecure.pdf.

211. Quest, *Reiki for Life*, 375.

212. Quest, *Reiki for Life*, 376.

• • • • • • •

that students be initiated to level two in a traditional system before beginning with level one in the Vajra Reiki system, known as Shokuden. In this level, students are taught hand positions, the Vajra Guru mantra, and four symbols; three attunements are given at this level. In the next level, Shinpiden, students receive one attunement and are given the Maha-Vajra Symbol. They also learn how to give Shokuden level attunements to others. Students must practice at this level for one year before progressing to the final level, the Vajra Raku-Kei Reiki Mastership. Master students are given one attunement and the Param-Agni Symbol ("ultimate fire"), and they learn how to conduct attunements for the previous two levels.[213]

Karuna Ki: Vincent P. Amador

Karuna Ki means "the way of compassionate energy," and the system centers around connecting to compassion as a pathway to healing self and others. It differs from Karuna Reiki through the introduction of new attunements, Karuna Ki Do meditations, and mudras. Like Karuna Reiki, Karuna Ki uses the symbols Zonar, Halu, Harth, Rama, Gnosa, Kriya, Shanti, Iava, Om, Fire Serpent, and the Tibetan Master Symbol. There are three levels of attunements given for those who are not already reiki masters in a traditional reiki system.

Karuna Reiki (Usui/Tibetan Reiki), Holy Fire Reiki: William Lee Rand

Training in these systems is available through the International Center for Reiki Training (ICRT) for those who have already completed a master-level training in a traditional system. There are two levels with two attunements, four "master symbols," and eight "treatment symbols." Please see chapter 12 for more information regarding Karuna symbols. The word *Karuna* can be translated as "compassionate action," and it focuses on self-healing and healing others as a means of diminishing the suffering of all beings.[214] The energy of Karuna is said to emanate from the Creator and lead one to the awareness that all beings are one.[215] Holy Fire Reiki was introduced by the ICRT in 2004, and it is said to be more refined and from a higher level of consciousness. It is included in the Karuna Reiki trainings.

Komyo Reiki Kai/Komyo ReikiDo: Hyakuten Inamoto

This system is based on the teachings of Chûjirô Hayashi as taught by Chiyoko Yamaguchi (see Jikiden Reiki), and it was developed in 1998 by Hyakuten Inamoto, a Pure Land Buddhist monk. There are four levels: shoden, chuden, okuden, and shinpiden. In shoden, students learn about

---

213. "The Unfolding," Vajra Reiki, accessed June 2, 2019, http://vajra-reiki.tripod.com/The_Unfolding.html.

214. "About Karuna Reiki," Karuna Reiki, accessed June 2, 2019, https://www.reiki.org/karunareiki/karuna homepage.html.

215. Gaia, *The Book on Karuna Reiki*, 9.

the history of reiki and the basics of hands-on healing. Four attunements are given at this level. In chuden, the symbols and their usage are taught, along with distance healing techniques. This level also includes four attunements. In okuden, the focus is on spiritual development. A fourth symbol is given, along with two attunements. Shinpiden is reserved for students who wish to become teachers, and according to the website, one must inquire about the necessary criteria before being permitted to enroll.[216] Inamoto is also the founder of Komyo ReikiDo International, which connects practitioners across the globe and provides a directory of certified teachers.

Newlife Reiki Seichim: Margot Deepa Slater

After studying traditional reiki and Traditional Seventh Facet Seichim, in 1991, Slater entered an altered state of consciousness and saw Mikao Usui and the deity Quan Yin, which led to the creation of Newlife Reiki Seichim. There are seven levels of instruction.

Osho Neo Reiki: Himani H. Gerber

This system was developed in the 1990s by a German reiki master, Himani H. Gerber, while she was living in an *Osho* commune in India. Osho was an Indian philosopher, guru, and mystic who lived from 1931 to 1990. Gerber studied reiki with Mary McFadyen (see page 351), receiving her master attunement in 1989. While teaching reiki in the commune, Gerber claims to have received a message from Osho that she was now to call this practice Osho Neo Reiki. In level one, students are taught the history of reiki, the basics of working with healing energy, hand positions for self-healing and treating others corresponding to the seven chakras, additional techniques for balancing the chakras, and two Osho meditations: Dynamic Meditation and Kundalini Meditation. They receive four attunements. In level two, students learn three symbols and how to use them in various ways, and they are given many tools to explore the seven levels of consciousness as they pertain to healing. The master level training is undertaken after a great deal of inner work, and the external experience is largely meant to honor and celebrate the inner transformation that has already occurred. It consists of a three-day preparation, including further teaching and shared meditation, followed by the master-level attunement.[217]

Rainbow Reiki: Walter Lübeck

The teachings of Rainbow Reiki are inspired by traditional reiki practices, with the addition of teachings from Zen Buddhism, Sufism, shamanism, Hermeticism, and Lübeck's personal

216. "Reiki Classes," Komyo ReikiDo, accessed June 2, 2019, http://www.komyoreikido.jp/english/e_class.html.

217. Oliver Klatt, *Reiki Systems of the World: One Heart—Many Beats* (Twin Lakes, WI: Lotus Press, 2006), 120–24.

philosophies, and many non-traditional techniques are incorporated, such as the Reiki Power-ball, chakra opening, inner child work, and "dynamization" of the aura. Prior to taking the first degree of Rainbow Reiki, one must receive four attunements from a "traditionally trained Reiki Master within the scope of a seminar on the First Degree."[218] For the second degree, one must first be attuned to the traditional three symbols and mantras.

Reido Reiki: Fuminori Aoki

Reido Reiki, a system created by Fuminori Aoki, means "to start again or be reborn," and its teachings are a blend of Japanese and Western techniques.[219] Aoki studied with Barbara Weber Ray and adopted the seven-level model of instruction. In addition to the four traditional symbols and mantras, the Koriki symbol, or Force of Happiness symbol, is used to bring about inner peace.[220]

Reiki Jin Kei Do: Ranga Premaratna

This system, created by Ranga Premaratna, claims lineage from Chûjirô Hayashi, but instead of being transmitted via Hawayo Takata, Premaratna says that he learned from two Buddhist monks who were students of Hayashi: the Venerable Takeuchi and the Venerable Seiji Takamori. The name has been translated as "the path of compassion and wisdom through Reiki," and it is sometimes referred to as *Usui Shin Kai*—the "core" or "heart" teachings of Usui.[221] It is said that during his travels in Nepal, Takamori met a group of monks who practiced an ancient system of healing that contained two reiki symbols, and he stayed with the monks for seven years, learning more about their healing and spiritual practices, which are referred to as Buddho Methods in *Reiki Jin Kei Do*, or the EnerSense System of Natural Healing. Takamori is said to have met Takata while traveling in the West, where he received a master attunement from her in order to experience an energy transmission from another one of Hayashi's students. Instruction is divided into three levels, with additional classes offered on advanced topics, such as deeper meanings of the symbols and special meditation techniques.[222]

Reiki TUMMO: Irmansyah Effendi

Created by Irmansyah Effendi, who studied the Usui system of reiki, Kundalini yoga, Tibetan meditation, and other spiritual practices, TUMMO is said to give a "better and bigger connec-

218. Walter Lübeck, *Rainbow Reiki: Expanding the Reiki System with Powerful Spiritual Abilities* (Delhi: Motilal Banarsidass, 1998), 13.

219. Quest, *Reiki for Life*, 378.

220. Stiene and Stiene, *The Reiki Sourcebook*, 210.

221. Klatt, *Reiki Systems of the World,* 126.

222. Reiki JKD Classes," Reiki Jin Kei Do and Buddho International, accessed September 4, 2019, https://www.reikijinkeidoandbuddhointernational.com/reiki-jkd-classes.html.

• • • • • • • •

tion to Divine energy" than traditional reiki. It is said to connect the recipient to "earth core energy" and remove knots residing in the chakras, which obstruct the flow of energy. It opens the sushumna, instantly awakening kundalini in a safe manner, and emphasizes connecting with the heart center. Teachings are divided into three levels, with additional classes offered in kundalini, meditation, and other techniques.[223]

Saku Reiki: Eric Bott

Information about this system comes from Bill Pentz, one of Bott's students.[224] Bott studied numerous spiritual traditions and methods, including Buddhism, Taoism, shamanism, Sufism, Bach flower essences, homeopathy, muscle testing, and reflexology. He learned under a number of reiki teachers, such as Kathleen Milner, William Lee Rand, and Frank Arjava Petter, and went on to create *Saku Reiki*, which is divided into six levels, with the possibility of progressing to the Saku Ascension Program and the Saku Teaching Master Apprenticeship Program.

Satya Reiki: Shingo Sakuma

Shingo Sakuma studied with a student of Toshiro Eguchi, who, in turn, was a student of Usui's and a well-known healer in his own right. Teachings are divided into three degrees, with anywhere from one to four attunements given, depending on the level. Four traditional symbols are used, and the system incorporates non-traditional techniques, such as chakras, morning prayer, symbol meditations, and counterclockwise energy spirals.[225]

Seichim: Patrick Zeigler

In 1980, Zeigler traveled to Egypt, where he spent a night in the Pyramid of Giza, experiencing what he describes as a "powerful initiation." He then traveled to Sudan, where he worked with a Sufi saint, and these experiences led to the creation of the Sekhem Energy System, also known as All-Love Sekhem, Seichem, Seichim, SKHM, Seichem-Reiki-SSR, and Isis Seichim. Initiation is said to connect the recipient to higher dimensions and reactivate the "eternal life breath," also known as *Ankh*, with the aim of opening the heart, harmonizing the entire energy system, and reconnecting the individual to Source. There are no levels to the instruction, and classes are offered in various formats, from one- to two-hour meditations to multiple-day retreats.[226]

223. "How Is Reiki TUMMO Different?" Padmacahaya, accessed June 2, 2019, http://www.padmacahaya.org/reiki-tummo/how-is-reiki-tummo-different.
224. "Mikao Usui's Reiki Principles," Bill's Reiki Page, last modified August 31, 2015, http://billpentz.com/reiki.htm#What%20is%20Saku%20Reiki.
225. Stiene and Stiene, *The Reiki Sourcebook*, 211.
226. "All-Love Sekhem," All-Love Sekhem, accessed June 2, 2019, https://www.all-love.com/.

Shamanic Reiki

There are various systems and practitioners operating under the umbrella of shamanic reiki, but here, I discuss the practices as outlined by Llyn Roberts, author of *Shamanic Reiki* and cofounder of Shamanic Reiki Worldwide. The system is divided into three practitioner levels, one teacher level and two "evolving master-teacher" levels. Shamanic Reiki blends traditional reiki practice with indigenous healing approaches, using methods such as accessing altered states of consciousness, removing and transforming energetic intrusions and energy cords, and using drums and rattles to release blocked energy.

Shamballa Multidimensional Healing/Reiki: John Armitage

This system was channeled by John Armitage from a being known as St. Germain, who is said to have brought reiki to earth during the time of Atlantis. Germain gave the energy to people living in what is now Tibet, but they kept the energy to themselves to enhance their own power. Shamballa claims to be the complete system, including the 352 symbols Germain learned during his time as a high priest in Atlantis (the current system has expanded to 1,024 symbols). Teachings are divided into four levels.[227]

Sun Li Chung Reiki: Yosef Sharon

This system originated in Israel and was channeled by Yosef Sharon. Instruction is divided into five levels, and it claims to have access to thousands of symbols, which are not given directly to the students, as they are expected to channel whichever symbols they need and receive attunement from their spirit guides.[228]

Tera Mai Reiki: Kathleen Milner

This system was developed by Kathleen Milner, a student of Helen Borth and Margarette Shelton, the latter of whom initiated her to the master level. She also received an initiation to Seichem by August Starr, one of Barbara Weber Ray's students, but felt that the energy needed to be stabilized, which led to the development of a type of Tera Mai known as Tera Mai Seichem. Milner says that she channeled her teachings from Buddha. Tera Mai Reiki and Tera Mai Seichem are divided into three primary levels, with the option to be initiated into an additional four levels upon completion of master training. Milner also offers classes in Tera Mai Sakara, again divided

---

227. Keth Luke, "Shamballa Multidimensional Healing," awakening-Healing.com, last modified December 31, 2013, https://www.awakening-healing.com/Healing/Shamballa_mdh1024.htm.

228. Quest, *Reiki for Life*, 379.

into three levels and connected to the elements of earth, water, fire, air, and ether; Tera Mai Cahokia, divided into ten initiatory levels; and various classes in shamanic techniques."[229]

Tibetan Reiki: Ralph White

This system is said to originate with Tschen Li, who is claimed to have taught Usui. There is a variation in the material taught, including the number of symbols. For example, one course lists eighteen symbols: Cho Ku Rei, Chakra Cho Ku Reiki Empowerment, Sei He Ki, Hon Sha Ze Sho Nen, En An Ra Hu, Crystal Heart, Crystal Cave, Fusion, Medulla Points, Flower of Life, DNA Activation, Tree of Life, Shiva's Drum, Eye of Horus, El Om, Star of David, Infinity Symbol, and Violet Fire.[230]

Usui Reiki Ryôhô: Frans and Bronwen Stiene

The Stienes are the founders of the International House of Reiki and Shibumi International Reiki. Frans is trained as a Gendai Reiki Ho Shihan (teacher) and a Kômyô Reiki Shihan; Bronwen's teachers include Hyakuten Inamoto, Kathleen Prasad, and Chris Marsh. Currently based in Australia, the Stienes' aim is to present reiki as it was originally taught by Usui. In addition to researching the origins of the reiki system, Frans studies Shintô, Shugendō, Tendai, and Shingon to understand more deeply what Usui was practicing when he developed his teachings. Bronwen's practice includes working with animals, through distance treatment sessions, fundraising, and activism. The Stienes have coauthored a number of books, such as *The Reiki Sourcebook* and *The Japanese Art of Reiki: A Practical Guide to Self-Healing*, and Frans is the author of *The Inner Heart of Reiki: Rediscovering Your True Self* and *Reiki Insights*. They offer in-person classes and retreats, online courses, treatments, and private teachings, as well as community with other practitioners via their international organizations.

Wei Chi Tibetan Reiki: Thomas A. Hensel, Kevin Rodd Emery

This system is divided into three practitioner levels and three teacher levels, and it is based on the channeled teachings of Wei Chi, who is said to have lived in Tibet 5,000 years ago. Wei Chi claims to have created the original system of reiki, which was lost until a small portion of the teachings was rediscovered in the nineteenth century.[231]

229. Kathleen Milner, "Kathleen Milner Home," accessed June 2, 2019. http://www.kathleenmilner.com/index.html.

230. Catherine Craig, "Tibetan Reiki Distance Course," Angelic Light, accessed June 2, 2019, https://www.angeliclight.co.uk/.

231. Stiene and Stiene, *The Reiki Sourcebook*, 220.

Reiki teachings have blossomed since their inception by Mikao Usui, and students and practitioners now have diverse options to choose from when looking for a school or reiki community. In spite of differences in approach, we are all united by the same fundamental energy of reiki, and it is truly a gift to have so many people with wide-ranging experiences contributing to this rich body of healing knowledge.

Recommended Resources

Client Communication

One of my favorite resources for effective communication is the Center for Nonviolent Communication (cnvc.org), and there are also wonderful books available, such as *Nonviolent Communication: A Language of Life* by Marshall Rosenberg, *Human Connection at Work* by Liv Larsson, and *Taking the War Out of Our Words* by Sharon Ellison.

Crystal Elixirs (Safety Precautions)

Gem Water by Joachim Goebel and Michael Gienger

Essential Oils

The Healing Power of Essential Oils by Eric Zielinski

The Complete Book of Essential Oils and Aromatherapy by Valerie Ann Wormwood

Essential oils and pregnancy precautions by the National Association for Holistic Aromatherapy: naha.org/explore-aromatherapy/safety

Feldenkrais

Visit feldenkrais.com for information on group classes and private sessions with Feldenkrais practitioners.

Awareness Through Movement: Easy-to-Do Health Exercises to Improve Your Posture, Vision, Imagination, and Personal Awareness by Moshé Feldenkrais

Feldenkrais Illustrated: The Art of Learning by Tiffany Sankary

· · · · · · · ·

Manuals for Reiki Teachers

The Reiki Manual: A Training Guide for Reiki Students, Practitioners, and Masters by Penelope Quest and Kathy Roberts

A Modern Method for Reiki Healing by Hiroshi Doi

Reflexology

Reflexology: Hands-On Treatment for Health and Vitality by Barbara and Kevin Kunz

The Reflexology Bible by Louise Keet

Working with Waka (Poetry)

In *The Spirit of Reiki*, Frank Arjava Petter includes all 125 waka traditionally used in Usui's teachings, translated by Petter's mother-in-law from an older form of Japanese into modern Japanese, and then by himself and his former wife, Chetna Kobayashi, into English.

• • • • • • • •

Glossary

akashic records: Thought to exist in the etheric plane of reality; a record of all human events, including actions, thoughts, and intents from the past, present, and future, that can be psychically accessed

anandamaya kosha: The fifth of the five koshas; sometimes called the "bliss layer" that connects us to our divine nature and a larger sense of self

annamaya kosha: The first of the five koshas; connected to the element of earth and the physical body; the level at which our energy, including thoughts and emotions, is manifested into physical form

aromatherapy: The practice of using essential oils for healing

Ascension Reiki: A ten-level reiki system developed by Jayson Suttkus

astral plane: A non-physical plane of reality that can be psychically accessed; believed by some to contain energetic blueprints for all things in physical existence

attunement: A ritualized process that opens the recipient to the flow of reiki or strengthens an already existing flow

aura: An energetic sheath surrounding and interpenetrating the body; divided into different layers with different yet complementary functions

Blue Star Reiki: A two-level reiki system created by Gary Jirauch; based on teachings and energy that are said to have originated in ancient Egypt

Breath of the Fire Dragon: Breathing technique used to circulate energy throughout the body; utilizes visualization, reiki symbols, and mantras

byôsen reikan hô: A technique for scanning the body with the hands, sensing for energetic areas of imbalance

Glossary

Celtic Reiki: A reiki system developed by Martyn Pentecost; incorporates the vibrations of certain trees and a personal development system

chakras: Energetic centers within the body that process and help distribute energy throughout the system

chakra kassei kokyû hô: A breathing technique designed to clear and balance the chakras

chiryô hô: A treatment, often used to refer to reiki healing techniques

Chiyoko Yamaguchi: A student of Chûjirô Hayashi; created Jikiden Reiki with her son, Tadao Yamaguchi

Choku Rei: The mantra associated with the first symbol in traditional Usui teachings; often connected to the qualities of power and focus and the element of earth

Chûjirô Hayashi: One of Usui's original master-level students and founder of a branch of reiki known as Hayashi Reiki Kenkyû Kai; he trained Hawayo Takata, the woman responsible for bringing reiki to the West

clairaudience: Literally, "clear hearing"; psychic ability to perceive via non-ordinary hearing sense

claircognizance: Literally, "clear knowing"; psychic ability to know something outside of ordinary thought channels

clairsentience: Literally, "clear feeling"; psychic ability to perceive via non-ordinary feeling senses

clairvoyance: Literally, "clear seeing"; psychic ability to perceive via non-ordinary visual sense

correspondence: In the context of distance healing, an object designated as a substitute for a recipient who is not physically present (e.g., a photo or teddy bear)

crown chakra: From the Hindu system, an energetic center related to connection with the Divine and higher consciousness

crystal grid: An intentional arrangement of crystals designed to direct the flow of energy for specific intentions, such as healing or cleansing

Dai Kômyô: The mantra associated with the fourth symbol in the Usui reiki system (although some sources argue that the fourth symbol was added to the teachings after Usui's death); sometimes referred to as the "master symbol" and associated with the quality of empowerment

Dento Reiki: Traditional reiki as taught by Mikao Usui

distance healing: The act of sending healing energy to recipients in another physical location or to situations in the past or future

dokukudashi: A technique used for detoxification of the body and energy system

energy channels: Pathways in the body and energy field for the transport of energy

energy cords: Energetic structures for transferring energy; typically used to refer to unhealthy energetic connections in which one or both parties are harmed by the energetic transfer

enkaku chiryô hô: A technique for sending reiki distantly

essential oils: Volatile, plant-derived aromatic oils used for healing and for their scents

extraordinary vessels: In Traditional Chinese Medicine, important energetic channels that connect the major meridians, organs, and other structures, facilitating a healthy flow of energy

five precepts: Also known as the "reiki precepts" or *gokai*; a set of maxims included in Usui's original teachings to aid in spiritual and personal development

flower essence: Sometimes referred to as "flower remedies"; made by steeping flowers in water and preserving the resulting liquid with alcohol, vinegar, or glycerin; different flowers are said to aid in healing various health issues

gasshô: A posture with palms of the hands together at the heart

Gendai Reiki Hô: System of reiki developed by Hiroshi Doi; intended to be a blending of traditional Usui teachings and modern reiki practices

Gokai: See *five precepts*

Golden Age Reiki: A reiki system developed by Maggie Larson, also known as Shamara; includes new symbols and a variation of elemental energy

gyôsei: Poetry, or *waka*, written by the emperor

gyôshi hô: A technique for sending reiki by staring with the eyes

hado kokyû hô: A breathing technique designed to boost the immune system, detoxify the body, raise energy, and cultivate a sense of calm

hara: A physical and energetic center below the belly button

hatsurei hô: A technique for increasing the flow of spiritual energy through the body

Hawayo Takata: A student of Chujirô Hayashi; credited with introducing reiki to the West

Hayashi Reiki Kenkyû Kai: System of reiki developed by Chûrô Hayashi, one of Usui's original master-level students

heart chakra: From the Hindu system, an energetic center related to love and relationships with self and others

Hermeticism: A philosophy and esoteric religious tradition based on writings attributed to Hermes Trismegistus

heso chiryô hô: Healing technique centered on the navel (belly button)

Hiroshi Doi: Founder of the Gendai Reiki system

holographic model: A model of reality stating that each individual part of a thing contains the whole

Holy Fire Reiki: A system of reiki developed by William L. Rand; said to be a more refined energy from a higher level of consciousness

Hon Sha Ze Sho Nen: The mantra associated with the third symbol in traditional Usui teachings

Hui Yin Breath: A breathing technique designed to connect to the Hui Yin acupuncture point

human energy field: Also referred to as the "aura"; a field of energy surrounding and interpenetrating the body, responsible for protecting the organism and mediating exchange with others and the environment

Ida: In Hindu philosophy, one of the primary energetic channels, or *nadis*, in the body; associated with the feminine and moon energy

implicate order: Theory developed by theoretical physicist David Bohm; presupposes an underlying pattern or fundamental ordering to all existence, known as the implicate order

jakikiri jôka hô: A technique for purifying inanimate objects

Jikiden Reiki: A system of reiki created by Chiyoko and Tadao Yamaguchi with the aim of presenting Chûjirô Hayashi's original teachings as accurately as possible

Jinlap Maitri Reiki: A five-level reiki system developed by Gary Jirauch; incorporates new symbols and the use of sounds, colors and elements for healing

Johrei Reiki: See *Vajra Reiki*

jôshin kokyû hô: A breathing technique used to purify the self, connect with reiki, and focus the mind

jumon: "Spell, incantation"; sometimes used synonymously with mantra or kotodama

kamiza: In a specific location, the area with the highest energy; in Jikiden Reiki, a scroll of the reiki precepts is placed in this spot

Karuna Ki: A system of reiki developed by Vincent P. Amador; incorporates new symbols, attunements, meditations, and mudras

Karuna Reiki: A system of reiki developed by William L. Rand meant to be taken after completing master-level training in a more traditional Usui system

kenyoku hô: Also known as "dry bathing"; a technique used to purify the body and energy field

Kirlian photography: A form of photography developed by Semyon Kirlian, said to capture the aura or energetic field surrounding living organisms and non-living objects

koketsuhô: Also known as "blood exchange"; a strengthening technique for chronic illness or recovery from a major illness or injury

koki hô: A technique for sending reiki using the breath

Komyo Reiki Kai / Komyo ReikiDo: A four-level system based on the teachings of Chûjirô Hayashi as taught by Chiyoko Yamaguchi; developed by Hyakuten Inamoto, a Pure Land Buddhist monk

kosha: In yogic philosophy, energetic sheaths or auras surrounding and interpenetrating the body

kotodama: "Words carrying spirit"; sometimes used synonymously with mantra or jumon

kyu: Degree; level of attainment

manomaya kosha: The third of five koshas; regulates and expresses emotional energy

MariEL: A system of reiki developed by Ethel Lombardi and named after Mary in the Christian tradition

meridian: In Traditional Chinese Medicine, a channel or pathway for energy to travel within the body

Mikao Usui: The founder of the healing system of reiki

morphogenetic field: Theory developed by Dr. Rupert Sheldrake; informational fields of energy, specific to individual species, that assist in directing development of the organism

mudra: A symbolic hand gesture

nadete chiryô hô: A stroking technique designed to treat the meridians and organs

nadi: In Hindu philosophy, energetic channels within the body responsible for distributing prana and other energies throughout the system

nadi shodhana: Alternate nostril breathing technique using a finger to seal one nostril while breathing in through the other and repeating on the opposite side

navel chakra: From the Hindu system, an energetic center related to the emotions, desire and sexuality

nentatsu: A technique for sending thoughts to a recipient with the intention of strengthening their willpower and ability to heal

Newlife Reiki Seichim: Seven-level reiki system developed by Margot Deepa Slater; inspired by spiritual visions of Mikao Usui and Quan Yin

oshite chiryô hô: A technique useful on stiff or tense areas; hand pressure is applied to the area while reiki is transmitted

Osho Neo Reiki: A three-level reiki system developed by Himani H. Gerber; incorporates chakra healing and Osho (an Indian philosopher and mystic) meditations

pingala: In Hindu philosophy, one of the primary energetic channels, or *nadis*, in the body; associated with the masculine and sun energy

pranamaya kosha: One of the five koshas; composed of prana or vital life force and intimately connected with the breath

Radiance Technique: A seven-level system of reiki created by Barbara Weber Ray, author of *The Reiki Factor*, who claims to be Hawayo Takata's successor

Rainbow Reiki: A system of reiki developed by Walter Lübeck; incorporates Zen Buddhism, Sufism, shamanism, Hermeticism, and other philosophies

Raku Kei Reiki: Also known as "the Way of the Fire Dragon," a four-level system of reiki created by Iris Ishikuro and Arthur Robertson

reflexology: The application of pressure to certain points on the hands and feet, said to correspond with different areas of and systems in the body to facilitate healing and energy flow

Reido Reiki: A seven-level system of reiki developed by Fuminori Aoki, a student of Barbara Weber Ray; a blending of traditional Usui teachings and Western practices

reiju: A spiritual offering or blessing; used to strengthen one's connection to and ability to channel spiritual energy; the basis for modern-day attunements

reiki: Spiritual energy; alternately thought to be the energy of all things, the energy of life, and the energy of love; the basis for the reiki system of healing

reiki boost: A technique for opening and balancing the chakras, promoting healthy energy flow throughout the entire body

Reiki Jin Kei Do: A system of reiki developed by Ranga Premaratna, who claims lineage from Chûjirô Hayashi via two Buddhist monks who were said to be students of Hayashi

reiki mawashi: The practice of creating an energetic current through practitioners, typically seated in a circle with hands touching or floating in close proximity

Reiki Ryôhô: Spiritual Energy Method

Reiki Ryôhô Hikkei: Spiritual Energy Method Manual; a sixty-eight-page manual divided into four sections published by the Usui Reiki Ryôhô Gakkai given to level one students of the Gakkai

Reiki Undô: The process of letting the body move naturally and uncontrolled, allowing any sounds, emotions, and other expressions to arise spontaneously

root chakra: From the Hindu system, an energetic center related to the physical body and tangible experience, and a sense of grounding and safety

Ryôhô Shishin: A healing guide; two of importance in reiki teachings are, one, the *Ryôhô Shishin* published by the Usui Reiki Ryôhô Gakkai and, two, the *Ryôhô Shishin* written by Chûjirô Hayashi

saibo kassei kokyû hô: A technique of scanning the body for imbalance and sending healing gratitude and reiki to those areas

Saku Reiki: A six-level system of reiki developed by Eric Bott

Satya Reiki: A three-level system of reiki developed by Shingo Sakuma

Seichim: A system of reiki developed by Patrick Zeigler who claims to have received an energetic transmission while spending the night in the Pyramid of Giza

seiheki chiryô hô: Treatment for healing mental patterns; utilizes mantras and symbols

Sei Heki: The mantra associated with the second symbol in traditional Usui teachings; sometimes referred to as the "mental-emotional symbol" and associated with harmony and the energy of heaven

seishin toitsu: A breathing technique used to purify the self, connect with reiki, and focus the mind

sekizui jôka ibuki hô: A technique for clearing energy flow along the spine and balancing the entire body

seventh-level technique: A process for activating and sending energy via an important energetic gateway located at the base of the skull

Shamanic Reiki: Various systems of reiki incorporating shamanic techniques, such as accessing an altered state of consciousness for healing and spirit communication and the use of drums and rattles for healing

Shamballa Reiki: A system of reiki developed by John Armitage; claims to have been channeled from a High Priest of Atlantis

shihan: Teacher or instructor

Shintô: "Way of the gods"; indigenous Japanese religion with diverse rituals, mythology, and beliefs; connected to the use of shrines for worshipping spirits and deities

shoden: The first level of instruction in traditional Usui reiki

shûchû reiki: Multiple practitioners treating one recipient, concentrating the spiritual energy

Shugendō: An esoteric form of Buddhism incorporating Taoist, Shintô, and shamanic practices; practitioners are known as yamabushi

six-point energy meditation: A technique to harmonize energy flow throughout the body

solar plexus chakra: From the Hindu system, an energetic center related to control, power, decision-making, and self-esteem

Sun Li Chung Reiki: A five-level system of reiki developed by Yosef Sharon with thousands of symbols, which are meant to be accessed via the student's spirit guides

sushumna: The central energy channel, or nadi, in Hindu philosophy; the seven primary chakras are aligned along the sushumna, which runs up the spinal column

Tadao Yamaguchi: Son of Chiyoko Yamaguchi, who studied under Chûjirô Hayashi; with his mother, he founded the system of Jikiden Reiki

tanden: A physical and energetic center below the belly button

tanden chiryô hô: A technique for energizing and strengthening willpower

Tera Mai Reiki: A three-level reiki system developed by Kathleen Milner, who claims her teachings were channeled from Buddha

third eye chakra: From the Hindu system, an energetic center related to intuition and clear seeing; also called the brow chakra

throat chakra: From the Hindu system, an energetic center related to communication, verbal and non-verbal, internal and external, and creativity and connection

TUMMO Reiki: A system of reiki developed by Irmansyah Effendi; blends Usui teachings, Kundalini yoga, Tibetan meditation, and other spiritual practices

uchite chiryô hô: A technique employing patting with the hands to clear the meridians and facilitate healing

· · · · · · · ·

Usui Reiki Ryôhô: A system of reiki taught by Frans and Bronwen Stiene of the International House of Reiki who aim to present the teachings as originally taught by Usui

Usui Reiki Ryôhô Gakkai: Society of the Usui Spiritual Energy Healing Method; said to have been created by Mikao Usui in Japan in 1922; still in existence today

Usui Shiki Ryôhô: Usui Way Healing Method; title used by Hawayo Takata on her certificates; the name has also been used to denote branches of reiki as taught by Phyllis Lei Furumoto, Beth Gray, and others

Vajra Reiki: Formerly Johrei Reiki; a three-level system based on the teachings of Mokichi Okada, using new symbols and mudras

vijnanamaya kosha: The fourth of five sheaths; the knowledge or wisdom layer, governing our ability to discern reality and truth

violet breath: A technique utilizing breath, visualization, and reiki symbols to facilitate energy flow throughout the body

waka: Poetry; in traditional Usui teachings, waka were used as a contemplation tool for spiritual development

Wei Chi Tibetan Reiki: Six-level system of reiki developed by Thomas A. Hensel and Kevin Rodd Emery; said to be channeled through Wei Chi, a Tibetan monk living 5,000 years ago

Bibliography

"About." Celtic Reiki. Accessed June 2, 2019. http://celtic-reiki.com/wp/index.php/about/.

"About." Ecstatic Dance. Accessed June 2, 2019. https://www.ecstaticdance.com/about/.

"About Karuna Reiki." Karuna Reiki. Accessed June 2, 2019. https://www.reiki.org/karuna reiki/karunahomepage.html.

Ahn, Andrew C., Agatha P. Colbert, Belinda J. Anderson, Ørjan G. Martinsen, Richard Hammerschlag, Steve Cina, Peter M. Wayne, and Helene M. Langevin. "Electrical Properties of Acupuncture Points and Meridians: A Systematic Review." *Bioelectromagnetics* 29, no. 4 (May 2008): 245–56. doi:10.1002/bem.20403.

Aitken, R. J., G. N. De Iuliis, Z. Gibb, and M. A. Baker. "The Simmet Lecture: New Horizons on an Old Landscape—Oxidative Stress, DNA Damage and Apoptosis in the Male Germ Line." *Reproduction in Domestic Animals* 47, no. 4 (August 2012): 7–14. doi:10.1111/j.1439 -0531.2012.02049.x.

"All-Love Sekhem." All-Love Sekhem. Accessed June 2, 2019. https://www.all-love.com/.

"Angelic RayKey—ARK." Of One Source. Accessed June 2, 2019. https://ofonesource.com /school/class-list/reiki-and-angelic-raykey.

"Ascension Reiki." Ascension Reiki. Accessed June 2, 2019. https://ascensionreiki.com /AscensionReiki-Introduction.html.

Beaulieu, John. *Polarity Therapy Workbook*. 2nd ed. Pennsauken, NJ: BookBaby, 2016.

Bohm, David. *The Essential David Bohm*. Edited by Lee Nichol. London: Routledge, 2008.

Brennan, Barbara Ann. *Hands of Light: A Guide to Healing through the Human Energy Field*. Toronto: Bantam Books, 1993.

Bibliography

Brown, Brené. *The Gifts of Imperfection.* Center City, MN: Hazelden, 2010.

Cairns, Rob A., Isaac S. Harris, and Tak W. Mak. "Regulation of Cancer Cell Metabolism." *Nature Reviews Cancer* 11, no. 2 (2011): 85–95. doi:10.1038/nrc2981.

Carney, Dana R., Amy J. C. Cuddy, and Andy J. Yap. "Power Posing: Brief Nonverbal Displays Affect Neuroendocrine Levels and Risk Tolerance." *Psychological Science* 21, no. 10 (September 2010): 1363–68. doi:10.1177/0956797610383437.

"Chapter 4: Coherence." HeartMath Institute. Accessed March 07, 2019. https://www.heart math.org/research/science-of-the-heart/coherence/.

Co, Stephen, Eric B. Robins, and John Merryman. *Your Hands Can Heal You: Pranic Healing Energy Remedies to Boost Vitality and Speed Recovery from Common Health Problems.* New York: Atria Paperback, 2002.

Cohen, Kenneth S. *The Way of Qigong.* New York: Random House International, 2000.

Cointreau, Maya. *The Practical Reiki Symbol Primer.* Self-published, CreateSpace, 2015.

Comish, Chris. *45 Free Reiki Attunements.* Self-published, Lulu.com, 2010.

Craig, Catherine. "Tibetan Reiki Distance Course." Angelic Light. Accessed June 2, 2019. https://www.angeliclight.co.uk/.

Dale, Cyndi. *The Complete Book of Chakra Healing: Activate the Transformative Power of Your Energy Centers.* Woodbury, MN: Llewellyn Publications, 2011.

———. *The Subtle Body: An Encyclopedia of Your Energetic Anatomy.* Boulder, CO: Sounds True, 2009.

Darras, J. C., P. Albarède, and P. de Vernejoul. "Nuclear Medicine Investigation of Transmission of Acupuncture Information." *Acupuncture in Medicine* 11, no. 1 (1993), 22–28. doi:10.1136/aim.11.1.22.

Dharmananda, Subhuti. "The Six Qi and Six Yin." November 2010. http://www.itmonline.org/articles/six_qi_six_yin/six_qi.htm.

Doi, Hiroshi. *A Modern Reiki Method for Healing.* Southfield, MI: Vision Publications, 2014.

Dreaminger, Jarandhel. "Corey Thorn's Reiki Symbols." WanderingPaths. Accessed April 27, 2019. http://wanderingpaths.dreamhart.org/reiki/coreysymbols.html.

Eden, Donna, and David Feinstein. *Energy Medicine.* New York: Penguin, 2008.

EFT and Tapping for Beginners: The Essential EFT Manual to Start Relieving Stress, Losing Weight, and Healing. Berkeley, CA: Rockridge Press, 2013.

Eversole, Finley, ed. *Energy Medicine Technologies: Ozone Healing, Microcrystals, Frequency Therapy, and the Future of Health.* Rochester, VT: Inner Traditions, 2013.

· · · · · · ·

Feldenkrais, Moshé. *Awareness through Movement: Health Exercises for Personal Growth.* New York: HarperCollins, 1990.

"Four Aspects." Usui Shiki Ryoho. Accessed June 2, 2019. https://www.usuishikiryohoreiki .com/usr-4%20aspects.htm.

Fueston, Robert N. *The History and System of Usui Shiki Reiki Ryoho.* Vol. 1 of *Reiki: Transmissions of Light.* Twin Lakes, WI: Lotus Press, 2017. Kobo.

Fulton, Elizabeth, and Kathleen Prasad. *Animal Reiki: Using Energy to Heal the Animals in Your Life.* Berkeley, CA: Ulysses Press, 2006.

Gaia, Laurelle Shanti. *The Book on Karuna Reiki: Advanced Healing Energy for Our Evolving World.* Hartsel, CO: Infinite Light Healing Studies Center, 2001.

Gerber, Richard. *Vibrational Medicine.* 3rd ed. Rochester, VT: Bear and Company, 2001.

Goldman, Jonathan, and Andi Goldman. *The Humming Effect: Sound Healing for Health and Happiness.* Rochester, VT: Healing Arts, 2017.

Goldman, Joshua, and Alec W. Sims. *Sound Healing for Beginners: Using Vibration to Harmonize Your Health and Wellness.* Woodbury, MN: Llewellyn, 2016.

Gordon, Richard. *Quantum-Touch: The Power to Heal.* Berkeley, CA: North Atlantic Books, 2006.

Gralton, Toni, and John F. Thie. *Touch for Health.* Camarillo, CA: DeVorss & Co., 2005.

Groner, Paul. *Saichō: The Establishment of the Japanese Tendai School.* Honolulu: University of Hawaii Press, 2002.

Haddad, Bob. *Thai Massage & Thai Healing Arts: Practice, Culture and Spirituality.* Chiang Mai, Thailand: Silkworm Books, 2013.

Harner, Michael. *The Way of the Shaman.* New York: HarperOne, 2011.

Hendricks, Gay. *The Big Leap: Conquer Your Hidden Fear and Take Life to the Next Level.* New York: HarperOne, 2010.

Hess, Katie. *Flowerevolution: Blooming into Your Full Potential with the Magic of Flowers.* Carlsbad, CA: Hay House, 2016.

"How Is Reiki TUMMO Different?" Padmacahaya. Accessed June 2, 2019. http://www.padma cahaya.org/reiki-tummo/how-is-reiki-tummo-different.

Iknoian, Therese, and Manny Fuentes. *Tai Chi for Dummies.* Hoboken, NJ: John Wiley & Sons, 2001.

Jacobsen, Nephyr. *Seven Peppercorns: Traditional Thai Medical Theory for Bodyworkers.* Forres, Scotland: Findhorn Press, 2015.

Jacobsen, Nephyr, C. Pierce Salguero, and Tracy Wells. *Thai Herbal Medicine: Traditional Recipes for Health & Harmony.* Forres, Scotland: Findhorn Press, 2014.

• • • • • • • •

Japanese American Living Legacy. "The Mystical World of Harry M. Kuboi: Reiki Master of Masters, Psychic and Professional Exorcist." News release, October 2010. http://www.ja livinglegacy.org/press/2010/12_Harry Kuboi.pdf.

"John Harvey Gray." The John Harvey Gray Center for Reiki Healing. Accessed June 2, 2019. https://learnreiki.org/reiki-master-teacher/john-harvey-gray/.

Judith, Anodea. *Wheels of Life: A User's Guide to the Chakra System*. 2nd ed. Woodbury, MN: Llewellyn Publications, 2016.

Kathleen Milner. "Kathleen Milner Home." Accessed June 2, 2019. http://www.kathleenmilner.com/index.html.

Katz, Debra Lynne. *You Are Psychic: The Art of Clairvoyant Reading & Healing*. Santa Barbara, CA: Living Dreams Press, 2015.

Klatt, Oliver. *Reiki Systems of the World: One Heart—Many Beats*. Twin Lakes, WI: Lotus Press, 2006.

Kluck-Ebbin, Michelle. *The Touch Remedy: Hands-On Solutions to De-Stress Your Life*. New York: HarperElixir, 2016.

Koshikidake, Shokai, and Martin Faulks. *Shugendō: The Way of the Mountain Monks*. Foreword by Steven K. Hayes. Faulks Books, 2015.

Kurzweil, Arthur. *Kabbalah For Dummies*. Hoboken, NJ: Wiley, 2007.

Kynes, Sandra. *Change at Hand: Balancing Your Energy through Palmistry, Chakras & Mudras*. Woodbury, MN: Llewellyn Publications, 2009.

"The Let Animals Lead Approach with Reiki." Animal Reiki Source. Accessed June 2, 2019. https://www.animalreikisource.com/animal-reiki-information/the-approach/.

Lipton, Bruce H. *The Biology of Belief: Unleashing the Power of Consciousness, Matter & Miracles*. Carlsbad, CA: Hay House, 2016.

Lübeck, Walter. *Rainbow Reiki: Expanding the Reiki System with Powerful Spiritual Abilities*. Delhi: Motilal Banarsidass, 1998.

Lübeck, Walter, Frank Arjava Petter, and William Lee Rand. *The Spirit of Reiki: The Complete Handbook of the Reiki System*. Translated by Christine M. Grimm. Twin Lakes, WI: Lotus Press, 2001.

Luke, Keth. "Shamballa Multidimensional Healing." Awakening-Healing.com. Last modified December 31, 2013. https://www.awakening-healing.com/Healing/Shamballa_mdh1024.htm.

Mallinson, James, and Mark Singleton, trans. and eds. *Roots of Yoga*. London: Penguin Books, 2017.

• • • • • • •

Maslow, Abraham H. *Religions, Values and Peak-Experiences*. New York: Penguin Compass, 1994. Kobo.

McKusick, Eileen Day. *Tuning the Human Biofield: Healing with Vibrational Sound Therapy*. Rochester, VT: Healing Arts Press, 2014.

Men, Hunbatz. *Secrets of Mayan Science/Religion*. Santa Fe, NM: Bear and Company, 1990.

Meyers, Bryant A. *PEMF—The Fifth Element of Health: Learn Why Pulsed Electromagnetic Field Therapy (PEMF) Supercharges Your Health Like Nothing Else!* Bloomington, IN: Balboa Press, 2014.

"Mikao Usui's Reiki Principles." Bill's Reiki Page. Last modified August 31, 2015. http://bill pentz.com/reiki.htm#What%20is%20Saku%20Reiki.

Milne, Hugh. *The Heart of Listening: A Visionary Approach to Craniosacral Work*. Vol. 1. Berkeley, CA: North Atlantic Books, 1998.

Muller, Florian L., Michael S. Lustgarten, Youngmok Jang, Arlan Richardson, and Holly Van Remmen. "Trends in Oxidative Aging Theories." *Free Radical Biology and Medicine* 43, no. 4 (2007): 477–503. doi:10.1016/j.freeradbiomed.2007.03.034.

Musser, George. *The Complete Idiot's Guide to String Theory*. New York: Alpha, 2008.

Myers, Thomas W. *Anatomy Trains: Myofascial Meridians for Manual and Movement Therapists*. Illustrated by Graeme Chambers, Debbie Maizels, and Philip Wilson. Edinburgh, UK: Churchill Livingstone, 2017.

Nishina, Masaki. *Reiki and Japan: A Cultural View of Western and Japanese Reiki*. Edited by Amanda Jayne. Self-published, CreateSpace, 2017.

Pacheco, Rebecca. *Do Your Om Thing: Bending Yoga Tradition to Fit Your Modern Life*. New York: Harper Wave, 2016.

Penczak, Christopher. *The Inner Temple of Witchcraft: Magick, Meditation, and Psychic Development*. Woodbury, MN: Llewellyn Publications, 2014.

———. *Magick of Reiki: Focused Energy for Healing, Ritual & Spiritual Development*. St. Paul, MN: Llewellyn Publications, 2004.

———. *The Outer Temple of Witchcraft: Circles, Spells, and Rituals*. Woodbury, MN: Llewellyn Publications, 2008.

———. *The Temple of High Witchcraft: Ceremonies, Spheres, and the Witches Qabalah*. Woodbury, MN: Llewellyn Publications, 2007.

———. *The Temple of Shamanic Witchcraft: Shadows, Spirits, and the Healing Journey*. Woodbury, MN: Llewellyn Publications, 2010.

Pert, Candace B. *Molecules of Emotion*. New York: Scribner, 2003.

• • • • • • •

Bibliography

Price, Shirley. *The Aromatherapy Workbook: Understanding Essential Oils from Plant to User.* London: Thorsons, 2000.

Quest, Penelope. *Reiki for Life: The Complete Guide to Reiki Practice for Levels 1, 2 & 3.* New York: TarcherPerigee, 2016.

Rand, William Lee. "Interview with Hiroshi Doi Sensei, Part One." *Reiki News Magazine*, spring 2014, 26–30. https://www.reiki.org/download/InterviewHiroshiDoiSecure.pdf.

Rebolini, Arianna. "What the Heck Happened to My Body During Reiki?" The Cut. September 25, 2017. https://www.thecut.com/2017/09/what-the-heck-happened-to-my-body-during-reiki.html.

"Reiki Classes." Komyo ReikiDo. Accessed June 2, 2019. http://www.komyoreikido.jp/english/e_class.html.

Reikifire Ministry. "Wagle Reiki Symbols Index." Reiki Spirit. Last modified January 4, 2005. http://reikispirit.net/church/sym.lib.wagle.html.

"Reiki Home: An Unfolding Journey." Reiki Home. Accessed June 2, 2019. https://reikihome.org/.

"Reiki JKD Classes." Reiki Jin Kei Do and Buddho International. Accessed September 4, 2019. https://www.reikijinkeidoandbuddhointernational.com/reiki-jkd-classes.html.

"Reiki 1 Class." The John Harvey Gray Center for Reiki Healing. Accessed June 2, 2019. https://learnreiki.org/reiki-classes/reiki-1-class/.

"Reiki Outreach International." The Reiki Association. Accessed June 2, 2019. https://www.reikiassociation.net/reiki-outreach-international.php.

Reiki Ryôhô no Shiori. Edited by Kazuwa Toyokazu. Tokyo, Japan: Usui Reiki Ryôhô Gakkai, 1974.

Rivard, Richard. *Reiki Ryoho Hikkei.* Last modified July 21, 2011. http://www.threshold.ca/reiki/Usui_Reiki_Hikkei.html.

Roberts, Llyn, and Robert Levy. *Shamanic Reiki: Expanded Ways of Working with Universal Life Force Energy.* Winchester, UK: O Books, 2008.

Roth, Gabrielle, and John Loudon. *Maps to Ecstasy: Teachings of an Urban Shaman.* London: Thorsons, 1995.

Salguero, C. Pierce, and David Roylance. *Encyclopedia of Thai Massage: A Complete Guide to Traditional Thai Massage Therapy and Acupressure.* Forres, Scotland: Findhorn, 2011.

Saso, Michael. *Tantric Art and Meditation.* Honolulu: Tendai Educational Foundation, 2000.

Shea, Michael J. *Biodynamic Craniosacral Therapy.* Vol. 1. Berkeley, CA: North Atlantic, 2007.

"Spiritual Practice Resources." Harry Potter and the Sacred Text. Accessed June 2, 2019. http:// www.harrypottersacredtext.com/spiritual-practice-resources.

Stibal, Vianna. *ThetaHealing: Introducing an Extraordinary Energy Healing Modality.* Carlsbad, CA: Hay House, 2012.

———. *Seven Planes of Existence: The Philosophy of the TheataHealing Technique.* London: Hay House, 2016.

Stiene, Bronwen, and Frans Stiene. *The Reiki Sourcebook.* Rev. ed. Ropley, UK: O Books, 2008.

Stiene, Frans. *The Inner Heart of Reiki: Rediscovering Your True Self.* Winchester, UK: Ayni Books, 2015.

Sun, Howard, and Dorothy Sun. *Colour Your Life: How to Use the Right Colours to Achieve Balance, Health and Happiness.* London: Piatkus, 2014.

"The Unfolding." Vajra Reiki. Accessed June 2, 2019. http://vajra-reiki.tripod.com/The _Unfolding.html.

"Usui Shiki Ryoho." The Reiki Alliance. Accessed March 22, 2019. http://www.reikialliance. com/en/article/usui-shiki-ryoho.

Villoldo, Alberto. *Shaman, Healer, Sage: How to Heal Yourself and Others with the Energy Medicine of the Americas.* London: Transworld Digital, 2010.

Walker, Lauren. *Energy Medicine Yoga: Amplify the Healing Power of Your Yoga Practice.* Boulder, CO: Sounds True, 2014.

Wangyal, Tenzin. *Healing with Form, Energy and Light: The Five Elements in Tibetan Shamanism, Tantra, and Dzogchen.* Edited by Mark Dahlby. New Delhi, India: New Age Books, 2003.

———. *Wonders of the Natural Mind: The Essence of Dzogchen in the Native Bon Tradition of Tibet.* New Delhi, India: New Age Books, 2004.

Wauters, Ambika. *The Complete Guide to Chakras: Unleash the Positive Power Within.* Hauppauge, NY: Barrons, 2010.

Wei, Haifeng, Lawrence Chung-Long Huang, and Jian Kong. "The Substrate and Properties of Meridians: A Review of Modern Research." *Acupuncture in Medicine* 17, no. 2 (1999): 134–39. doi:10.1136/aim.17.2.134.

Westcott, William Wynn, trans. *Sepher Yetzirah: The Book of Formation with Fifty Gates of Intelligence and the Thirty-Two Paths of Wisdom.* London: J. M. Watkins, 1911.

Yamaguchi, Tadao. *Light on the Origins of Reiki: A Handbook for Practicing the Original Reiki of Usui and Hayashi.* Translated by Ikuko Hirota. Edited by Neehar Douglass. Twin Lakes, WI: Lotus Press, 2007.

Zehr, Leslie. *The Alchemy of Dance: Sacred Dance as a Path to the Universal Dancer.* New York: iUniverse, 2008.

· · · · · · ·

Index

• • • • • • •

U
uchite chiryô hô, 232, 357
University of Chicago, 89
Usui, Makao, 73, 76, 79, 81–84, 87, 89–93,
99–102, 107, 109, 115, 152, 158, 165, 193,
217, 221, 222, 227, 229, 249, 265, 285,
333–338, 340–345, 347, 348, 350, 352–358
Usui Reiki Ryôhô, 82, 83, 89, 91, 100, 115, 337,
340, 341, 347, 356, 358
Usui Reiki Ryôhô Gakkai, 82, 83, 89, 91, 100,
115, 337, 340, 341, 356, 358
Usui Shiki Ryôhô, 334, 335, 338, 358

V
Vajra Reiki, 341, 342, 354, 358
vajrini, 35
vijnanamaya kosha, 24, 25, 358
yagyu ryu, 81
yin-yang theory, 32, 36

W
waka, 82, 222, 229, 322, 350, 353, 358
Weber, Barbara, 88, 89, 91, 335, 336, 344, 346,
355, 356
Wei Chi Tibetan Reiki, 347, 358
White, Ralph, 347

Y
yamabushi, 83, 357
Yamaguchi, Chiyoko, 85, 333, 337, 342, 352,
354, 357
Yamaguchi, Tadao, 84–86, 115, 221, 333, 352,
354, 357
Yamashita, Kay, 88, 338

Z
zaike, 82
Zeigler, Patrick, 345, 356
zentô bu, 110